The Justice and the Mare's Ale

For Iris Macfarlane, my mother, who first
introduced me to Kirkby Lonsdale documents.

The Justice
and
the Mare's Ale

*Law and disorder
in seventeenth-century England*

Alan Macfarlane
in collaboration with Sarah Harrison

BASIL BLACKWELL · OXFORD

©Alan Macfarlane and Sarah Harrison 1981

First published in 1981 by
Basil Blackwell Publisher
108 Cowley Road
Oxford OX4 1JF
England

British Library Cataloguing in Publication Data

Macfarlane, Alan
    The justice and the mare's ale.
    1. Cumbria, Eng. — Social life and customs
    I. Title   II. Harrison, Sarah
    942.7'8'06   DA670.C93
ISBN 0–631–12681–3

Printed in Great Britain by
Billing and Sons Ltd,
London, Guildford, Oxford and Worcester.

Contents

List of Maps

List of Illustrations

Acknowledgements

The following read all of the manuscript and made so many useful comments that it has been impossible to acknowledge every suggestion in the text: Dr John Baker, Cherry Bryant, Richard Jenkins, Jessica King, Iris Macfarlane, John Tarring. I am enormously grateful to all of them. Dr John Morrill kindly read the introduction and conclusion. The help of Mr and Mrs C, and J. Mason has been acknowledged in the text, but I would like to add general thanks for their co-operation in tracking down the legends of the Smorthwaits. Sheila Macpherson and Bruce Jones of the Kendal and Carlisle branches of the Cumbria Record Office helpfully answered queries and the staff of these two record offices and the Lancashire Record Office at Preston once again provided indispensable assistance, as did the staff of the Public Record Office in London. Mary Wraith efficiently and speedily typed the manuscript. The Social Science Research Council made it possible to carry out the detailed parish study through a project grant. The Department of Social Anthropology, Cambridge University, and particularly Professor Jack Goody, provided support and stimulus.

Mr and Mrs H. Harrison-Beck kindly put a number of Middleton deeds at our disposal and Monica Tarring helped to arrange this and other matters. The portrait of Sir Daniel Fleming is reproduced by kind permission of Lord Inglewood and with the help of Mary Burkett, that of Sir George Jeffreys by kind permission of the National Portrait Gallery, the cover portrait by kind permission of the Tate Gallery. The endpapers were reproduced from a drawing by Mr A. Wainwright in his *Lune Sketchbook*, by kind permission of Mr Wainwright.

Transcriptions and photographic reproductions of Crown-copyright material in the Public Record Office appear by permission of the Controller of HM Stationery Office. Transcripts of documents at Preston are published by kind permission of the Lancashire Record Office. Transcripts and photographic reproductions of documents at Kendal are published by kind permission of the Cumbria Record Office. Reproduction of material from the Fleming letters and papers (WD/Ry) is by kind permission of Mrs J. I. H. Curwen of Rydal and Mrs D. E. Stockley of Charles, near Barnstaple.

Finally, we are grateful to John Davey, Fay Sharman and Maureen Verity who have all helped with the production of this book and given good advice.

Ivy Farm Barn,
Lode,
April 1980   *near Cambridge*

Some of the Principal Characters

(*Note*: Gentleman and yeoman denote status; husbandman denotes status and also occupation — in agriculture; farmer denotes occupation in agriculture. All places are in Westmorland unless otherwise stated.)

Edward Bainbridge of Mansergh: burglar and coin clipper; yeoman and farmer.

John Bainbridge of Mansergh: elder brother of Edward and suspected accomplice.

Margaret Bainbridge of Middleton: victim of burglary; widow of gentleman; related through her husband to Edward and John Bainbridge.

Edward Bradrick of Leeds, Yorkshire: highwayman and coin clipper; gentleman.

Margaret Bradrick: wife of Edward.

James Dawson of Old Hutton: a chief witness and arbitrator; whitesmith.

Joseph Dawson of Old Hutton: suspected accomplice of coin clippers; whitesmith, son of James Dawson.

Henry Dixon of Middleton and Bentham, Yorkshire: suspected accomplice of Bainbridge and Smorthwait; married to widow Alice Smorthwait, mother of William.

Sir Daniel Fleming of Rydal Hall: Justice of the Peace and chief investigator; gentleman.

William Foster of Tatham, Lancashire: coin clipper; gentleman.

John Jackson of Old Hutton; suspected burglar; yeoman and miller.

John Jackson of Mansergh: suspected burglar and accomplice; husbandman; possibly the same person as the other John Jackson.

Sir George Jeffreys of London: Chief Justice of England and Northern Assize Judge.

Edmund Lodge of Old Hutton and Clapham, Yorkshire: suspected coin clipper and accomplice of thieves; curate, schoolmaster and vicar.

Margaret Lodge: wife of Edmund.

Robert Robinson of Old Hutton: victim of burglary; gentleman and sometime High Constable.

Thomas Robinson: son of Robert.

George Scaif of Old and New Hutton: pickpocket and accomplice of burglars;
tailor.

Thomas Scaif of Hutton in the Hay: witness, husbandman; brother of George
Scaif.

Gerard Scaif of Thornton, Yorkshire: suspected receiver of stolen goods; not
known to be related to George and Thomas Scaif.

William Smorthwait of Middleton and Austwick, Yorkshire: burglar, highwayman and coin clipper; gentleman and farmer, sometime High Constable.

Henry Smorthwait of Middleton and New Hutton: burglar, highwayman and
coin clipper; yeoman and farmer; younger brother of William Smorthwait.

Alice Smorthwait of Middleton and Bentham, Yorkshire: mother of William
and Henry Smorthwait and later married to Henry Dixon (see above).

Bryan Thompson of Kirkby Lonsdale: burglar and receiver of stolen goods;
glazier, farmer and alehouse keeper.

Thomas Wilson of New Hutton: witness; his daughter married to Henry
Smorthwait.

Abbreviations and Conventions

Place of publication of all books is London, unless otherwise specified.

CRO   Cumberland Record Office, now Cumbria Record Office, Carlisle

LRO   Lancashire Record Office, Preston

PRO   Public Record Office, London

WRO   Westmorland Record Office, now Cumbria Record Office, Kendal

TCWAAS   *Transactions of the Cumberland and Westmorland Archaeological and Antiquarian Society*

Spelling, punctuation and capitalization have been modernized in all the quotations. Place and personal names have been standardized and made to conform with modern usage, and dates are in new style, with the year starting on 1st January. Abbreviations have been expanded, except in the quotations from the notes kept by Daniel Fleming.

Since much of the material comes from legal depositions, where there is a good deal of repetition and semi-redundant wording, the following alterations and omissions have been made: 'this examinate' is changed to 'he' or 'she', unless the meaning is ambiguous; 'said' and 'aforesaid' are omitted; the residence and county are omitted if they have already been specified.

Ordinary parentheses in quotations are in the original document; square brackets indicate insertions by the author. Obscure and technical terms are listed in the glossary.

The old counties of Westmorland, Cumberland and the West Riding of Yorkshire are constantly referred to, though much of this area is now within the newly fabricated county of Cumbria.

The old form of coinage, with 12 pence (*d*) to the shilling (*s*) and 20 shillings to the pound (£), has been retained. One pound is now worth less than a thirtieth of what it was in the 1680s.

How were men tried? There is no better touchstone for a social system than this question.

Marc Bloch, *Feudal Society*

Certainly to any one who has an eye for historic greatness it is a very marvellous institution, this Commission of the Peace, growing so steadily, elaborating itself into ever new forms, providing for ever new wants, expressing ever new ideas, and yet never losing its identity. . . We shall hardly find any other political entity which has had so eventful and yet so perfectly continuous a life. And then it is so purely English, perhaps the most distinctively English part of all our governmental organization.

F. W. Maitland, *Collected Papers*

More than this, the notion of the regulation and reconciliation of conflicts through the rule of law . . . seems to me a cultural achievement of universal significance. . . And since some part of the inheritance from this cultural moment may still be found, within greatly changed contexts, within the United States or India or certain African countries, it is important to re-examine the pretensions of the imperialist donor.

E. P. Thompson, *Whigs and Hunters: the Origins of the Black Act*

There is no jewel in the world comparable to learning; no learning so excellent both for prince and subject, as knowledge of laws; and no knowledge of any laws (I speak of human) so necessary for all estates and for all causes, concerning goods, lands, or life, as the common laws of England. If the beauty of other countries be faded and wasted with bloody wars, thank God for the admirable peace, wherein this realm hath long flourished under the due administration of these laws; if thou readest of the tyranny of other nations, wherein powerful will and pleasure stands for law and reason, and where, upon conceit of mislike, men are suddenly poisoned, or otherwise murdered, and never called to answer; praise God for the justice of thy gracious Sovereign.

Sir Edward Coke, *The Second Part of the Reports*

Introduction: The Rediscovery of Violence

The apparently rising tide of physical violence at the national and inter-national level today gives the historical study of crime and social control a special relevance. For those who wish to investigate patterns over a long period of time the history of England is a particularly fruitful area for study. England is unique in two ways. Firstly, its judicial records stretch in an unbroken and magnificent series back to the thirteenth century; they are more complete and of longer duration than those for any nation in the world, with the possible exception of Japan. Secondly, England is generally acknowledged to have been the first 'modern' centralized nation-state, which means that it was the first to establish the rule of law and to control violence. If we were able to determine how and when this happened and to use these unsurpassed records for a study of patterns of crime, we would make a contribution to the understanding of problems which are still of importance.

It is now widely believed that the major turning point — the final eradication of endemic violence and the personality changes associated with it — has only occurred recently, probably during the period between 1700 and 1850. But it is only during the last half century that historians have rediscovered this great truth, although there have long been those who were aware of it. In the later eighteenth century the great historians and philosophers of the Scottish Enlightenment came to find that only in their own century did England finally escape from the barbarities and unlicensed violence of that feudal age into which Europe had sunk after the destruction of Rome. According to Adam Smith and David Hume, for example, feudal England was in a state of perpetual war, of decentralized anarchy:

> After the institution of feudal subordination, the king was as incapable of restraining the violence of the great lords as before. They still continued

to make war according to their own discretion, almost continually upon one another and very frequently upon the king; and the open country still continued to be a scene of violence, rapine, and disorder.[1]

The change occurred gradually between the late fifteenth and eighteenth centuries and was caused by the rise of a market economy: 'Commerce and manufactures gradually introduced order and good government, and with them, the liberty and security of individuals, among the inhabitants of the country, who had before lived almost in a continual state of war with their neighbours, and of servile dependency upon their superiors.'[2] Thus the eradication of violence and the rise of what would later be called 'capitalism' were seen to be linked even then.

Another early historian who seems to have been well aware of the great transformation and of the fact that endemic violence was stamped out very late was Lord Macaulay. The savagery which had been widespread all over England in the dark days before the Glorious Revolution of 1688 lingered on longest in the outlying parts of the country, for civility and civilization only gradually spread outwards from London. One vignette which epitomizes this realization may be quoted.

> In truth a large part of the country beyond Trent was, down to the eighteenth century, in a state of barbarism. Physical and moral causes had concurred to prevent civilization from spreading to that region. . . . In the reign of Charles the Second, the traces left by ages of slaughter and pillage were still distinctly perceptible, many miles south of the Tweed, in the face of the country and in the lawless manners of the people. There was still a large class of mosstroopers, whose calling was to plunder dwellings and to drive away whole herds of cattle. . . . The seats of the gentry and the larger farmhouses were fortified. Oxen were penned at night beneath the overhanging battlements of the residence, which was known by the name of Peel. The inmates slept with arms at their sides. . . . No traveller ventured into that country without making his will. . . . The irregular vigour with which criminal justice was administered shocked observers whose life had been passed in more tranquil districts. Juries, animated by hatred and by a sense of common danger, convicted housebreakers and cattle stealers with the promptitude of a court martial in a mutiny; and the convicts were hurried by scores to the gallows.[3]

---

[1] Adam Smith, *An Inquiry into the Nature and Causes of the Wealth of Nations* (5th edn, 1789; University of Chicago Press, 1976), edited by Edwin Cannan, I, p. 437. For Hume's views see David Hume, *The History of England from the Invasion of Julius Caesar to the Revolution in 1688* (1754–61; University of Chicago Press, 1975), abridged edn, introduction by R. W. Kilcup, pp. xl, 13, 40, 86–8.
[2] Smith, *Wealth of Nations* I, p. 433.
[3] Thomas Babington Macaulay, *History of England* 1848; (Everyman edn, 1906) I, pp. 213–14.

Northumberland and the borders were the location of the extreme and lingering remains of the earlier state of affairs, whose brutishness and boorishness are widely described in Macaulay's works. His view was based on contemporary sources and was to be substantiated by the publication of contemporary legal records. In the preface to an edition of northern Assize depositions for the seventeenth century, James Raine wrote:

> Of the social position and character of the people of the north during the seventeenth century it is impossible to speak with commendation. The depositions give us a very unvarnished tale. . . . The convulsions in the state had shattered the foundations of society, and many vices had sprung up which were congenial to the period, and which the rulers treated with that unequal justice that is so detrimental to the morals and happiness of the people.

In Cumberland and Northumberland, for example, 'every village had its party of thieves; every family had its own feuds and wrongs to avenge. No one could go to rest with the certainty of finding his cattle in his fold when he arose in the morning.'[4] There had thus been a revolution in sentiments and structure, from a 'pre-modern' society to the world which Smith, Hume and Macaulay found themselves living in.

During the second half of the nineteenth century it appears that there was a growing divergence between professional historians, primarily interested in national institutions, and amateur historians or antiquarians, some of whom concentrated on local records. Throughout the period and during the first years of the twentieth century a number of local record societies published sets of records in which the editors continued in the same vein as James Raine. In other words, they continued to be shocked by and disapproving of the violence which they found in the records of Quarter Sessions and other jurisdictions.[5] At the same time, the chairs of history were held by men whose work began to imply a different view. Exploring the treasure of the Public Record Office rather than local records, they were struck less by the violence and brutality and strangeness of the past than by the enormous order, centralization and continuity between past and present. Their research was never directly concerned with violence as such and it is therefore difficult to infer from their silence their views on this matter. But what is striking in the work of the greatest of these historians, namely

---

[4] *Depositions from the Castle of York, relating to offences committed in the North Counties in the Seventeenth Century* (Surtees Society, XL, 1861), pp. xiii–xiv, xi.

[5] I owe this point to Dr J. S. Morrill: for another example see J. W. Bund(ed.), *Worcestershire County Records: Calendar of Quarter Session Papers, 1591–1643* (Worcester County Council, 1900). Not all Victorian antiquarians were prepared to infer the presence of widespread violence from these records alone; for example, see John Lister (ed.), *West Riding Sessions Rolls, 1598–1602* (Yorkshire Archaelogical and Topographical Association, Records Series, III, 1888), preface, especially p. xxxix.

Stubbs and Maitland, is that they give very little impression of a revolutionary break between past and present. They accepted of course, that there was continuous change, but their work gives no sense of a recognition that one kind of uncivilized and violent society had suddenly given way in the sixteenth and seventeenth centuries to a civilized and non-violent one. Bearing in mind that we are discussing only an indirect impression, a negative feature of their work deduced from what they did concentrate on, let us pause briefly to examine their views.

William Stubbs (1825–1901), bishop of Oxford and Regius Professor of Modern History at Oxford, was a man of great erudition. As the leading authorities on his work have written:

> All that we know of Stubbs inspires confidence, confidence in the solidity and extent of his knowledge, the honesty of his criticism, the sureness of his judgement, the depth of his practical experience of men and things. . . . The *Constitutional History* . . . is the fruit of prodigious labour, of a thorough investigation of the printed sources which a historian could consult. . . . It is an admirable storehouse of facts, well chosen, and set forth with scrupulous good faith.[6]

Petit-Dutaillis and Lefebvre have amended his work in a number of ways, but his major interpretation has been left unchallenged. This interpretation stresses the continuity of the linguistic, constitutional and legal features of England. The basic structure of England, Stubbs believed, was laid down very early, by the thirteenth century at least. He writes that 'The great characteristic of the English constitutional system is the continuous development of representative institutions from the first elementary stage. . . . The nation becomes one and realizes its oneness. . . . It is completed under Henry II and his sons.'[7] He recognized, of course, that there were considerable turmoils and political changes ahead. But he believed that the basic nature of the nation did not change:

> The constitution . . . reached its formal and definite maturity under Edward I. . . . The continuity of life, and the continuity of national purpose, never fails: even the great struggle of all [sic], the long labour that extends from the Reformation to the Revolution [i.e. 1688], leaves the organization, the origins of which we have been tracing, unbroken in its conscious identity, stronger in the strength which it has preserved, and grown mightier through trial.[8]

[6] Ch. Petit-Dutaillis and Georges Lefebvre, *Studies and Notes Supplementary to Stubbs' Constitutional History* (Manchester, 1930), p. v.
[7] William Stubbs, *The Constitutional History of England in its Origin and Development* (5th edn, Oxford, 1891) I, pp. 584–5.
[8] *ibid.* I, p. 682.

There is no notion here or elsewhere of a basic shift from one kind of society to another, from a world where people thought and felt in one way, to a 'modern' world where they think, feel and act in another. This was not because Stubbs was blind to change. He acknowledged that the sixteenth and seventeenth centuries 'witnessed a series of changes in national life, mind, and character, in the relations of the classes, and in the balance of political forces, far greater than the English race had gone through since the Norman Conquest.'[9] These he listed as the Reformation, the change from the baronage to a nobility, and the 'recovered strength of the monarchic principle'. But he did not seem to be aware of a revolutionary change in character or in the nature of political integration.

If we turn to Stubbs's occasional speculations on social structure, he again stresses continuity, especially among the bulk of the population.

> As we descend in the scale of social rank the differences between medieval and modern life rapidly diminish; the habits of a modern nobleman differ from those of his fifteenth-century ancestor far more widely than those of the peasantry of to-day from those of the middle ages, even when the increase of comfort and culture has been fairly frequent throughout.[10]

His picture of medieval life suggests a world very similar to that of the eighteenth century, divided into gentry, tradesmen and yeomanry, with a great deal of social and geographical mobility, wealth, markets, wage labour and security. Perhaps most significant is the style of his writing and his omissions. There is no hint that he looked on people in the past as living in a violent and lawless society. Nor does it seem to have entered his head that either in terms of mind or emotions they were somehow basically a different, a 'lower' species, more brutal, instinctual, simple-minded. The insights of Hume and Macaulay were lost.

A man who should have been even better placed than Stubbs to see the great divide was F. W. Maitland. Like Stubbs, he was fully conversant with work written in German and French and knew a great deal both about England and the Continent. He was familiar with contemporary anthropology and prodigiously learned. He is widely regarded as one of the greatest of English historians: as K. B. McFarlane graphically wrote, 'As we look back over the whole range [of past historians] from a distance, we can see that the summit of Mount Maitland overtops them all. What other English historian has combined such exact scholarship with so much imaginative insight, intellectual grasp, and brilliance of exposition?'[11] Yet we seek in vain for traces of the realization that England had changed from one kind of society to another, and that English character had changed with

[9] *ibid.* III, p. 3.
[10] *ibid.* III, p. 570.
[11] K. B. McFarlane, 'Mount Maitland', in *New Statesman*, 4 June 1965, p. 882.

it. Maitland seems convinced throughout his works that by the thirteenth century, at least, the legal and hence the social structure of England is of the same nature as that some five centuries later. For example, by the time of the death of Henry II (1272), 'English law is modern in its uniformity, its simplicity, its certainty.'[12] The whole basic structure of law was laid out early. The continuity of English laws means that 'the law of the later middle ages has never been forgotten among us. It has never passed utterly outside the cognizance of our courts and our practising lawyers. We have never had to disinter and reconstruct it in that laborious and tentative manner in which German historians of the present day have disinterred and reconstructed the law of medieval Germany.'[13] He made no modifications in his *Constitutional History* to Stubbs's general vision of the continuity of the political structure since the later middle ages. 'Take any institution that exists at the end of the middle ages, any that exists in 1800 — be it parliament, or privy council, or any of the courts of law — we can trace it back through a series of definite changes as far as Edward's reign.'[14] Maitland's picture of later medieval England is diametrically opposed to that implied by Hume and Macaulay. He viewed it as a society dominated by contract, by common law, by powerful central government. The ground-plan of constitutional, legal, political and social history had early been laid down. Given this similarity with the present, he does not discuss the possibility that the ordinary people who lived in that world were basically more brutal, violent or 'simple', that their family system, mentality, social structure was somehow that of a 'pre-modern' kind, totally different from that of his own world. Maitland's vision of the thirteenth century has been summarized by the foremost exponent of his work as follows:

> The world into which Maitland's real actions fit is essentially a flat world, inhabited by equal neighbours. Lordship is little more than a servitude over the land of another, and its content is fixed and economic. The services and incidents are important, but the law relating to them is self-contained, unrelated to other questions; and distress of chattels is all that is left of direct seignorial control. To the creation and protection of rights over land in general, the Lord is fundamentally irrelevant.[15]

This picture is one which minimizes the political power of lords and stresses the strength of economic and governmental ties.

[12] Sir F. Pollock and F. W. Maitland, *History of English Law before the Time of Edward I* (2nd edn, Cambridge, 1968) I, p. 225.
[13] *ibid.* I, p. civ.
[14] F. W. Maitland, *The Constitutional History of England* (Cambridge, 1919), p. 20.
[15] Milsom in Pollock and Maitland, *History of English Law*, I, p. xlvii.

It took the next seventy years after the death of Maitland in 1906 to rediscover the full violence and degraded brutality of the inhabitants of England up to the eighteenth century. This rediscovery was made possible by the combination of new ideas of how societies work, derived from the discipline of sociology, with the use of new records by national historians. In a sense, it could be argued that the gap between national and local or antiquarian history which had opened up in the later nineteenth century has been closed. National historians began to make increasing use of the records of Quarter Sessions and other courts which dealt with violence. Thus there had been a shift in interest, in expectations about the past, and in the nature of the material used. Although it is always invidious to do so, perhaps we may select a few of the studies completed during the last seventy years, which show us how it has been possible to return to a Macaulayite vision of the past, but at the same time illustrate how the shadow of the great Victorians lay over the earlier social historians. For a while, therefore, their works were somewhat hesitant and inconsistent, as if they were looking in two directions — towards an idea of continuity and a past inhabited by sophisticated and complex individuals, and yet more and more towards an idea of a major revolution in structure and sentiment. The latter concept, most powerfully embodied in the thought of the great German and French sociologists. Marx, Weber and Durkheim, increasingly made historians aware that one kind of special system, 'pre-capitalist' or 'feudal' or 'peasant', had turned into another, 'capitalist' or 'modern'. With this structural change there was bound to be a vast change in law, in the patterns of crime and violence, and in human mentality and emotions.

Our first illustration of shifts in historical perception can be taken from a work which explored in a national context just those records which antiquarians had edited and found full of so much violence. In a book published in 1919, Eleanor Trotter based a general account of parish life very considerably on the records of the Justices of the Peace, particularly those of the North Riding of Yorkshire. In most of the book, Trotter described in great detail a system of highly regulated and, on the whole, efficient and centralized justice and administration. It was not a new system and it suggested a law-abiding and largely non-violent society. She showed the many tasks and duties of the churchwardens, the overseers of the poor, the petty constables. Everything appeared to be carefully regulated and violence and corruption were kept at an amazingly low level. It is a world conforming more to Maitland's vision than to Macaulay's. But suddenly, in a chapter entitled 'Rogues and Vagabonds', the author presents a different interpretation. We are reminded that 'undoubtedly the seventeenth century inherited a train of vagabonds who were the product of the sixteenth. . . . The period was one of transition; the growth of capitalism in manufacture and the system of enclosure of land were hurtful to the small farmer or trader, though possibly beneficial to this community.'[16] The dislocation, and the image of a disintegrating feudal world, is shown elsewhere:

> These vagrants were a terror to rich and poor; in an age when the larger half of mankind was emerging from a state of serfdom, when passions were fierce and uncontrolled, the bands of wandering beggars were as great a terror to country districts as if they had been brigands. The cause of their existence was in large measure due to unemployment.[17]

Rather curiously, Trotter then reverts to the theme of order and efficiency, discussing the intricate system of local justice executed by the Justices of the Peace. The passions which were so 'fierce and uncontrolled' are forgotten.

The sources were further expanded in another pioneering work, first published in 1942. Mildred Campbell made extensive use of diaries, account books and contemporary pamphlets to supplement the local records of the courts. There is the same hesitation and inconsistency in the final product. Most of the book is devoted to showing how affluent, sophisticated, organized and self-disciplined were the middling ranks of England in the sixteenth and seventeenth centuries. When the author reflects directly on the question of violence and order, she continues partly in this vein.

'Country roads and village streets after dark were probably safer than they had ever been in England. . . . There were laws, and courts where wrongs might be righted, and where a man could be held to his bargain if it were in writing.'[18] But alongside this, a new dimension emerges suddenly, of violence and disorder. We are told that the Elizabethan yeomen 'were no self-controlled, submissive lot.' Despite the preceding remark about the safety of the roads, we are assured that 'nobody trusted too much to this. . . . A yeoman riding to and from fairs and markets, or on other business, usually carried a pike, staff, or other weapon, particularly if he were alone.' This was because although 'the preservation of the king's peace was a fairly well-established ideal . . . life was held rather cheap and quarrels and brawls that resulted in bloodshed were a commonplace.' We are then given a 'typical' description of a local disorder, with a group of men and their servants and womenfolk assembling armed with pitchforks and other weapons and entering someone's property.[19] These were rough times, when 'physical injuries, and not infrequently loss of life, were the toll of neighbourhood quarrels and local drinking bouts.' A number of brawls are

[16] Eleanor Trotter, *Seventeenth-Century Life in the Country Parish, with Special Reference to Local Government* (Cambridge, 1919), p. 176.
[17] *ibid.* p. 163.
[18] Mildred Campbell, *The English Yeoman Under Elizabeth and the Early Stuarts* (New Haven, 1942), p. 364.
[19] *idem.*

then described and the theme of rural peasants and their family vendettas is emphasized. We are told that 'a good deal of the feud element was still present in neighbourhood relationships. Country memories are long, and grudges carefully nursed were handed down from father to son.'[20]

The author's hesitation, and the general impression which the book conveys of an orderly and affluent society, probably arises from the fact that, after a very considerable amount of research on primary materials for a nation of several million persons over a period of eighty years, she found very few cases of physical violence and brutality. The yeomanry she was studying were in the front line of the assault by capitalism on the older feudal social structure; they were also among the victims of this attack. Yet their account books, diaries and appearances in court seem to give only a rather limited amount of evidence to confirm the view of turbulent transition and violence which the author half expected to find. Nor does she seem to have regarded her subjects as somehow of an inferior, more degraded and brutal race than herself. It needed imagination, combined with a greater acquaintance with sociology and with legal records, to enable historians to rediscover the great transition.

One of the earliest to make the rediscovery was Wallace Notestein, a scholar with a good knowledge of constitutional history, diaries and legal records. In his work we see, for the first time since Macaulay, the full idea that not only was life before the eighteenth century taking place in a world of endemic violence, but that this was related to the fact that people were somehow different in their character structure at that time. In his widely read textbook published in 1954 he portrays a society which would have been familiar to Macaulay. England was still a very violent place. Although 'violence on a large scale was out of the question', he believed that 'petty violence was not far under the surface of life in some place.' This was especially the case in the north, as Macaulay had realized: 'In the Yorkshire dales an old Norse fury would break forth and groups of more-or-less armed men would march across the moors to attack a house or to occupy fields of which they claimed ownership; occasionally they were able to terrorize justices and to frighten sheriffs.'[21] The explanation of this violence is related to both the character of the people and to the general poverty and backwardness of the society. Notestein had discovered that 'a lack of compassion was characteristic of many. People gathered by hundreds to watch executions. . . . The interest of common men and women in the whipping of vagrants and in the ducking of miserable women was unwholesome.' Whole villages were inhabited by 'backward' and 'criminal' types. Notestein

[20] *ibid.* pp. 365 ff.
[21] Wallace Notestein, *The English People on the Eve of Colonization, 1603–1630* (1954; Harper Torchbook edn, 1962), pp. 13–14.

regrets that 'of some villages, indeed, little good can be said.' To be more specific, 'many hamlets in Gloucestershire and Worcestershire, in the moorlands of the north, and even in the counties near the capital abounded in rude people who lived miserably and were up to little good.'[22]

Yet we should not be too harsh on them, for, as Notestein argues, they were a brutalized and pre-modern type of man. 'These remote villagers must not be judged by modern standards. Serfdom and numbing poverty had been the lot of their ancestors, and they themselves were seldom better off.' Their physical impoverishment explains their mental childishness, he argues. 'They had little to think about except their beasts, their fields, and the common; the neighbour and the wrong he had done. Their minds had been too much occupied with small matters to look at things from another's point of view.'[23] Their childishness was not just shown in their violence, but in their whole personality. They lacked individual characteristics and sophistication. On the basis of paintings and diaries, Notestein had come to the conclusion in an earlier work that of people in the seventeenth century in general it could be said:

> Their philosophy was standardized and of a piece; the individual had not yet — or rarely — made his own attempt at truth and unity. Their faith was more readily useful than ours, their passions were immediate and more easily shifted, like those of the young; their codes more black and white, their aspirations more in a straight line, their pleasures less sophisticated and often childlike.[24]

Of course there were exceptions, fictional creatures such as Hamlet or real people like Brilliana Harley's brother. But these exceptions were a strange mutation; indeed, if it were not absolutely certain, we would be tempted to believe that the proof of their conception or existence at that early date were forgeries. Thus Dorothy Osborne 'left letters so whimsical and full of implications that the doubting historian looks again and again at her handwriting in the British Museum to make sure that he has not been tricked. She fits into no formulas and belongs in no regular seventeenth century frame.'[25]

It is not just that the rural villagers are violent and pre-modern: all those living before the eighteenth century are strangers. Notestein compares the portraits of seventeenth- and eighteenth-century people. In the nineteenth century, one is in a period where there is 'much subtlety and sophistication and fineness of spirit', for these men and women belonged 'to a highly civilized society'. But when Notestein looks at the portraits of the sixteenth

[22] *ibid.* pp. 14–15.
[23] *ibid.* p. 15.
[24] Wallace Notestein, *English Folk: a Book of Characters* (1938), p. 30.
[25] *idem.*

and seventeenth centuries, 'you are in another England and among strangers.' Like the proverbial Chinese to the western eye, they all look alike: 'The men of that time look more like one another. . . . They are less English than the men on the first floor.'[26] This is a view confirmed by diaries and autobiographies. After studying them at length, Notestein concluded that 'about all those seventeenth century figures there is a kind of grayness apparent even to one long familiar with them.' Notestein dismisses the argument that this is the result of an inability to express complexities in canvas or on paper. It is because people in the seventeenth century were basically not 'as complicated creatures as we'.[27] Modern man's greater complexity and sophistication, the fact that we have 'ampler and more variegated personalities', can be linked to a number of factors, Notestein thinks. Particularly, it is due to 'the complexity of modern life', which means that, as compared to people in the seventeenth century and before, 'We have new sensitiveness, new types of unselfishness, new forms of high-mindedness, of which neither our forefathers nor their imaginary creations ever dreamed.'[28]

Notestein was only one of those who had discovered the simplicity, violence and difference of life before the eighteenth century. Another very widely read author of the time was A. L. Rowse who, in a general book published in 1950, basing himself on sources fairly like those of Notestein, came to a similar conclusion concerning the prevalence of violence. Writing about the functions of the Justice of the Peace, Rowse stated that 'one cannot overestimate the violence latent in society; and in the palpitating, ragged, vigorous life of the Elizabethan age, just emerged from the insecurity and endemic strife of medieval society, the violence of men's impulses was as often as not uninhibited and released.' This violence stretched from top to bottom of society and led to very high rates of crime. 'Stealing and robbery were endemic. . . . Murder and manslaughter were frequent, there were constant fights and affrays ending in wounding or death.' The reasons for this widespread brutality are clear to Rowse: 'Life in a world where pestilence and famine were regular, was indeed very cheap.' For an analogy with such a world, Rowse suggests that we take the supposedly bloodthirsty society of an east Mediterranean society. 'Those who know the Middle East today know what the middle ages were like in these respects with us.' Thus Rowse warns us not to be 'surprised at the brutality of the world, outside the happier West', for 'it is the human condition; it was once our own.'[29]

[26] Notestein, *English People on the Eve of Colonization*, p. 34. Notestein is talking of the portraits in the National Portrait Gallery in London; hence the reference to 'the first floor' is to the nineteenth-century portraits, then displayed on that floor.

[27] *ibid.* p. 35.

[28] *idem.*

[29] A. L. Rowse, *The England of Elizabeth* (1950), pp. 344, 345, 348.

Between 1950 and the late 1960s the amount of accessible legal records, especially those of the Sessions of the Peace, increased even more with the establishment and reorganization of local record offices and publication of further documents. Thus when C. Bridenbaugh examined the same question as Notestein and Rowse, namely what kind of society was England in the later sixteenth and early seventeenth centuries, he was able to base his account on an even wider range of materials than his predecessors. In a work published in 1968, he documented the side-effects of the great transition from one kind of economy to another. 'The half-century after 1590 was a time of profound, unprecedented, and often frightening social ferment for the people of England', for 'although conditions were steadily improving — these were the years in which England was developing a capitalistic economy — the old undeveloped, agrarian society did not adjust with sufficient rapidity to provide employment for the thousands of labouring poor.'[30] Thus during this period, 'War, enclosures, political grievances, uneven application of the law, combined with depressions, epidemic diseases, and food shortages, manifested themselves like boils on an otherwise sound body politic.' Reacting to these 'boils', the 'hard-pressed people were frustrated, desperate, restive.' There was a general 'loosening' of the social fabric, 'of family and church ties'. and the result was that 'drunkenness and immorality increased along with crime and violence as idleness and mischance forced helpless thousands down into the ranks of the defenceless poor.'[31] It was this desperation that brutalized people: 'Even those who themselves were sorely troubled and suffering greatly exhibited a callous indifference to the misery and anxieties of their fellow men.' Although the author concedes that 'the bulk of the people, even in the cities, were honest, moral, law-abiding, well-behaved, decent and relatively pious',[32] a large part of the book is concerned with chronicling the rise in fraud and cheating, the widespread drunkenness, the increase in sexual immorality. Poverty was at the root of much of this, especially the widespread thieving. 'If anyone of that day had reflected on the extreme want apparent in every village and town, he should not have been surprised at the amount of petty thievery, breaking and entering, and robbery on the highways.' It was a violent society, filled with rogues and vagabonds. 'Of particular concern to rural villages were "the Roaring Country Lads", able-bodied males who crowded the highways and, during their wanderings, infested the highways and attended markets and fairs.'[33] The 'rough conduct on the part of both men and women', which was 'a familiar feature of daily life in England', was 'crowned by crimes of violence.'[34] This turbulence was clearly a

[30] Carl Bridenbaugh, *Vexed and Troubled Englishmen 1590–1642* (Oxford, 1968), p. 355.
[31] *ibid*. p. 356.
[32] *ibid*. p. 361.
[33] *ibid*. pp. 379, 386.
[34] *ibid*. p. 387.

side-effect of commercialization and capitalism. In fact it was this poverty and violence that led to the emigration to America, according to Bridenbaugh.[35]

Both Notestein and Bridenbaugh depended heavily on the exceptional legal records of the county of Essex, which are not only the earliest for England but the best organized. Two recent studies of the Essex records lend support to their views. One is by Joel Samaha, and is largely a statistical analysis of Assize records for the Elizabethan period.[36] He finds that 'A plethora of legal records which begin in the reign of Philip and Mary verifies the general impressions that contemporary critics and modern historians have portrayed — a society of growing lawlessness measured by swelling felony statistics.'[37] Elizabethan felons 'tended to follow the rhythm of the seasons and the agricultural year in this criminal behaviour.'[38] The rising crime rates were a result of a shift to a market economy, where the falling standard of labourers, growing proletarianization led to many desperate crimes.[39] Summarizing the central conclusion of the work, Samaha states that 'the crimes committed and the punishments suffered by ordinary men and women in Essex mirror the pain that was attendant in the beginning of the great transformation of England from a pre-industrial to a modern society.'[40]

Samaha is mainly concerned with figures. A much more striking impression is created by the work of F. G. Emmison, who deals with the court leet cases. He reminds us that 'it goes without saying that the human tendency towards assault is well represented', and gives a sample of the 'thousands of routine assault cases'.[41] In his book on *Elizabethan Life: Morals and the Church Courts* (1973), extensive quotations from the plentiful ecclesiastical court records gives further evidence of sexual violence and brutality. But the central work concerned with violence is based on the unique Quarter Sessions records, on the calendar of Assize Rolls and on pleas in Queen's Bench. This work of over 300 pages, mostly devoted to giving summaries and extracts from the records, covers a county of more than 50,000 persons for a period of over forty years. Thus the author admits that 'Essex is a large county, and Elizabeth's reign was a long one.'[42] Yet, even taking this into consideration, the impression created by the extracts is indeed one of violence and disorder. As well as numerous minor assaults, there were brutal murders and homicides. Emmison narrates a number of cases of homicide, which are, he believes 'all violent cases, but typical, we may

[35] *ibid.* p. 394.
[36] Joel Samaha, *Law and Order in Historical Perspective: the Case of Elizabethan Essex* (1974).
[37] *ibid.* p. 13.
[38] *ibid.* p. 23.
[39] *ibid.* pp. 32, 34–5.
[40] *ibid.* p. 113.
[41] F. G. Emmison, *Elizabethan Life: Home, Work and Land* (Chelmsford, 1976), pp. 223–4.
[42] F. G. Emmison, *Elizabethan Life: Disorder* (Chelmsford, 1970), p. 129.

assume, of what was happening all over the country in every decade of Elizabeth's reign.'[43] Libel and slander were 'a ubiquitous and everyday feature of Elizabethan life', even though they seldom led to indictments at the Quarter Sessions and Assizes.[44] Again, 'infanticide was woefully common',[45] a fact known not from the mere thirty cases recorded in the records over these years, but from the deduction that these were only the tip of the iceberg: 'There were probably many other violent deaths by smothering or bruising which were concealed from the coroner.'[46] And, although highway robbery is largely absent from the formal records, yet 'how many people were robbed without the rascals being charged must, of course, be a matter of pure speculation. A number between five and ten times greater is perhaps a fair estimate.'[47] The high (invisible) rate of violence and crime was related to the ineffectiveness of the policing system. 'Many constables were of course ignorant fellows. . . . The majority probably loathed their term of office. . . . Assaults on them and on the bailiffs . . . form a vital element in Elizabethan disorder.'[48] Thus, through a very detailed study of all the local records, Emmison is able to convey a picture of disorder, violence, hot tempers and lack of control as central features of Elizabethan village life. The cumulative evidence of numerous stories of assault and theft, the figures of 'the vast number of cases of larceny, housebreaking, burglary, closebreaking and highway robbery' add considerable weight to the earlier speculations of the authors we have examined.[49]

In this way, through an increased use of the documents for social history, account books, diaries, legal and local records, two main things have been rediscovered. First, that the sixteenth and seventeenth centuries were a time of violent upsurge, with high crime rates, physical brutality, a breakdown of law and order. This is true not just of the outlying regions of the north or west, but even in those areas near London which were the first to suffer the penetration of the new social and economic forces of capitalism. Secondly, this was not just a surface matter concerned with institutions, but was related to the fact that people before the eighteenth century were somehow different from us. This is clearly linked to violence. The insecurities of the world, particularly poverty and sudden death, made people brutal, and they then added to the insecurities by their sadistic and uncontrollable anger. This connection between generalized violence and the

[43] *ibid.* p. 148.
[44] *ibid.* p. 66.
[45] *ibid.* p. 156.
[46] *idem.*
[47] *ibid.* p. 275.
[48] *ibid.* p. 179.
[49] *ibid.* p. 256.

brutalization of the personality is most persuasively shown in the work of Lawrence Stone.

In the chapter on 'Power' in his *The Crisis of the Aristocracy* we are given a portrait of the transition from the endemic violence of the medieval period to the orderly society of the eighteenth century. The Tudors managed to control the upper levels of the society, but lower down, among the mass of yeomen and below, it was not until the growth of a police force in the ninteenth century that centralized control became 'effective in the greatest cities and the smallest villages. In the early twentieth century even the lower classes lost the habits of violence.'[50] The problem for the Tudors was that 'In the sixteenth and seventeenth centuries tempers were short and weapons to hand. The behaviour of the propertied classes, like that of the poor, was characterized by the ferocity, childishness, and lack of self-control of the Homeric age.'[51] The violence was partly a result of notions of honour and generosity inculcated by the educational and social system, partly a result of physiological causes. One reason may have been illness: people in the sixteenth century 'were so exceedingly irritable . . . possibly because they were nearly always ill.' Another may have been bad diet: 'The poor were victims of chronic malnutrition, the rich of chronic dyspepsia from over-indulgence in an ill-balanced diet: neither condition is conducive to calm and good humour.'[52]

The endemic lawlessness and violence were eliminated from the centre; they lingered longest in the more remote upland regions of England. In the sixteenth century in the 'Highland' zones, people 'still preferred traditional methods of settling disputes to obedience to the law. . . . The blood feud and blood-money remained an important element in the pattern of human relationships, operating quite outside any only partly effective legal machinery.'[53] The process is one of the gradual elimination of traditional violence: the 'irresponsible violence of word and deed, controlled hardly at all by the forces of order' of the medieval period was gradually brought under control, particularly the 'problem of feudal disorder in the Highland Zone'.[54] Violence was only directed into new channels: 'A consequence of the decline of violence was an astonishing growth in litigation. Societies being weaned from habits of private revenge always turn to the law with intemperate enthusiasm.'[55] In general Stone is charting the political dimension of the transition from 'feudalism' to 'capitalism' in this volume, with an exclusive emphasis upon the wealthiest

[50] Lawrence Stone, *The Crisis of the Aristocracy, 1558–1641* (abridged edn, Oxford, 1967), p. 97.
[51] *ibid.* p. 108.
[52] *idem.*
[53] *ibid.* p. 110.
[54] *ibid.* p. 113.
[55] *ibid.* p. 117.

and most powerful one per cent of the population. But continued violence was as prevalent among the lower orders and Stone has documented this in a more recent work.

There are frequent references to brutality and violence throughout this later work. For example, we are told that 'the late sixteenth and early seventeenth centuries were for England the great flogging age; every town and every village had its whipping-post, which was in constant use as a means of preserving social order.'[56] Stone refers to 'the extraordinary amount of casual inter-personal physical and verbal violence as recorded in legal and others records', which is evidence that 'at all levels men and women were extremely short-tempered.' This meant that 'the most trivial disagreements tended to lead rapidly to blows' and, since 'most people carried a potential weapon, if only a knife to cut their meat', the courts 'were clogged with cases of assault and battery.'[57] This violence was not confined to cities. 'In some villages throughout the sixteenth and much of the seventeenth centuries, both feuding among kin factions and personal hostility of one individual towards another were so intense that in the more backward areas it proved impossible to impose the normal discipline of parish worship.'[58] In this face-to-face world, 'it was possible for expressions of hatred to reach levels of frequency, intensity and duration which are rarely seen today.'[59] These 'habits of casual violence' were not balanced by friendliness or hospitality or love, 'for the violence of everyday life seems to have been accompanied by much mutual suspicion and a low general level of emotional interaction and commitment.'[60] The state of affairs is summed up in a description of a bitter and intolerant local community, which ends thus: 'The Elizabethan village was a place filled with malice and hatred, its only unifying bond being the occasional episode of mass hysteria, which temporarily bound together the majority in order to harry and persecute the local witch.'[61] But this coldness and hostility does not mean that emotions were absent, just that they were negative. 'Tempers were short, and both casual violence and venomous and mutually exhausting litigation against neighbours were extremely common' and this 'soaked up much psychic energy.' Also, 'from time to time emotional tensions obtained release in collective acts of persecution of some scapegoat, denounced as a witch or a heretic.' Stone summarizes the new vision of the sixteenth and seventeenth centuries, the triumph of the rediscovery of violence, as follows: 'What is being postulated for the sixteenth and early seventeenth centuries

---

[56] Lawrence Stone, *The Family, Sex and Marriage in England, 1500–1800* (1977), pp. 170–71.
[57] *ibid.* p. 93.
[58] *ibid.* p. 94.
[59] *ibid.* p.95.
[60] *idem.*
[61] *ibid.* p. 98.

is a society in which a majority of the individuals that composed it found it very difficult to establish close emotional ties to any other person. Children were neglected, brutally treated, and even killed; adults treated each other with suspicion and hostility; affect was low, and hard to find.'[62]

This view of a violent and brutal period is now widely accepted, for the rediscovery of the truth of Macaulay's views fits very well with the general theories of transition, from a disorderly feudal world through a period of crisis and violence, as a new type of society emerged and finally became calm again in the eighteenth century. As J. S. Cockburn writes, 'Historians have in general accepted this broad impression of a violent and increasingly delinquent society.'[63] Just two out of many instances can be given. Leslie Clarkson has written that:

> Violence was a general feature of pre-industrial society. . . . The occasions for blood-letting were endless, whether they were drunken brawls, matrimonial quarrels or economic disputes. In the countryside uncertainties about field boundaries or unreasonable claims for tithes from the clergy caused endless friction which sometimes flared into violence. . . . Economic hardship was at the bottom of much aggression. . . . The reasons why personal quarrels, economic deprivation, or differences of opinion over religion or politics so often took a violent turn were various. The regular processes of the law for settling disputes must have seemed to many people too remote, too slow, or too expensive. . . . The widespread habit of wearing daggers and swords meant that a rush of temper was all too often followed by a rush of blood. There was no regular police force to curb acts of aggression.[64]

A similar picture, citing Clarkson and Stone, is given by G. R. Quaife.

> In these tense troubled communities that made up the rural villages of seventeenth century England violence was always just below the surface, and frequently erupted. Almost every occasion had potential for blood-letting. . . . Stone hints at why dearth should find its outlet in part in violence, much of it pointless. He suggests that the childhood of most peasants, separated from their parents at an early age and subjected to brutal discipline, produced cruel, cold and suspicious adults liable to outbursts of aggressive hostility towards each other. He concludes that the average peasant was a short-tempered, malicious character who flared into physical violence on the flimsiest excuse. On the other hand these sudden outbursts may have provided a safety valve for frustrated

---

[62] *ibid.* p. 99.
[63] J. S. Cockburn (ed.), *Crime in England 1550–1800* (1977), p. 50.
[64] Leslie Clarkson, *Death, Disease and Famine in Pre-Industrial England* (1975), pp. 114–15.

men locked into their place in the hierarchy and subject to a multitude of pressures which they could not control.[65]

The violence is so striking a feature of society that we may be surprised at its apparent invisibility to the great Victorian historians. Furthermore, its full dimensions seem to have escaped even the earlier social historians, such as Trotter and Campbell from whom we quoted, while other great social and economic historians such as R. H. Tawney seem to have been only dimly aware of the fact that the sixteenth and seventeenth centuries were filled with a violent and brutalized peasantry and nobility.[66] We may therefore ask the question, why has it taken historians so long to realize such an obvious fact about the past?

There are a number of reasons. One stems from the underlying theories concerning the whole development of English society. Those who believed strongly in the continuity of English history were unlikely to expect or to see a period of violence and revolution as one type of society was shattered by another. On the other hand, those who have a general model of the emergence of modern capitalism and the nation state in the sixteenth century have a theory which predicts violence in the transition, and this makes it easier to find. They also have a view that people were basically 'peasants' up to the seventeenth century, and analogies with other peasantries have suggested to them that peasants are often characterized by mutual suspicion, hostility, physical violence. In other words, it has only been with the widespread acceptance of sociological theories of the great transition from 'traditional', 'peasant' societies to 'modern' and 'capitalist' ones that historians have really been able to approach the documents with expectations of violence and brutality. They knew what to find and the rediscovery of past violence has therefore directly paralleled the rediscovery of a great watershed in English history. This rediscovery has not been made easier by the nature of English historical sources which, on the surface, appeared for a long time to point in the opposite direction.

It seems that most of those who lived in the violent and turbulent world of the sixteenth and seventeenth centuries were poor observers of their own society and were singularly unaware of the coldness and simmering aggression around them. For example, the many who travelled through England

---

[65] G. R. Quaife, *Wanton Wenches and Wayward Wives* (1979), p. 25.

[66] Despite his belief in a massive transition, there is little evidence in Tawney's many works that he considered sixteenth-century 'peasants' as somehow more brutal and violent than modern folk. In fact, he believed that we would never really know their innermost thoughts and feelings: 'What manner of men these were in that personal life of which economics is but the squalid scaffolding . . . of the hopes and fears and aspirations of the men who tilled the fields . . . we know hardly more than of the Roman plebs, far less than of the democracy of Athens.' R. H. Tawney, *The Agrarian Problem in the Sixteenth Century* (1912; Harper Torchbook edn, 1967), p. 121.

in the late sixteenth and seventeenth centuries give a strong impression of an orderly, controlled and non-violent society.[67] Even those, like 'Drunken Barnabee,' who specialized in frequenting the most likely scenes of aggression — the pubs — noted scarcely any physical or verbal violence.[68] They often travelled alone and over long distances, sometimes through the supposedly wild north. Yet they were curiously blind to the facts which modern historians have discovered about their society. Those who wrote autobiographies and diaries during the period also show an almost complete ignorance of the violence that soaked their world, whether in the city like Pepys, or in a country village like Josselin, whether at the level of the gentry like Thomas Whythorne, or that of the apprentice like Roger Lowe or the journeyman tailor Wheatcroft. The very strong impression these autobiographical works give is of a society in which people were not moved by irrational anger and fury, where people did not live or travel in fear, where despite physical hardships there was a great deal of tenderness and affection.[69] This strange self-image of their own society has made it difficult for historians to see it as it really was.

They have been helped by a few general descriptions of the lawlessness of the times. But even these are not as helpful as they might be. For example, Macaulay, Stone and other historians have relied very heavily on a famous passage describing the wild state of the northern border written by a contemporary, Roger North.[70] Unfortunately, as North states, he is describing a vanished state of affairs, before 1603 and the Union of the crowns; furthermore he is explicitly describing Northumberland and it would be unsafe to generalize to other parts of the country. Another contemporary often quoted, the Essex vicar William Harrison who wrote his *Description of England* in 1587, also has to be treated with caution. Where his remarks can be checked, it is clear that he has resorted to hyperbole. For example, he stresses the assaults and thefts by rogues and vagabonds in Essex. Yet Emmison's recent study of the Essex records for the Elizabethan

---

[67] For example, Fynes Moryson, *An Itinerary* (1617; Glasgow, 1908), 4 vols; Jane M. Ewbank (ed.), *Antiquary on Horseback: the Collections of the Rev. Thos. Machell* (Kendal, 1963), written mainly in 1692; Christopher Morris (ed.), *The Journeys of Celia Fiennes* (1947), compiled mainly in 1702.

[68] *Barnabee's Journal* (7th edn. 1818), originally published in the first half of the seventeenth century, and probably written by the Kendal Justice of the Peace Richard Braithwait, who took the nickname 'Drunken Barnabee.'

[69] *The Diary of Samuel Pepys* (1970 onwards, in progress), edited by Robert Latham and William Matthews; *The Diary of Ralph Josselin 1616–1683* (British Academy, Records of Economic and Social History, n.s. III, 1976), edited by Alan Macfarlane; *The Autobiography of Thomas Whythorne* (1962), edited by James M. Osborn; *The Diary of Roger Lowe of Ashton-in-Makerfield, Lancashire, 1663–74* (1938), edited by William L. Sachse; Rev. C. Kerry, 'Leonard Wheatcroft, of Ashover' and 'The Autobiography of Leonard Wheatcroft' in *Journal of the Derbyshire Archeaological and Natural History Society* XVIII, XXI (1896, 1899).

[70] Hon. Roger North, *The Lives of the Right Hon. Francis North, Baron Guildford . . .* (1742; 1890 edn) edited by Augustus Jessop, I, p. 178.

period only cites two certain incidents of assaults by vagrants in the whole county for forty years.[71] It would appear that Harrison has multiplied the number of 'rogues' excuted each year, which he puts at about three or four hundred, by a factor of at least ten.

The difficulties of finding contemporary material is shown in the meagre evidence which Stone quotes in support of his views concerning village violence. For the level below the gentry for the 200 years between 1500 and 1700 in England, Stone's evidence is as follows: some information from a mid sixteenth century minister in the exceptional border lands of Northumberland and the works of F. G. Emmison on the church courts. A promising further line of enquiry would seem to be intensive local studies. Even if there is very little about violence in contemporary autobiographical material, the recent upsurge of detailed local studies should document it. The fact that none of these studies is cited by Stone and others who have rediscovered the violence of the past might be explained by the fact that once again they generally give an impression contrary to that which such historians would expect to find. We may cite a few examples.

Old-style local histories of particular parishes or lordships tend to portray sophisticated, highly regulated and property-conscious societies with little violence.[72] Thus, writing of Hawkshead in north Lancashire, H. S. Cowper concluded that 'crime of any sort was rare, as it is now, through all the dales of Cumberland, Westmorland, and Furness. . . . Little acts of meanness and petty theft were hardly known.'[73] More recently, the new studies of the economy and society in particular parishes also give an impression of little physical violence.[74] Certainly the villages are described as going through great economic change, rising problems of poverty, and religious divisions. But while the poor are present, criminals, deviants, brigands and feuds are almost totally absent. This could be accounted for by the nature of the local documents used by these historians. Land records, wills, parish registers and other documents usually show a highly intricate, continuous and effective governmental machine and a great deal of control and organization. Thus, as one of the greatest local historians, J. Horsfall Turner, wrote after printing numerous records for the Halifax area, 'the reader may be struck with one thing, the glamour of romance and unreality has to give place to a matter-of-fact life very little different from that of the

---

[71] Emmison, *Elizabethan Life: Disorder*, p. 151; William Harrison, *The Description of England* (1587; New York, 1968), edited by Georges Edelen, p. 193.

[72] For examples of this genre, Percy Millican, *A History of Horstead and Stanninghall Norfolk* (privately printed, 1937); Lord Rennell of Rodd, *Valley on the March: a History of a Group of Manors on the Herefordshire March of Wales* (1958).

[73] Henry S. Cowper, *Hawkshead: its History, Archaeology, Industries . . .* (1899), pp. 199, 224.

[74] Two notable examples of this approach are W. G. Hoskins, *The Midland Peasant: the Economic and Social History of a Leicestershire Village* (1957) and Margaret Spufford, *Contrasting Communities: English Villagers in the Sixteenth and Seventeenth Centuries* (Cambridge, 1974).

public life of to-day.'[75] In fact, we will only find the added dimension of violence if we use legal records, as a number of historians have recently done.

F. West studied the Lincolnshire village of Wrangle for the period 1603–32. He used the Quarter Sessions records, yet even so he came to the conclusion that 'a study of the cases at the sessions gives the impression that not only Wrangle, but Holland as a whole, was remarkably free of serious crime.'[76] What is even more surprising is the very small amount of petty crime that is presented, an absence which West puts down to the inefficiency of the petty constables. This 'dark figure' of real but undetected or unpresented crime is a perennial problem for the historian of violence, and it is one to which we shall return later. If we turn to other specific studies of crime and violence at the village level, they also fail to confirm the general expectations concerning a blood-spilling society. In a recent study of crime in Elizabethan Essex, J. Walker discovered that 'there were only a handful of parishes which experienced a felony as frequently as once a year, while there were more than 25 parishes with no record of felonies during the whole 45 years of Elizabeth's reign.'[77] In his study of the Essex parish of Kelvedon, J. A. Sharpe examined a population of roughly 500 persons over the period 1600–1640. He found twenty-four cases of theft, burglary and breaking and entering, but in terms of violent physical assaults, there was only one case of manslaughter and two of infanticide (one of them by a girl in a neighbouring village).[78] A study of the parish of Earls Colne in Essex over the longer period 1560–1750, using all types of local and criminal records, gives some suggestion of the amount of violent assault within a population of very roughly 800 persons over nearly two centuries. One woman was hanged for killing her child in 1608, another woman was acquitted on the charge of poisoning her husband in 1626, a man was branded for killing his stepson in 1667 and the following year a man was found guilty of homicide and was transported. The acquitted woman subsequently married again. The branded man four years later signed a petition as one of the chief inhabitants of Earls Colne, asking for a school-master, and the transported felon later returned to live in the village.[79] Since it is a difficult to conceal a dead body, these probably constitute most of the cases of violence. In the nearby parish of Terling, with a population of

[75] J. Horsfall Turner, *The History of Brighouse, Rastrick, and Hipperholme* (Bingley, Yorks., 1893), p. 238.
[76] F. West, 'The Social and Economic History of the East Fen Village of Wrangle, 1603–1637' (University of Leicester PhD, 1966), p. 25.
[77] J. C. M. Walker, 'Crime and Capital Punishment in Elizabethan Essex' (BA thesis, copy in Essex Record Office), p. 47. I am grateful to Mr Walker for permission to quote from his thesis.
[78] In Cockburn (ed.), *Crime in England*, pp. 100, 109.
[79] The sources and methodology of this study are described in Alan Macfarlane, Sarah Harrison and Charles Jardine, *Reconstructing Historical Communities* (Cambridge, 1977).

roughly half the size, over the 140 years from 1560 to 1699, there was one reported infanticide by a mentally unstable woman and one reported homicide.[80] No comparable study of an English village over the last one or two centuries has been undertaken, but it is difficult to envisage that the number of cases would be much lower.

The fact that detailed village studies fail to confirm the general historical theories could be explained away, partly through the distortion created by failures to detect violence and crime, partly through the destruction of records. There are various ways we might hope to get round these problems, one of them being to use other sources which give an insight into what went on outside the official records. The account books and notebooks of petty law-enforcement officers, constables, High Constables, bailiffs are one such source, but again, in the few examples I have seen, they are strangely negative.[82] For instance, Arthur Raistrick has summarized the contents of an account book kept by Richard Wigglesworth in the 1690s in the honour of Skipton in Yorkshire. Wigglesworth acted as constable, churchwarden, pinder in charge of the village pound, bylawman and overseer of the poor. There are plenty of records of the detaining of stray animals, of the loading and transporting of poor vagrants, of the carrying out of local by-laws. Given all these law-enforcement activities, we would have expected that in this remote and wild area there would have been a good deal of opposition to his activities. Raistrick concludes, however, that 'in the years when he has served as constable his duties varied, but the area was peaceful, so his journal has no record of violence or theft.'[83]

Another promising source would be contemporary accounts of village life. The best of these is the famous description of the Shropshire parish of Myddle, written in 1700 by Richard Gough.[84] It is based on Gough's experience of life in the parish back to the first half of the seventeenth century. The extraordinary value of this account has been increased by a detailed local study by David Hey, which puts this account into the context of other records.[86] Myddle was a parish of small pastoral farmers and

[80] Keith Wrightson and David Levine, *Poverty and Piety in an English Village: Terling, 1525–1700* (1979), pp. 116–17.
[81] J. A. Sharpe, 'Crime in the County of Essex, 1620–1680: a Study of Offences and Offenders at the Assizes and Quarter Sessions' (University of Oxford DPhil thesis, 1978).
[82] An example is R. S. France, 'A High Constable's Register, 1681', *Transactions of the Historic Society of Lancashire and Chesire* CVII (1956), pp. 55–87.
[83] Arthur Raistrick, *Old Yorkshire Dales* (1967), pp. 62–71.
[84] Richard Gough, *Antiquities and Memoirs of the Parish of Myddle, County of Salop* (Shrewsbury, 1875).
[85] David G. Hey, *An English Rural Community, Myddle, under the Tudors and Stuarts* (Leicester, 1974).
[86] *ibid.* p. 224.

tenants, with a population of about 600 persons. It is ideally situated for the study of past violence, for several reasons. It was only a few miles from the Welsh border, and hence on the margins of English society. Furthermore, a number of contemporaries in the seventeenth century stressed that of all of England, the woodland areas like Myddle were the most 'idle and lawless.'[87] And Gough is a perfect chronicler, for, as Hey remarks, he was 'attracted by the sensational'.[87] Over a fifty-year period, from memory and experience, Gough did indeed find violent incidents. He reported a homicide with a peat spade and a murder of an infant, as well as the attempts of several women who were 'weary of their husbands' to poison them.[88] He also mentions some suicides and a certain amount of theft, a good deal of it petty, and cases of bastardy and drunkenness. But the major and almost sole instance of physically violent behaviour apart from this was in the case of a man called William Tyler, who was a considerable trouble to the village. He resisted arrest, but was finally taken to gaol. Despite various serious crimes, he was released. During these sixty years, two persons from the community were sentenced to death, according to Gough — a thief and a murderer. Hey comments that 'vicious crime' was 'unusual.'[89] Indeed, Hey's impression is that, although there were some notorious individuals and families, on the whole 'the crime rate seems to have been lower, and the moral code more strictly observed, than is the case in much of the England of today.'[90] Obviously such a statement, to be proven, would require not only that the criminal records for Myddle should have survived and been analysed, but also that they should be carefully compared with those for the present. Nevertheless, it is an interesting impression, which tends once again to fit badly with our expectations. In fact, standing back from Gough's account, it is the absences which are most interesting: witchcraft, feuds and factions, highway robbers, mob violence and sadism are nowhere to be seen. There is very little recorded interpersonal violence, and there is a great deal of counter-evidence in his work of warmth, humour, tolerance and kindliness, love and affection, both within the family and between neighbours.

We are thus in a curious position. We must suppose, from historical accounts and from general theories of the past, that people were living in a period of unprecedented upheaval. We are told that they were still largely 'pre-modern' in their mentality and feelings, brutalized by their physical and social world. Yet the contemporary evidence, on the whole, points in an opposite direction. This is what seems to have confused some earlier historians. How can we possibly go beneath the surface, find out what it was really like to live in a sixteenth- or seventeenth-century village with its feuds,

[87] *ibid.* p. 188.
[88] Gough, *Myddle*, pp. 30, 72, 91.
[89] Hey, *An English Rural Community*, p. 225.
[90] *ibid.* p. 224.

simmering violence and frequent bloodshed? How can we go behind the formal end process which is all that is recorded in the legal records of presentments and indictments? We can occasionally get a glimpse through a pamphlet account of a trial, or through a literary description of the underworld.[91] But this is a frustrating experience, for the trial pamphlets never give us enough detail about local community reactions and the literary accounts are always written as fiction.

One other solution is to draw on two types of materials which have hitherto been little used by social historians, namely the despositions taken in criminal trials and the informal documents preserved by Justices of the Peace. Combined with local documents, these allow us to go beyond mere numbers of cases to the level of how violence was controlled and contained. They enable us furthermore to see how violence was perceived and the degree to which it permeated thought and action.

A unique set of documents, concerning several robbers in the 1680s, has survived and allows us to enter the everyday world at that time. It provides a 'social drama' which, as anthropologists have urged, enables us to see into the heart of a society. Such an 'extended case study' of a particular set of events provides 'a limited area of transparency on the otherwise opaque surface of regular, uneventful social life. Through it we are enabled to observe the crucial principles of the social structure in their operation.'[92] The events occurred in the region of the Lake District and the western Yorkshire Pennines — an area generally thought to be one of the most lawless and violent in England. Not only was it near the Scottish border, so that criminals could more easily escape, but it is widely believed that poverty was greatest in this area. Furthermore, the pastoral economy of the region meant considerable underemployment and the need for other, often criminal, bi-employments. Family feuds were especially likely to be present in an area which is usually described as being dominated by wide kinship groups. Moreover, though the period is a late one, the 1680s are a time of exceptional political upheaval. The supposed Popish Plot of 1679 was succeeded by many other threatened risings, one of the most serious occurring in 1683 with the Rye House Plot. These political uncertainties culminated in Monmouth's rebellion and the final expulsion of James II. Such national insecurity, with divisions among the ruling elites, provided a vacuum within which violence and forms of social banditry would be most likely to thrive, and it was exacerbated by terrible weather affecting the crops. A local diarist, William Stout of Lancaster, wrote of 1682 that 'the

---

[91] An excellent example is Richard Head and Francis Kirkman, *The English Rogue, Described in the Life of Meriton Latroon* . . . (1665; 1928).
[92] V. W. Turner, *Schism and Continuity in an African Society* (Manchester, 1957), p. 67. A general description of this approach is given by J. Van Velsen, 'The Extended-Case Method and Situational Analysis' in A. L. Epstein (ed.), *The Craft of Social Anthropology* (1967).

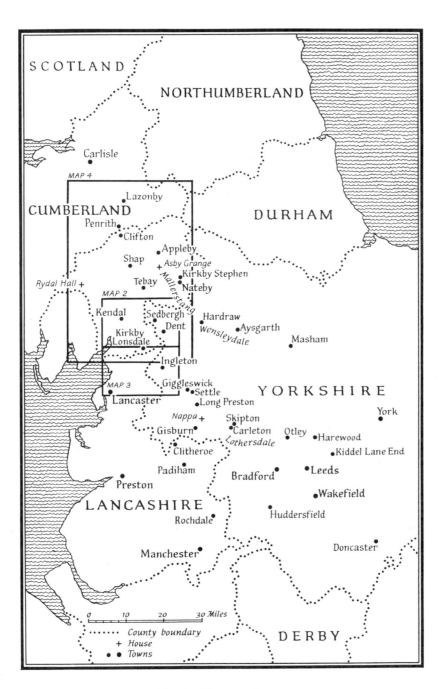

SCOTLAND

NORTHUMBERLAND

Carlisle

MAP 4

CUMBERLAND
Lazonby

Penrith
Clifton

DURHAM

Shap
Appleby
Asby Grange
Kirkby Stephen
Tebay
Nateby

Rydal Hall
MAP 2
Kendal
Sedbergh
Dent
Hardraw
Aysgarth
Masham
Wensleydale

Kirkby
Lonsdale
Ingleton

MAP 3
Giggleswick
Settle
YORKSHIRE
Lancaster
Long Preston

York
Nappa
Skipton
Gisburn
Carleton
Otley
Harewood
Lothersdale
Clitheroe
Kiddel Lane End

Padiham
Bradford
Leeds

Preston
Wakefield

LANCASHIRE
Huddersfield
Rochdale

Manchester
Doncaster

0   10   20   30 Miles

County boundary
+   House
• • Towns

DERBY

Map 1   The general region.

winter this year proved very scarce of fodder, straw being short and the grass burnt up in summer, so that little hay was got. People were very much straitened to keep their cattle alive, and many starved.'[93] The winter of 1682–3 was even worse, a 'long and sharp frost' continuing from November to the end of January, 'to the great hardship and mortality of many people. It was the longest and sharpest frost with snow that had been in the memory of any man then living; killed many sheep and cattle, all rivers and fresh waters being frozen, so that water was scarce to serve cattle and necessary occasions.'[94]

The place and the times might therefore be regarded as abnormal. This is compounded by the nature of the sources. It is clear that a study largely centred on the criminal records of a contemporary society would tend to emphasize the level of violence. This book is based on the depositions returned to the court which dealt with the most serious cases of violence, namely the Assizes. But even within this exceptional source, we are taking a singular example. A search of all the records within the general class of northern Assize depositions for the period 1650–1750 indicates that no other set of events attracted as much attention as those to be described. This impression is reinforced by the fact that the most active Justice of the Peace involved, whose private papers have been used, clearly came across no other happenings of a similar kind during his forty years as a Justice for Cumberland, Westmorland and Lancashire. By any standards the case is exceptional. Yet such has been our failure to find supporting evidence for the general thesis now accepted by many social historians that we must make use of such material, while recognizing that it will tend to give a distorted impression. Once we have established the full dimensions of past violence, we will be able to set it within the context of studies of other societies to see how it should be regarded.

[93] J. D. Marshall (ed.), *The Autobiography of William Stout of Lancaster, 1665–1752* (Manchester, 1967), p. 79.
[94] *ibid.* p. 80.

1
'A Black and Terrible Troop'

Some inhabitants of the country of Westmorland in 1680 warned the Justices of the Peace of the 'great danger they were in, occasioned by some persons who ride armed and with vizards.' The Justices thus 'being informed that divers persons ride armed with vizards to the terror of his Majesty's subjects', issued orders that a search be made 'by night and day in places suspected twice a week at least'.[1] In early 1683 the Justices began a formal investigation of the activities of these masked men. They were urged on by some of the local gentry, who wrote praising their preliminary activities 'in order to the bringing to light of one of the horrible and dark deeds of that black and terrible troop of notorious malefactors by which this part of the county . . . hath been intolerably infested.'[2] The Justices were warned that these 'insolent and formidable felons . . . were so hardened in their impious actions that they were neither ashamed nor afraid implicitly to glory in their treasonable and felonious feats', so that 'few had the courage (although they had done them mischief) to give information thereof, some of them giving dangerous hints what they would do to men's persons or houses if complaint were made.' During the next eighteen months we witness a battle between the law and this 'black and terrible troop.'

The physical appearance of the region where this drama occurred has changed less than in many areas of England (see illus. 4,6). Travellers to the Lake District and the western dales of the Yorkshire Pennines will recall the bracken-covered hills rising to a little over two thousand feet. The centre of the events was the large parish of Kirkby Lonsdale in southern Westmorland, or Cumbria as it is now called. This parish included the eight chapelries or townships of Hutton Roof, Lupton, Killington, Mansergh, Firbank, Middleton, Barbon and Casterton, and numbered about

[1] Kendal Indictment and Order Book 1669–91, p. 266, 8 October 1680 (WRO).
[2] Fleming Letter 2635 (WRO).

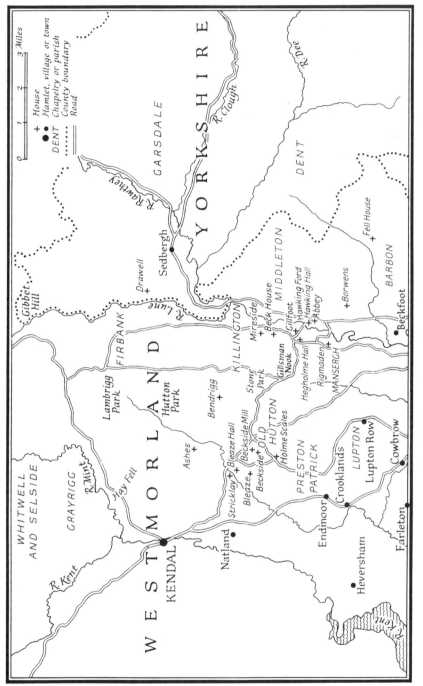

Map 2   The northern part of the central area.

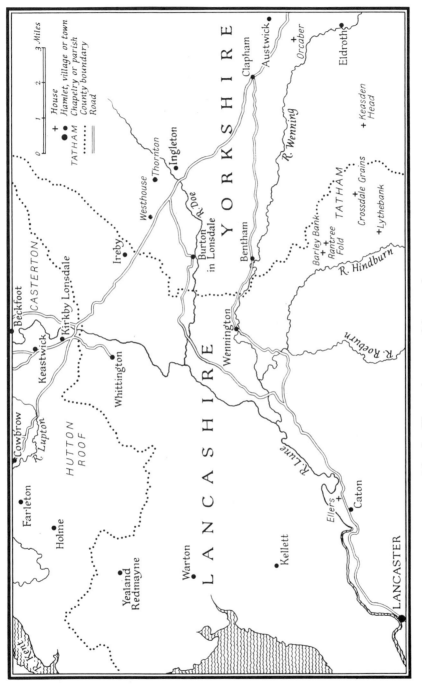

Map 3   The southern part of the central area.

2,400 persons altogether (see maps 1–3 for places mentioned in the text). There was also the town of Kirkby Lonsdale, the second largest market town in Westmorland at the time, with a population of about 600 persons. The parish straddled the four main physical zones, the rounded Pennines of the east, the craggy moorlands typical of the Lake District to the west, the empty heaths to the north and the flat lush lands of north Lancashire to the south. Most of the population outside the market town lived in scattered hamlets or single stone-built farmhouses. They grew oats and barley, fattened cattle and raised sheep. Many combined this with small trading and artisan activities. Similar parishes lay on all sides. To the south there was much flatter and richer land in the lower Lune valley stretching towards Lancashire. To the west were Old Hutton and, a few miles beyond, the market town of Kendal, where the cloth and other knitted products of Kirkby Lonsdale and neighbouring parishes were sold. To the east was the large Pennine parish comprising Sedbergh, Garsdale and Dent.

The machinery of criminal justice administered in this time and region may be simplified to a system with three levels. At the most exalted level were the Assizes whereby judges travelled around 'circuits', trying serious felonies and undertaking a 'delivery' of the local gaols. This was a system of great antiquity, well established by the middle of the thirteenth century.[3] Although there had been developments, expansions and refinements, what we are witnessing in Westmorland in the 1680s is a process which could have occurred at any time in the five hundred years between 1300 and 1800. It was not only ancient, but national. The northern Assize circuit was one of six in England and included the counties of York, Durham, Northumberland, Cumberland, Westmorland and Lancashire.[4] The judges who travelled this circuit also travelled the other five and applied a national law. Records from elsewhere, for instance those for the home circuit which have been extensively studied and published,[5] indicate that an identical legal system was in operation in, for example, Essex and Westmorland. Types of offence or the nature of personnel might vary, but the basic machinery of justice and the principles upon which it rested were uniform, and the example of Westmorland therefore throws light on judicial process throughout England.

The Assize courts on the crown or criminal side were 'chiefly occupied

[3] A. P. Brydson, 'Notes on the Westmorland Assize Roll of AD 1256', *TCWAAS*, n.s., XIII (1913). For details about the antiquity of a system stretching back until at least the eleventh century, see J. S. Cockburn, *A History of English Assizes 1558–1714* (Cambridge, 1972), pp. 15–22.

[4] For a more detailed account of the extremely complex jurisdictions, including the Palatinate rights of Durham and Lancashire, see Cockburn, *History of Assizes*, pp. 38–46.

[5] The home circuit indictments have now been published by Her Majesty's Stationery Office, edited by J. S. Cockburn. A preliminary analysis of the incidence of crime in these circuits is made in chapter 2 of J. S. Cockburn (ed.), *Crime in England, 1550–1800* (1977).

with murder, robbery, burglary and grand larceny, together with other serious offences such as rape, coining and witchcraft.'[6] Most of the documentation of what went on in these courts has been destroyed.[7] For all but the northern Assizes, the only evidence we have comes from the gaol calendars and from the short formal accusations known generally as 'indictments', with the supporting recognizances for appearance at court.[8] Historians have consequently been forced to base their general conclusions upon these documents. We may wonder what impression we would gain of criminal activities in Westmorland if we had only such sources.

A study of such documents alone would suggest that Westmorland in the twenty years leading up to the events of 1680 was almost without any serious crime. The few surviving gaol calendars show that it was unusual for there to be more than half a dozen prisoners awaiting the judges in the gaol. Most of those in prison were accused of minor thefts. As a small example of the apparent absence of serious disturbance and crime we may look at the parish of Kirkby Lonsdale. Over the period 1660–79 there was only one indictment, for the theft of a horse. In the fifteen years from 1685–99 there was one indictment, for the theft of a silver tankard and spoons. Even allowing for the fact that perhaps half the indictments for Westmorland have been lost, the impression of absence of serious crime is overwhelming. But there were two unusual years. In 1683 there were six indictments which involved people said to be of the parish of Kirkby Lonsdale. The amount of information contained is extremely limited. We are given three names of inhabitants of the parish who were accused and the names of several witnesses and victims. The description of their offences was as follows: 'for stealing of a coat worth 24s'; 'for stealing a quarter of veal'; 'for clipping twenty shillings of half crowns, twenty shillings of one shillings, and twenty shillings of sixpences;' 'for robbing of Robert Robinson of Old Hutton, gent, and taking from him forty-three pounds in silver, three silver spoons, a pair of shoes, a pair of silver weights and a pewter bottle, the third day of November 1680 about two o'clock in the morning in the dwelling place of Robert Robinson, the said Robert Robinson then being within & put in fear and dread by the same'; 'for stealing of an heifer'. A bundle of recognizances show that many witnesses were called, but if there were no despositions we would know nothing else about the case. The following year we find two people of the same name, but now said to be of parishes outside Kirkby Lonsdale, accused of further

---

[6] J. H. Baker in Cockburn (ed.), *Crime in England*, p. 28. The article by Baker provides a very useful introduction to criminal procedure in England between 1550 and 1800.

[7] 'Of this mountain of material, precious little remains.' J. S. Cockburn, 'Early Modern Assize Records as Historical Evidence', *Journal of the Society of Archivists* V, no. 4 (October 1975), p. 216.

[8] The meaning of 'indictment' and of other technical legal words, as well as obscure and archaic words, is explained in the glossary, p. 219.

offences, and one extra man from Kirkby Lonsdale town also involved. The offences were: that certain men 'did feloniously and burglariously break and enter the mansion house of Richard Hindson at Ling and take £9 in money'; that the same persons took 18*d* from Andrew Bell; that certain men 'between the hours of 10 and 12 in the night, with force and arms at Farleton, did break and enter the mansion house of Henry Preston, with the intention of committing a burglary, putting him in fear'; exactly the same people at the same date, 'for wounding Henry Preston with a falchion'. Clearly something exceptional happened in 1683–4. It was presumably connected with the remarks about a 'black and terrible troop'. Throughout nearly the whole of England for most centuries until the middle of the eighteenth, we would be able to progress little further, for we would only have evidence such as this.

One place we might hope to find further evidence would be in the records of the next level of machinery, the Sessions of the Peace. While major felonies were, on the whole, dealt with finally by the Assizes, the Justices of the Peace at the Sessions often dealt with the first stage of the criminal process. Furthermore, the Quarter Sessions records often give details concerning the keeping of the peace in general, dealing with minor thefts and assaults. The Justices of the Peace for the area we are concerned with met at Kendal and Appleby, again working within a system that was both ancient and universal within England. The machinery which suddenly becomes illuminated in Westmorland, by the chance survival of records in some quantity after 1655, had been operating in a roughly similar fashion for at least three hundred years before that date. As Sheila Macpherson, the County Archivist at Kendal, has stated, we can now read about offences that occurred in the 1650s, 'but there must have been many of a similar nature in the period of almost 300 years prior to 1655 — a period about which we know little or nothing because unfortunately the records have not survived.'[9] As Maitland wrote, 'that most thoroughly English of English institutions, the Commission of the Peace' we 'owe to the fourteenth century.'[10] We are again dealing with a system that could be observed at any period from the fourteenth century onwards. Similarly, it was a uniform national system. The very extensive printed and unpublished Quarter Sessions records for many parts of England from the sixteenth century indicate a similar process and largely similar content throughout the land.[11]

[9] Typescript guide to 'Westmorland Quarter Sessions, 1361–1971' (WRO).
[10] F. W. Maitland, *Justice and Police* (1885), p. 79. For the medieval origins, see Esther Moir, *The Justice of the Peace* (Penguin, 1969), chapter 1.
[11] An early survey of printed and unprinted Quarter Sessions material for the whole of England is F. G. Emmison and Irvine Gray, *County Records* (Historical Association Pamphlet, no. S.3, 1948). A more recent list of records and some extracts, are given in John West, *Village Records* (1962), pp. 84–91, and see W. B. Stephens, *Sources for English Local History* (Manchester, 1973), pp. 54–6.

Naturally, local conditions would influence the number and proportions of certain kinds of offence. Likewise, though the Justices used the same manuals and had been educated at the same universities and Inns of Court, the personnel varied over time and space. But if we compare, for example, the Sessions records for Westmoreland with those for Essex during a similar period, it is immediately clear that we are dealing with a unified system.

We may wonder what impression the records of these Sessions on their own would give, concerning crime in general and the activities of the notorious malefactors in particular. We may again take the sample parish of Kirkby Lonsdale, with its population of about 3,000 during the period 1660–99. During this period there were some twenty-two cases of minor assault, or a little over one every two years. There were twenty-one cases of trespass on private property. There were eight accusations of theft, in which there is no recorded verdict for four persons, not guilty for three, and only one person was found guilty. It seems to be a picture of general orderliness, with the total absence of violent crimes such as rape, murder, burglary, or of more insidious ones such as clipping the edges off coins. As for the affairs of the early 1680s, we would learn very little about what happened. Apart from the order to the constables to search for armed men, already quoted, there were only indirect hints that something was happening. All we have are eight recognizances of persons outside Kirkby Lonsdale, who are ordered to give evidence in a case unspecified, and one indictment against a Kirkby Lonsdale town man for resisting the constables who were trying to make a search of his house. It is clear that we could not get behind what was happening at the Assizes by using this source, though it should be noted that the order book of the Justices is missing for the period April 1682 to April 1686.

Another possible source of further information lies at the third level, that of the village. The countryside was policed by the inhabitants themselves, through a system of mutual responsibility and by constables appointed by the manor court leet or Quarter Sessions. In some areas of England there still survived active manorial courts known as leet courts, which tried minor assaults, thefts and other misdemeanours in which the penalty could be a fine of up to £5. They were often combined with a system of 'frankpledge', in which every male resident aged over twelve years owed suit to the court — in other words had to attend and take an oath to maintain the peace and present evildoers. Again, this was very old and a very widespread system of social control, which could be traced directly from the Anglo-Saxon system of justice before the Conquest, and flourished through the middle ages. Its antiquity and wide scope may be illustrated from the manor of Kirkby Lonsdale itself, for in a decree of 1569 the lord and lady of the manor successfully claimed that certain liberties had been granted to the lord of this manor in the year 1217 and had been confirmed and re-confirmed many times since.[12] Many of these rights, including the holding of the court leet, the appointment of officers, and the right to regulate markets and fairs, continued until at least the end of the eighteenth century. Not only are we dealing with an institution that flourished through half a millennium, but it is also clear from the published records of numerous manors in various parts of the country that the courts leet of the various parts of England were almost identical.[13] The stewards of all these manors used the same hand-books and applied the same customary law. Of course there were minor variations, depending on local conditions, but the general principles were universal. Thus again when we look into one manor, to a certain extent we look into them all, and when we look at the late seventeenth century we also learn something of the preceding several centuries. It is only the chance survival of records or the limits of our expertise which make us believe otherwise.

In the manor of Kirkby Lonsdale, with a population of about 600 persons plus the frequent additions of larger numbers brought in by the market and fairs, there was an average of two minor assaults presented a year during the period 1660–99. There were no reported thefts, major riots or other offences. There is no reflection of the strange events of 1683–4, but a strong impression of discipline and order.

A final source, which shows the way in which the various levels were interconnected, was the constable's presentment. The constables were appointed by the court leet or Justices, and were responsible to the Justices and through them to the Assizes. In order to ensure the presentment of crimes and misdemeanours, constables were obliged to return a set of answers to specific questions to the Quarter Sessions, stating what disturbances there had been in their small area and what action they had taken. If they failed in their duties, it was the obligation of both High Constables and Justices to prosecute them.[14] This supervision of popular order may be illustrated by one set of constable's presentments for 1665 from a chapelry in Kirkby Lonsdale, namely Firbank with a population of about 150 persons.[15]

---

[12] A copy of this Common Pleas document is D/Lons/1/K.L./1(CRO).

[13] The old but standard survey of manorial records is Nathaniel J. Hone, *The Manor and Manorial Records* (1906). Since Hone, numerous court rolls have been published by local record societies. Many of these publications up to the mid-1950s are listed in E. L .C. Mullins, *Texts and Calendars* (Royal Historical Society, 1958).

[14] Some argued that the constables make their presentments *ex officio*, without precepts being issued on each occasion by the High Constable; see R. S. France, 'A High Constable's Register, 1681', *Transactions of the Historic Society of Lancashire and Cheshire* CVII (1956), p. 72.

[15] The presentment is in ASSI/44/13 at the PRO. The population figures for Firbank and Kirkby Lonsdale have been calculated from a listing of the inhabitants made in 1695 and from earlier hearth taxes, supplemented with information from wills, parish registers and other documents. For a description of the sources used in the study of the sample parish, see appendix D.

1   The persons inhabiting in the hamlet and forbearing to repair to the church according to the law are Thomas Aray and Thomas Wilson, called Quakers: sojourners there is none, neither any who have neglected to resort to hear divine service whereby the penalty of twelve pence becomes due.

2   There have been no felonies nor robberies committed within the hamlet since the last Assizes.

3   Vagrant persons or rogues there have been none apprehended nor none let pass unpunished.

4   No cottages erected, nor inmates entertained, within the hamlet.

5   Taverns there is none, alehousekeeper William Fawcett, licensed by his Majesty's Justices of the Peace, and lives in a convenient place, of civil carriage, entertaining no lewd persons.

6   To this article [i.e. unlawful weights and measures] I have nothing to present.

7   Ingrossers, forestallers or regrators, there is none in the hamlet.

8   Constable for the hamlet is hereunto subscribed, sworn and allowed by his Majesty's Justices of the Peace and more there is none.

9   Servants there is none in the hamlet who have been put off of their service before their due time expired.

10   Bridges and highways and causies [causeways] are in good repair.

11   Stock for the poor we have none: and bastards we have had none born.

12   To this article [concerning profane swearers or cursers] I have nothing to present.

13   Riots, routs, or other unlawful assemblies none have been committed or done within the hamlet.

14   No neglect by the constable in punishing rogues.

In the same year the constables for all the chapelries in Kirkby Lonsdale including Firbank (except Middleton and Killington which are missing) reported eighteen Quakers, one Catholic and four vagrants whipped and sent on to the next constable. In answer to explicit questions, they reported no robberies, riots or serious offences. Unfortunately, the constable's presentments for other years have disappeared for this parish. But the few that survive for other Westmorland townships during this period also give a picture of little disorder or crime.

The apparent absence of disorder and crime might lead one to start theorizing about the causes for such tranquillity. As well as the elaborate system of overlapping courts, from Westminster to the local court leet, one might note the multiplicity of local officers to patrol the population. The constable was only one among many such officers. In Kirkby Lonsdale manor, for example, with an eligible adult male population of roughly 200 persons, in the year 1664 the court records mention the following officers: four assessors of the poor relief, one overseer for the poor, four guardians of the lordship stock of money for the poor, four men in charge of weights and measures, two to seal leather, two 'becklookers' to prevent poaching and pollution of the streams, four 'bylawmen' to see that the village bylaws were obeyed, two 'swinelookers', four surveyors of the common, two surveyors for the highways, two for the regulation of the measures and quality of bread and ale. At the following court a 'pounder' to look after confiscated stray animals, and a constable were appointed. If we add to these the two churchwardens, we have thirty-five separate officers.

Before we start to build theories as to why, with the exception of some events about which we can learn little in the early 1680s, southern Westmorland was so devoid of crime and disorder, it is important to be certain that this was indeed the case. Normally we could not do this. A number of historians have pointed out that what is really intriguing and unknowable is what went on behind the formal and highly uninformative indictments. Do the normal legal records reflect reality at all accurately? And by what process were people brought to court and tried? Geoffrey Elton has pointed out that 'in a trial for felony . . . it is usually easy to discover the court that tried the case, the names and descriptions of accused and victims, the type of crime alleged, the names of the jurors, the fact of conviction or acquittal. We cannot learn from the record the particulars of the crime, the details of what went on in court, or — more surprisingly — quite often whether the sentence was carried out.'[16] This is true both of the Assize courts and also of the great central criminal courts, particularly King's Bench. In the voluminous plea rolls 'all entries follow common form and tell almost nothing of the personal or individual facts behind a case: one will be told the name of the parties and usually their employment or status, and one is likely to discover the cause alleged in dispute, but that is all.'[17] We are consequently warned that 'we need to learn a lot more about how information came to be gathered, processed and introduced. . . . Since we urgently need to comprehend why some people were sucked into the machinery of criminal process while others, who had committed the same offences, were not, we want more searching concentration on that first stage of the process.'[18] But where can we find such information, in order to test the accuracy of the impression given by Assize indictments, Quarter Sessions and leet records?

In a few selected cases, particularly famous treason trials or sensational trials of witches, murderers or highwayman, a contemporary pamphlet

---

[16] In Cockburn (ed.), *Crime in England*, p. 11.

[17] G. R. Elton, *England, 1200–1640* (1969), p. 59.

[18] Elton in Cockburn (ed.), *Crime in England*, p. 8. There is a useful discussion of the defects of indictments by John Beattie, 'Towards a Study of Crime in Eighteenth Century England: a Note on Indictments', especially pp. 302–3, in D. Williams and P. Fritz (eds), *The Triumph of Culture: Eighteenth Century Perspectives* (Toronto, 1972).

account was published of the actual trial.[19] These enable us to see what went on in court and often include detailed depositions by witnesses which give some of the background of the trial. Sometimes we glean facts from the early ballads of the lives and deaths of notorious criminals.[20] But those sources are limited, partly because they only reproduce a fraction of the evidence, partly because they give no information concerning the stages of the judicial process itself. We would appear to be at an impasse. This would indeed be the case for all England up to 1640, and for nine tenths of the population until the nineteenth century. But there is something special about the northern Assize circuit.[21]

By an act of 1555 it was stated that all Justices of the Peace were to take a written examination of all persons brought before them suspected of manslaughter and felony, and of those who brought them in. They were to certify their having done this at the next Assizes.[22] Unfortunately, as J. C. Cockburn observes, these depositions 'were not, legally speaking, documents "of record" . . . a fact which possibly accounts for their wholesale destruction.'[23] For while they have existed for the whole country the only Assize circuit for which they survive before 1719 is the northern Assize, and here only in some quantity after 1640.[24] These informal depositions taken by Justices have been little used by legal and social historians. A very abbreviated selection from this class was published nearly one hundred and twenty years ago by James Raine, when the depositions were at York Castle.[25] But partly because they have only very recently been

[19] A helpful compilation of often verbatim reports is contained in T. B. Howell (ed.), *A Complete Collection of State Trials* (1816–31), 31 volumes. A brief comparison of evidence from indictments and pamphlet accounts of trials in relation to witchcraft trials is given in Cockburn (ed.), *Crime in England*, pp. 77–8.

[20] H. E. Rollins (ed.), *The Pepys Ballads* (Cambridge, Mass., 1929 ff.) is a useful collection of printed ballads, but the eight volumes contain only about a quarter of the ballads now in the Pepys Library, Magdalen College, Cambridge. I am grateful to the Pepys Librarian, R. C. Latham, for enabling me to see the full collection. Examples of confessions of highwaymen and coin clippers are published in Rollins, III, no. 115 and VII, no. 445.

[21] Apart from the northern circuit and Palatinate of Lancaster, the only Assize depositions for the period before 1800 are for the Oxford circuit, starting in 1719.

[22] Statutes of the Realm, 2 & 3 Philip and Mary, cap, 10. For an excellent discussion of the statute and its background, see John H. Langbein, *Prosecuting Crime in the Renaissance* (Cambridge, Mass., 1974).

[23] Cockburn, 'Early Modern Assize Records', p. 216. It seems likely that a number of these depositions have survived in the papers of gentry families of the period. For example, a few are to be found in the papers of Sir Nathaniel Bacon of Norfolk; see Camden Society Miscellany, 3rd ser., LII (1936), pp. vii, 21–2. others survived among Quarter Sessions papers, occasionally, in borough archives, and in lawyers' notes; see Langbein, *Prosecuting Crime*, pp. 81 ff, 91–5 and *ibid.* p. 39.

[24] Now in the Public Record Office, class ASSI 45. A more complete description of these and other documents is given in appendix D, p. 215.

[25] James Raine (ed.), *Depositions from the Castle of York, relating to offences in the Northern Counties in the Seventeenth Century* (Surtees Society, XL, 1861). The highly selective nature of Raine's extracts is shown by the fact that there is no mention in them of the affairs discussed in this book.

sorted and listed at the Public Record Office, little other use has been made of them. Raine himself published them because he was fully aware of their great value for social history and Cockburn has again stressed the 'considerable interest of depositions to social historians'.[26] As the same author notes, it is ironic that 'these halting, colloquial statements should reflect more accurately the facts of a case than the precise, stylized forms of the indictment.'[27] Having examined all the northern circuit Assize depositions for the period 1640–1750, one set of depositions, concerning a case which continued over two Assizes, stood out among this wealth of material as perhaps the most voluminous and detailed. By chance, these happened to concern the background of the bald indictments which we have already quoted. They thus enable us to see how accurate the normal legal records are, and they partly enable to us piece together the process of prosecution. But even depositions of eye-witnesses have their defects. Two may be mentioned.

Firstly, they tell us little about the people involved, outside their criminal activities or involvement. We see a person for a year or two, but where he came from or what happened to him, what his other relationships were, his family and neighbourly background, are only rarely and indirectly revealed. This deficiency can partly be overcome in this case by using work on the other surviving records for the parish of Kirkby Lonsdale.[28] The second limitation is that the examinations still tell us only a limited amount about the judicial process. We know when and where they were taken, and they tell us about the activities of constables and witnesses. But how the informations were gathered, how the suspects were apprehended and taken to gaol, we are unable to piece together. Here we are extremely fortunate, for the papers of the most active of the Justices of the Peace in this area survived and have been deposited in the local record office.[29] Again they have remained largely unused, partly because they are bulky and only partially listed. Thus by combining the formal legal records available throughout England with special sources for Kirkby Lonsdale, for the northern Assizes, and from a Justice's papers, we are able to gain some impression of how the English legal system worked at this time. We are hence able to throw some light on a system which has had a large influence in shaping the legal framework of many parts of the world.

A judicial system can be described abstractly, but it is only as good or as bad as those who operate it. We therefore need to know what kind of people inhabited the landscape we have begun to portray and particularly the officers who made the machinery work. We may choose for a very brief

[26] Cockburn, 'Early Modern Assize Records,' p. 216.
[27] *idem.*
[28] For a summary of the sources used in this study, see appendix D, p. 215.
[29] The papers of Sir Daniel Fleming, which are described in the note on sources.

description five people who would all be concerned with the events of 1683–4. They have been chosen for two main reasons. They span a wide spectrum of power and social position in England, from a man who became the second most powerful figure in England, Lord Chancellor and baron, down to a village glazier who ended his life as a pauper. Secondly, each of them represented the overlapping roles of law-enforcer and law-opposer. All five were legal officers — the Lord Chief Justice of England, a Justice of the Peace, a High Constable and two constables. But one ended his life in the Tower of London with many calling for his execution for treason, a second later entered into a conspiracy against the king, two more were tried for high treason and other felonies, and the fifth was tried on at least four occasions for capital offences. In August 1684 their lives would come together briefly, one as judge, one as major instigator, one as chief crown witness and two as accused of burglary and assault.

At the level of the Assizes, the highest officer was the Judge. On the northern circuit in 1684 one of the two judges was the recently appointed Chief Justice of the King's Bench, Sir George Jeffreys (see illus. 1). A brilliant man of forty when he toured the northern circuit, he already had considerable experience as Recorder of London, Chief Justice of Chester, and Judge on the western circuit. As the author of a recent biography has written, 'Had [he] died at the end of the summer term, 1685 . . . the name of Jeffreys would have been transmitted to posterity as that of a great judge, of strong convictions and unusual range of intellect, who was a believer in the royal prerogative . . . who had made some notable contributions to the practice of English common law in the brief period of this Chief Justice-ship.'[30] Instead, he was involved in the suppression of the Monmouth Rebellion in the autumn of 1685 at the 'Bloody Assizes' and became one of the most vilified of all characters in English history as 'Bloody Judge Jeffreys'. As Keeton points out, he was a man of vast energy, immense legal knowledge and swift intelligence. Having dealt with the criminal world of London for several years, he was an appropriate man to try the 'formidable felons' who had terrorized parts of the north.

His task would have been impossible, however, without the work of the chief officer of the next level of the law, the Justice of the Peace who acted through the Quarter Sessions. Of the half dozen Justices who took a major hand in opposing the armed and disguised 'troop', one particularly merits our attention, Sir Daniel Fleming of Rydal Hall (see page 41, illustration 2). Born in 1633, he was aged forty-seven when the first rumours of masked men reached him in 1680. He had taken over the family estate at the age of nineteen on the death of his father, after a brief education at Oxford and the

[30] G. W. Keeton, *Lord Chancellor Jeffreys and the Stuart Cause* (1965). This is by far the most sympathetic and thorough study of Jeffreys.

1 Sir George Jeffreys, Lord Chief Justice and one of the Judges on the northern Assize circuit in 1684. Painting attributed to W. Claret, c.1678–80.

2 *Sir Daniel Fleming of Rydal Hall, Westmorland.*

Inns of Court in London. In 1655 he had married the sister of Sir George
Fletcher, a Justice and Member for Cumberland. He was the first sheriff of
Cumberland after the restoration of Charles the Second and acted as a
Justice for Cumberland, Westmorland and Lancashire. He was knighted
by Charles in 1681 and was elected a burgess for Parliament in 1685. Later,
he joined with other northern gentry in the successful conspiracy to invite
William of Orange to England. His voluminous personal papers show him
to be a truly remarkable man. He combined great intelligence, vast
erudition, immense curiosity and great energy, with a love of documents.
When his papers were deposited in the Cumbria Record Office in the 1960s
they comprised about seventy manilla boxes. There were also roughly 6,000
letters to and from him. There are copies of love letters, books of jokes, series
of grocers' bills, payments to harvest workers and many other items. Just
the letters concerning the education of his children, when published, filled
three bulky volumes.[31] His immense energy and organization is shown in an
account book he kept which, if fully published, would run to many volumes.
His legal learning is illustrated by his letters and book purchases, but one
particularly strong indication is the annotated copy of the *Statutes of the Peace*
which he kept with him in his judicial business. The first 286 pages are a
printed abstract of the legal position in relation to alphabetically arranged
subjects such as 'Alehouses', 'Archery', 'Arrests'. These first pages are
densely annotated with added topics, modifications, amplifications from all
the current legal writers. Not content with this, Fleming then proceeded to
fill a further 482 pages in his tiny handwriting with annotations and
explanations, with the forms of writs and warrants, with the statutes
concerning taxation and the poor, and numerous other topics.

Fleming's curiosity and energy showed itself in other ways. He was an
early antiquary, writing one of the first descriptions of Cumberland and
Westmorland in the seventeenth century, and corresponding with several
noted antiquaries. He kept or copied out public papers such as listings of
inhabitants and hearth taxes for parts of Westmorland in the seventeenth
century, which would otherwise have been lost. He not only kept copies of
letters to himself, but, in the days before carbon paper, energetically made
copies in his own hand of important legal letters, warrants and other
messages from himself. There were all duly filed away and among his
papers is a list showing how he had organized what amounted to a small
record repository, in which his great account book was duly shelved as
'Ms.U'. All this was combined with a vigorous belief in the importance of

---

[31] J. R. Magrath (ed.), *The Flemings in Oxford. . . .1650–1700* (Oxford Historical Society, XLIV,
LXII, LXXIX, 1904, 1913, 1924). Only the letters relating to Oxford and education in general are
printed, yet these, with critical apparatus, occupy 1,568 pages. The only, very incomplete, list
of the letters is in the seventh part of the *Appendix to the 12th Report of the Historical Manuscripts
Commission* (1890).

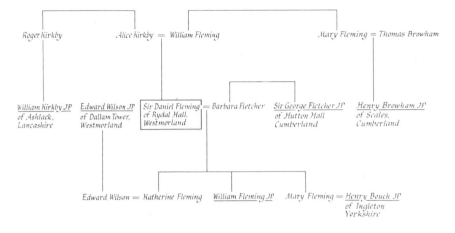

3 Sir Daniel Fleming's family links to other Justices of the Peace.

justice and order which made him a powerful prosecutor of the Quakers and of all other malefactors. His family connections, and ties of kinship to other local Justices (see illustration 3) were particularly useful in the prosecution of offences which occurred over wide distances or in different counties. When the threat of disguised robbers arose in south Westmorland and they lighted on the house of an old acquaintance of Sir Daniel's for their first major burglary, they chose a redoubtable foe. It would have been impossible to write this book without Fleming for we would have had no detailed records of what happened.

The chief official under the Justice, apart from the sheriff, was the High Constable. The Justices operated at the county level, while each county was divided into wards. Westmorland was divided into four parts, one of which was the Lonsdale ward. The person responsible for each of these was the High Constable. The duties of this officer were summarized at the time.[32]

> The High Constable has the direction of the petty constables, head-boroughs, and tithingmen, within his hundred: his duty is to keep the peace, and apprehend felons, rioters &c. and to make hue and cry after felons; and take care that the watch be duly kept in his hundred; and that the statutes for punishing rogues and vagrants to put in execution. He ought to present unlawful games; tipling, and drunkenness; bloodshed, affrays &c. He is to execute precepts and warrants, directed to him by Justices of the Peace, and make returns to the Sessions of the Peace to all the articles contained in his oath, or that concern his office.

[32] Giles Jacob, *A New Law Dictionary* (5th edn, 1744), under 'Constable'.

They were clearly men of power and responsibility, chosen by the Justices.[33] One of those selected for this key position in the Lonsdale ward was a man named William Smorthwait. Born in the same year as Sir George Jeffreys, Smorthwait was thirty-six in 1680, when he was described as a 'tall, proper man'. His grandfather moved to Middleton from Dent in the early seventeenth century. His father was a feltmaker but obviously a prosperous one for he was styled 'gent.' in 1667, and was important enough to sit on the Quarter Sessions jury and also acted as High Constable in 1667. He had two sons, William and Henry, to whom he left his goods when he died in 1670. To William he also left Abbey Farm in Middleton (see illustration 4). Smorthwait's mother remarried a man of bad reputation. William married in about 1673 and proceeded to have several children baptized between then and 1677. He was rated on a relatively large four-hearth house in 1674. In 1679 or 1680 he moved outside the parish boundary into Yorkshire, to the township of Clapham. He was not only comparatively wealthy, but also inherited his father's legal roles. He was a juror at the Quarter Sessions at Kendal in 1673 and 1677, and was chosen

4 Abbey Farm in Middleton, long the home of the Smorthwait family.

[33] For interesting accounts of two High Constables in this area, see R. S. France, 'A High Constable's Register' and M. A. Logie, 'Benjamin Browne of Troutbeck, High Constable of Kendal Ward, 1711–1732', *TCWAAS*, n.s., LXXI (1971).

High Constable for the ward in 1677–8. He seems to have performed this role somewhat negligently, for in October 1678 a warrant was made out for his good behaviour and 'for not paying the public moneys in his hands according to a former order of the Justices'.[34] What lay behind this note is disclosed in Fleming's papers in a 'Memoirs' on Smorthwait.

> Will. Smor. being High Constable for Lonsdale ward 1678, had of the countries money in his hand, which he refusing to pay unto his successor, he was ordered to do it by the Quarter Sessions at Kendal. But he contemptuously disobeying that order, the Justices of the Peace issued out their warrant for his good behaviour, and upon his refusal, for the conveying of him to gaol. Jo. Bainbridge constable of Middleton arrested him in Middleton & pursued him into Barbon May 24 1679, where taking him with the assistance of Joseph Gibson, Thos. Ellis & Rich. Cragg conveyed him unto Appleby gaol May 25 1679, where he stayed until he had paid the countries money, which was soon after.

We thus have a picture of a yeoman, aspiring to minor gentry, with a large farm, a wife and family, and a tendency to abuse his office. Fuller details of his life and that of his younger brother are given later, for this was the man who would be the ringleader of the 'black and terrible troop'.

At the local level the preservation of order depended on the constables. One of the many constables for one of the nine townships in Kirkby Lonsdale was a certain Edward Bainbridge. He too came from a long-established local family, going back to the sixteenth century and having some connection with a Master and also a Senior Fellow of Christ's College, Cambridge.[35] The family had lived at Gillfoot in Mansergh since at least 1629 and Edward's father was clearly a substantial man, styled a gentle-man and a freeholder with rights to vote in 1640. Both parents were still alive in 1680 when Edward, born in the same year as Smorthwait and Judge Jeffreys, was aged thirty-six. He was five years younger than his brother John and, like his brother, was still unmarried. Their house was comfort-ably furnished as successive inventories of possessions show and both brothers were able to sign their names. They were clearly farmers, raising cattle and sheep on a medium-sized farm. On at least one occasion Edward was constable of Mansergh, for in 1674 the hearth tax list was signed by him as constable. He was described as 'a tall man, with sad coloured hair'. On one occasion he wore a 'whitish stuff coat and bright buttons', on another he

---

[34] Kendal Indictment Book, p. 245 (WRO).

[35] Christopher Bainbridge, Senior Fellow of Christ's, had a younger brother Thomas, who left a widow Margaret. She stated in a deposition to be quoted later that Edward Bainbridge was a kinsman of her husband. For a contemporary genealogy of the family of the Master of Christ's, see Jane M. Ewbank, *Antiquary on Horseback* (Kendal, 1963), p. 33. One of Christopher's uncles, Thomas Bainbridge, was Master of the College and Milton's tutor.

'had a white hat on his head, with a broad belt about his middle buckled before, and sad coloured clothes.' Details concerning his family, his farming life and house appear in local documents. None of them would have enabled one to predict in 1680 that Bainbridge would appear for separate offences, each carrying the death penalty, in 1682, 1683, 1684 and 1686, or that Fleming would one day write a special letter to Judge Jeffreys interceding on his behalf.

The constable's task of maintaining order was lightened by the numerous other officers in the village. One man, who during his life was not only constable but also in charge of weights and measures, becklooker, swine-looker and bylawman, was Bryan Thompson of Kirkby Lonsdale. Just as Bainbridge represents the middling yeoman farmer, so Thompson may be taken to represent a middling artisan, who gradually became poorer during his life. Thompson's family had been in Kirkby since at least the middle of the century. The family seems to have been a reasonably affluent one, with a three-hearth house which had become a five-hearth one by 1674. Thompson's father styled himself a 'yeoman' in his will and both mother and father signed their wills. From the property they left, it appears that they were farmers. Bryan, who was the third son, continued to farm part of the time but combined this with work as a glazier and running an alehouse. He had been born in 1647 and was thus aged thirty-three in 1680. He married in 1670 a woman who shortly after gave birth to a premaritally conceived child. A further five children were baptized before 1680, three of whom were still living at home when the family was listed in 1695. Thompson frequently undertook glazing jobs on the local church in his early years. Both Thompson and his wife were presented for minor assaults and affrays before 1680, Thompson on three occasions, his wife once. They also infringed the local by-laws in various other ways — by leaving a dead horse in the highway, keeping unringed pigs, not making fences, playing cards in a neighbour's house at 'unseasonable' times. But other inhabitants in Kirkby Lonsdale were presented for similar offences. It would again have been extremely difficult to have guessed that Thompson would play a major role, as receiver of stolen property, informer as to the whereabouts of valuables to be stolen, coin clipper, thief, and as a burglar involved in a serious assault.

We now have some idea of the principal actors and of the physical and legal world within which they would move. The interaction between personalities and structures over the next four years enables us to see behind the formal legal documents. The affair which started the whole process occurred in November 1680.

2
'The Stoutest Deed that ever Man Did'

The first hint of the impending dramatic conflict is recorded in a later 'Memoirs' by Daniel Fleming, which we have briefly cited.

> Mr Henry Bateman, and other honest and able persons in, or near, Old Hutton in the said country, acquainting the Justices of Peace with the great fear and danger they were in, occasioned by some persons who rid armed and with vizards; there was an order made at Michaelmas Quarter Sessions 1680, for the making of search twice every week at the least, and for the disarming of all suspicious persons, and warrants were sent out by the High Constables accordingly in Nov. 1680.[1]

A copy of the warrant which the Justices sent out is recorded in the Quarter Sessions order book.[2]

> The court being informed that divers persons ride armed with vizards to the terror of his Majesty's subjects. It is therefore ordered that the High Constables of Kendal and Lonsdale wards do issue out their warrants to the petty constables within both their wards to make private search, as well by night as by day, in places suspected twice a week at least. And also to make search for all arms, and if they find any such like men to bring before the next Justice of Peace there for to be examined and also all the armour they so find to bring them to the next Justice of Peace.

The order was then passed on to the constables by the High Constable. Fleming kept a rough copy of the order made by John Browham, High Constable of Kendal ward, on 20 November 1680.[3]

---

[1] The quotation is from the Fleming manuscripts. All quotations in the text with no specific reference can be assumed to be from these manuscripts or, in the case of Assize despositions, from the class ASSIZES 45 in the Public Record Office, London. A detailed description is given in appendix D, p. 215.
[2] Kendal Indictment and Order Book 1669–91, p. 266, 8 October 1680 (WRO).
[3] Fleming Letters, 2337.

By virtue of an order of the last Quarter Sessions holden at Kendal:
These are in his Majesty's name to command you that you make search
twice every week at the least (as well by night as by day) in all suspicious
houses and places within your constablewick. And if you shall find any
person or persons therein that you know or suspect to ride armed, or with
vizards, to the fear of his Majesty's liege people, that you forthwith
apprehend them and convey them before some of his Majesty's Justices
of the Peace for the county, to be examined and dealt withal according to
law. And you are likewise to seize upon such arms as you shall find in any
of the houses or places aforesaid, or possessed by any of the said persons
and deliver them to some Justice of the Peace, to be disposed according
to law. And hereof fail not at your peril.

The menace was real enough, for in that month, six armed men, some of
them wearing masks, broke into a house at the very same Old Hutton from
which the warning had come, and stole £43 and other goods from an aged,
half blind gentleman named Robert Robinson. This was the act which one
of the robbers, Edward Bainbridge, described as 'the stoutest deed that ever
man did'. In the absence of the depositions and Fleming's notes, all that we
would know about the event would be contained in one draft bill.[4]

William Smorthwait late of Clapham in Yorks, yeoman, Henry Smorthwait late of New Hutton in Westmorland, yeoman, Edward Bainbridge
later of Mansergh in Westmorland, yeoman, and William Manning
junior late of Holmescales in Westmorland, tailor, for robbing of Robert
Robinson of Old Hutton, gent., and taking from him forty-three pounds
in silver, three silver spoons, a pair of shoes, a pair of silver weights and a
pewter bottle, the third day of November 1680 about two o'clock in the
morning in the dwelling place of Robert Robinson, the said Robert
Robinson then being within & put him in fear and dread by the same.
Witnesses: Robert Robinson, Thomas Robinson, Margaret Dickonson,
Dorothy Stainbank, John Jackson, George Holme, James Dawson,
Robert Ward, John Barker.

This is relatively detailed for an indictment, yet it still leaves us with a
shadowy picture of what happened at the event which proved to be the
centre of the subsequent prosecutions. Fortunately, we can amplify the
picture from the evidence Fleming collected.

The burglary itself seems to have been something of an accident, for the
robbers had originally planned to steal the money on the highway. After the
affair, one of Edward Bainbridge's neighbours, John Barker,

---

[4] ASSI/44/31 (PRO).

desired earnestly of him to know whether Mr Edmund Lodge[5] was anyway guilty concerning the robbing of Mr Robert Robinson; to which Edward Bainbridge falling upon his knees answered, Woe be unto him, for he was the ruin of us all; saying further that Mr Lodge had sent several times for them before they could go; and he acquainted them that if they delayed coming Robert Robinson's money would be disposed of. Edward Bainbridge did then further confess to this examinate, that Mr Lodge did give them, Edward Bainbridge and William Smorthwait, notice of a prize; Mr Lodge being to travel over a moor with his friend, who had charge of money about him. But Edward Bainbridge and William Smorthwait drinking too long at an alehouse missed the opportunity of meeting with them.

It may have been after this misadventure that the conspirators had to replan the more serious matter of the break-in. Their planning session does not seem to have been very effectively carried out, for it was witnessed. It was clearly important for Lodge not to be seen in the company of people who would be suspects, yet he met with the others in a house in Kendal a fortnight before the break-in. Margaret Blakeling told how 'being a servant unto Mr John French in Kendal did see Edmund Lodge, Henry Smorthwait and three other men whom she knew not, in the house of Mr French about a fortnight before Martinmas gone two years, and she did fill them ale in the parlour of the house: but doth not remember what discourse they then had.' She was more cautious in her examination than she had been at the time, according to two other witnesses. George Holme said that she had told him that 'she did there see the two Smorthwaits, Ned Bainbridge and Mr Lodge all drinking about a fortnight before Robert Robinson of Old Hutton gentleman was robbed, and going suddenly into the room amongst them she said they were talking of strange things.' This was corroborated by Richard Rigg, a waller of Old Hutton, to whom Margaret had also spoken, and added that the event occurred on Kendal fair day, and that having heard 'very strange discourse amongst them' she had 'looked there would be nought that was good amongst them, before she heard of Robert Robinson's house breaking.' We begin to see why the neighbours very soon suspected Bainbridge and the others.

Fleming believed that this burglary was the most important and well witnessed of the crimes of the disguised robbers. Consequently, a large part of the depositions gathered in 1683 concerned this case. Eleven people gave evidence concerning the burglary: six were within the house when it was

---

[5] Edmund Lodge was one of the occupants of the house. He was also curate and schoolmaster of Old Hutton. His name does not appear in either of the standard biographical registers of graduates of Oxford and Cambridge by Foster and Venn. He was later vicar of Clapham, 1684–96.

attacked, two of the suspected burglars and three neighbours also gave evidence. The location of those who were asleep or pretending to be so at the point when the burglary occurred, and their relationship to each other, is shown in illustration 5.

The house itself was part of a small hamlet of three or four houses lying about half a mile from the main centre of Old Hutton. As well as the Robinson house, there was a mill-house occupied by the Jackson family, situated about fifty yards to the north by a small stream.

It it perhaps easiest to reconstruct what happened if we see it first through the eyes of the central character, Edward Bainbridge. He described how it started, by

> Mr Lodge minister of Old Hutton acquainting John Jackson of Old Hutton that forty pounds and upward was lying in a chest ready to be taken away in Robert Robinson's house. John Jackson acquainted William Smorthwait, Henry Smorthwait, William Manning junior and this examinate therewith. And William Smorthwait, Henry Smorthwait,

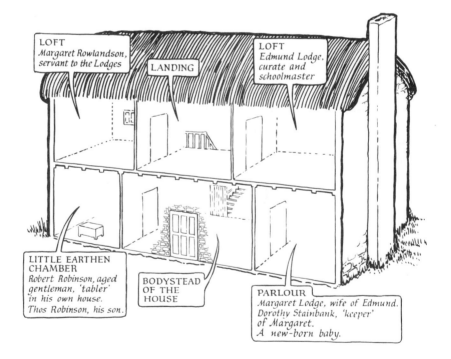

5 *Reconstruction of Beckside, Old Hutton, at the time of the burglary on 3 November 1680.*

William Manning and this examinate did meet upon Hutton fell upon Monday the first day of November 1680 and going all together to Beckside mill in Old Hutton where John Jackson was, with a design to rob the house of Robert Robinson, but William Manning and John Jackson being then both drunk it was deferred till the Wednesday night following. And then all the persons meeting together a little within the fell yeat did go to the house of Robert Robinson late in the night, and then this examinate tumbling a great many sheaves of brackens to a window on one story high, did hold the same till William Manning (who knew the house) did get in at a window thereof. And he opening the out-door, William Smorthwait and Henry Smorthwait did go into the same and did rob Robert Robinson of about forty pounds with some plate and other things, their faces being disguised with masks or vizards. And during the robbery he did hold their horses (but whether John Jackson was then in the said house or no this examinate knows not). After which robbery William Smorthwait, Henry Smorthwait, William Manning, John Jackson and he did all forthwith go to their several homes, and all the money and plate then taken from Robert Robinson, William and Henry Smorthwait did carry away the same. And the said money was so clipped by William Smorthwait and Henry Smorthwait (as this examinate believes) as this examinate and John Jackson's shares thereof could hardly be offered in payment.

Bainbridge in a further examination confessed

that after he had holden the horses a while near the house of Robert Robinson he did go in at the window of the house after William Manning, and Manning going down the stairs fell down some of them and William Smorthwait did hold a Bible to Robert Robinson to swear whether he had any more gold or silver than what they had taken from him. And this examinate heard that Robert Robinson did then swear he had no more and that Mr Lodge did laugh when he heard Robert Robinson sworn. He also saith, that he hath heard William Smorthwait say that Mr Lodge had part of the money taken from Robert Robinson.

The chief victim of the burglary was Robert Robinson, who said that

The third day of November 1680 about two of the clock in the morning, there came about six persons in vizards and riding coats (unknown to this deponent) and broke into his house and broke open a chest in the chamber, and took forth forty-three pounds in silver, three silver spoons, a pair of shoes, a pair of silver weights and a pewter bottle and other goods of this informant. And he saith that he believes one of the said felons break a staincher [stanchion] of a window and so got into the house. And opened the door and let in there into the house; and the persons had their swords drawn, and one of them run this deponent into the finger.

In a second deposition Robinson stated that he suspected William and Henry Smorthwait, Edward Bainbridge, John Jackson and William Manning of robbing him. This provides the stark outline of what was taken. Further details of what Robinson witnessed are given indirectly by a neighbour, James Dawson of Old Hutton, who said

> that the very morning next after Robert Robinson of Old Hutton was robbed, Robert came to him at his house in Old Hutton and acquainted him that about twelve of the clock in the night Mr Lodge's maid was called up (who lay in bed near the window where the robbers or some of them came into the house) which maid went into the parlour where her mistress lay in child-bed and was there kept in that room whilst the robbery was committed, which continued until about one of the clock in the morning, whilst the robbers were in the house. That two or three of the robbers came into Robert Robinson's chamber where he lay that night, and demanded of him his money, acquainting him that they were come for it, to which Robert answered that he had little money, save what was in the country.[6] And that Thomas Robinson son of Robert lying in another bed in the same room, and one of the robbers pricking him with a sword, called to his father and said pray tell them where your money is, upon which Robert acquainted the robbers that his money was in a chest within the same room. And Robert Robinson did then further acquaint this examinant that the robbers broke open a cupboard placed in the wall near the fire in the house and did take away the money that was therein. And that there was in the same room a large cupboard with divers galls or divisions therein, all which belonged to Mr Lodge save one, in which Robert usually laid some papers, which gall was broken open by the robbers, and the other not meddled with by them. And that about the going away of the robbers, some of them returned back and enquired of Robert for his gold and that Mr Lodge made little or no assistance during the time of the robbery, only at their going away, he called upon his son Thomas to help to look after them. And that none of the goods belonging to Mr Lodge was taken away by the robbers.

Dawson ended by describing the malefactors thus: 'William Smorthwait is a tall, proper man, Henry Smorthwait a middle sized man, with yellowish hair, and Edward Bainbridge is a tall man, with sad coloured hair.'

Sharing Robert Robinson's room on the night of the break-in was his son Thomas. He described how

---

[6] In other words, out on loan or invested in trade.

About the third day of November 1680, when his father Robert Robinson
and he were lying in two several [i.e. separate] beds in one room within
his father's house in Old Hutton, between one and two of the clock in the
night, about five men rushed into the room with drawn swords or
rapiers, and with something over their faces. Who demanded of this
examinate's father where his money was, and the robbers also threatening him he spoke to his father to acquaint them where his money lay, who
told them that it was in a chest at his bed foot, and they thereupon broke
it open, and did take away his money. That some of the thieves wounded
him in the neck with one of their rapiers, which was often run through his
bed-clothes. That some of the thieves did also break open a cupboard in
the body-stead of the house belonging to this examinate's father, and
took some money, as he believes, out of it. He also saith that the robbers
did take away from his father about forty-three pounds, with divers
other things, as he verily believeth; and that they, or some of them, came
in at an old window, an heap of bracken being laid on the outside thereof.
That when the thieves were gone, he got up, and would have gone out at
the door, but they having locked it on the outside, he did go out at the old
window and opened the door, and then Mr Lodge came out of the same
and he and this examinate acquainted some of the neighbours with this
burglary. He also saith that he heard his father say that Mrs Lodge
should [i.e. did] acquaint him that the night before the burglary was
committed she was sore afraid of robbers and troubled with the clapping
of the window leaves; whereupon this examinate did in the evening
following make fast the leaves of the old window, which were opened as
he hath heard before Mr Lodge's maid servant did go to bed that night
when the robbers came in, but who opened them he knows not. He also saith
that on a Sunday after, he did see William Smorthwait in the chapel of
Old Hutton and looking very much at him, thought him to be one of the
said robbers; he being like to the tallest of them, who threatened most
this examinate and his father, and stayed the longest in the room. He also
saith that all the rest of the robbers were such like persons as Henry
Smorthwait, Edward Bainbridge, John Jackson & William Manning
junior, but they all being then disguised, and altering their voices, he did
not certainly know them.

Edmund Lodge and his wife were also in the house. Implicated as an
accomplice, Lodge's examination and that of his wife, are among the most
interesting in the whole set. Lodge said

that about Candlemas 1678 he did take a messuage and some lands
thereunto adjoining in Old Hutton of Robert Robinson gentleman, for
the term of three years then next following, which he enjoyed accordingly. That he did take Robert Robinson and Thomas Robinson his son

during the same term of three years to table[7] and Robert and Thomas did usually lie in a little earthen room called the little chamber in the messuage. That his wife did fall sick and was brought in bed of a son upon Wednesday the twenty seventh day of October 1680. That he was in Mr John French's house in Kendal with Henry Smorthwait where he stayed until Robert Robinson called of him; but doth not well remember the day when it was. He further saith that having been at Kellet and Whittington in the county of Lancaster, he came home upon Tuesday the second day of November 1680, about the sun setting, and having been from home one night or two, and wanting [i.e. lacking] his usual rest, did go to bed that night (about nine of the clock) sooner than his accustomed time. He being asleep was awaked by his wife's calling upon her maid (then called Margery Rowlandson, now the wife of John Dickonson of Lupton Row, yeoman) who laid in the loft over where Robert Robinson and Thomas, his son did lie that night. And the maid not answering her mistress, called her up, and she thereupon did go downstairs into the parlour where her mistress lay in childbed. After which he did sleep about one hour, and was then suddenly awaked by the noise of a man below the stairs speaking out loud these words: Your house is surrounded, where is your money, You have thousands of pounds by you; and he did also then hear Robert Robinson make him an answer, whereupon he did leap out of his bed in the loft above the parlour, and did go in his shirt unto the stair head, and cried out what is the matter, and who is there; upon which a lusty man at the stairs foot with his face covered with white and with a drawn sword in his hand answered him saying, Damn you for a dog, hold your peace or I will cut your flesh from your bones. And he pausing a while, called upon Margaret Rowlandson in the parlour to open the casement and to cry out for help, upon which one of the disguised persons below, said, You dog be at quiet, or else I will let a brace of bullets into your belly. Whereupon he was silent and looking down through a hole above the stair foot door did see two men (of above a middle stature with horseman's coats on tied about the waist, one of the coats of a white grey, one with white, and the other with black, with their faces covered) standing in the body-stead of the house, with their swords drawn, and either with a lighted candle in his hand close by the cupboard. And after they had whispered together, they did break open the locker in the room. He further saith that he

---

[7] The meaning of 'tabling' in someone's house was explained in a letter from Robert Robinson to Daniel Fleming shortly after the start of the trials (Fleming Letters, 2623): 'Sir, I had let the house and four closes of ground to farm for three years to one Edmund Lodge our school-master, and I was but a tabler with him. I had no command in the house, but only of myself. He might entertain friends or whom he would and never make me acquainted, it being his house during his lease.'

believes there were four of the robbers in the house; he seeing one of them keep his stand at the stair-foot, two in the body-stead of the house, and he heard the voice of a fourth in the little chamber where Robert Robinson and his son did lie, who in a threatening manner asked Robert where was the bladder.[8] He also said that during this time he heard his wife to make great lamentations, and desired him to hold his peace, whereupon one of the robbers calling her whore, bid her hold her peace or he would nail her to her bed. So soon as he did see the robbers put out their candles and make away, he called upon Thomas Robinson and bid him make ready to follow them, who going with him to the door found it locked on the outside. Whereupon Thomas Robinson did go out at the window where the robbers broke in, as he believes, who opening the door he and Thomas did go together to call up some of the neighbours, he going to the house of Richard Jackson[9] a miller, where calling at a window three times John Jackson asked what was the matter. Which, when this examinate had told him, he came to the door in his shirt and let in this examinate and Thomas. And after that John Jackson and other neighbours did go into the house lately robbed and there abode until it was daylight. He further says that Robert Robinson received a prick with a sword in one of his fingers, as he believes, by one of the robbers, and Thomas Robinson also affirmed that he had received a prick with a sword by some of them. He further says the he believes that Robert Robinson had then taken from him to the value of forty pounds or upwards, three silver spoons, a pair of new shoes, divers hooks and eyes, and a pewter brandy-bottle. He also says that none of the robbers came into the room where he was above the stairs, nor hath he heard that any of them did go into the parlour where his wife lay that night. He also says that Dorothy Stainbank of Killington, spinster, did lie at night with his wife.

It seems likely that Lodge's desire to distance himself from the robbers had made him report as much of their violence, particularly in speech, as possible. Their reputed threats would not only help to preserve his innocence but explain why he took so little action, Lodge mentions three women who were also present in the house, his wife, his servant, and a woman who was acting as a 'keeper' to his wife after her delivery of a child. Margaret Lodge said that she

being in child-bed the third of November 1680, and having a desire to drink, acquainted Dorothy Stainbank then her keeper therewith, who

---

[8] Money was often kept in a dried animal's bladder.
[9] Richard Jackson is correct; John Jackson later said that he was living in his father's house and Fleming made a note: 'Richard Jackson of Old Hutton, miller, the robbers being in the mill, get his son to confess.'

laid that night with her and was very sleepy having waked four or five nights before. Whereupon this examinate called upon Margaret Row-landson her then servant, who laid in a chamber over the room where Robert Robinson did then lie, and who came down presently to her, Margaret having laid upon the bed in her clothes that night. A little after, about one of the clock in the morning, she heard a dog bark very much, and soon after heard the noise of one going down the stairs, upon which she bid Margaret go forth to see what the matter was, who going to the parlour door could not pull it open it being made fast, or some holding it on the other side. Immediately after this a great noise this examinate heard in the house. And Dorothy Stainbank calling upon this examinate's husband, he forthwith leapt out of his bed and came into the stairs in his shirt, and one of the robbers prodding at him with his sword, he bid Margaret Rowlandson call out of the window for help; upon which she going towards the window one opened the parlour door, and swore he would run her to the heart if she said a word. She did see him who opened the door, and who had a white thing over his face, his hair appeared to be of a flaxen colour, and he had a white hat on his head, with a broad belt about his middle buckled before, and sad coloured clothes; he stood at the door with a lighted candle in his left hand, and a drawn sword or rapier in his right. He did not come into the parlour. She also saith, that she heard Margaret say that the man who stood at the parlour door has a pair of grey stockings on, and was then without his shoes. She believes that two of the robbers came in at the window near the bed where Margaret used to lie, and one of them held the parlour door and the other opened the out-door which was usually barred with an iron gavelock. She further saith, that she heard one of the robbers call aloud unto Robert Robinson, saying, Old Rogue where is thy money, but did not hear what answer he gave him; and she also heard Dorothy Stainbank whilst the robbers were in the house, say that she believed the voice of one of the robbers was very like unto the voice of Edward Bainbridge of Mansergh. She also saith, that the robbers left the house soon after two of the clock in the morning taking away none of the goods belonging to her husband or herself, and only cutting and bruising a new pewter tankard.

The details match the other accounts very well.

A further witness was Margaret Rowlandson, the maidservant. She de-scribed how

being a servant unto Edmund Lodge, the second day of November 1680, did go to bed between nine and ten of the clock that evening but did not put off her clothes being to rise early next morning to wash. And she also saith, that about eleven of the clock that night her master Mr Lodge did call her up to go down unto his wife in the parlour, which she forthwith did, and the dogs beginning to bark her mistress bid her go forth to see the occasion thereof. Whereupon she did go out of the parlour, but being somewhat afraid, durst not open the entry door (which was usually barred with an iron gavelock) without a lighted candle, upon which she returned into the parlour, and lighting a candle she heard the entry door open and the gavelock fall down, which made her forbear to go to the door, and to sit her down in a chair. Soon after this the dogs gave over barking and her mistress bid her again to go forth to see what the matter was. Whereupon, lighting a candle, she did go to the parlour door, but could not get it opened, some holding the same, which, telling her mistress, the robbers called forth that the house was set round, they were come for money, and money they would have. Hereupon she called upon her master, who leapt out of bed, and came down the stairs in his shirt, and he lifting up the sneck of the door at the foot of the stairs, one of the robbers (with a drawn sword in one hand and a lighted candle in the other) said Sirrah stand, he would have his flesh off his bones if he came one foot further. Hereupon Mr Lodge running up the stairs called to her to open the casement and call for help. But this robber at the door of the parlour threatening her, she durst not open the casement nor make any noise. She also saith that she heard some of the robbers very much threaten Robert Robinson who lay in a little ground-chamber, and which so affrighted her, that she desired her mistress to give her leave to lie upon the bed by her. She further said, that her bed was over the chamber where Robert Robinson did lie, and was within a yard of the window, where the robbers or some of them came in; they having laid (as she believes) a great many brackens to the outside of the window, which were found there the next morning. She also saith that she believes the robbers came into the house between twelve and one of the clock that night and did go away soon after two. That she did see the robber which stood at the parlour door to have a pair of grey stockings on, without his shoes, a white hat, and a horseman's coat. . . . She also saith that she believes the robbers, or some of them, had wounded Robert Robinson: for that he affirmed the same, and she found the sheets bloody when she made his bed the next day. That not any of the robbers came into the parlour; there being none there save Mrs Lodge, Dorothy Stainbank (who lay with Mrs Lodge that night) a young child and this examinate.

The final direct witness was Dorothy Stainbank, who corroborated the details:

That being keeper to Mrs Lodge, wife of Edmund Lodge, Mrs Lodge had a desire to have her maid Margaret Rowlandson called, which this examinate did several times, and she not hearing, this examinate called

then upon Mr Lodge, who calling upon the maid, she forthwith came
into the parlour, where Mrs Lodge and this examinate were in bed
together, she having waked near a week before. That the robbers came
into the house about one of the clock in the morning and continued there
about one hour. . . . That she heard the robbers make a great noise with
threatening, swearing, cursing & clattering of their swords. That she
said unto Mrs Lodge, Woe be unto Edward Bainbridge if he come hither
to affright me.

Some further information on the affair is also contained in the various
depositions by, and concerning, the man who lived in the adjoining house,
John Jackson. One of those first suspected, William Speight of Old Hutton,
said that he had met John Jackson in the alehouse in Old Hutton at
Christmas 1680, and Jackson had confessed to taking part in the robbery
and had given the names of the robbers. A few days later, Speight told this
to James Dawson and 'desired him to acquaint Robert Robinson of the
same.' Dawson delivered to Fleming at Rydal Hall a more detailed information from Speight. This survives in Fleming's manuscripts, but was not
sent to the Assize Clerk, perhaps to shield Speight who was a useful witness.
Speight said that

About the month of November 1680 there was a robbery committed in
the night time at the house of Robert Robinson, by the confession of
Robert Robinson, forty pounds of money or other goods to the value
thereof and upwards carried away, proper goods of Robert Robinson.
And he further maketh oath that, about the 10th day of January next
following the robbery, he met with John Jackson of the Beckside in
Hutton and went with him to the house of Henry Guy, alehouse keeper
and there falling into discourse about the robbery, Jackson did then and
there affirm that it was no sin to take money from Robert Robinson, and
after a while called this informant out of the house and said to him that if
he would not discover it he would tell him who took away Robinson's
money and committed the robbery. He did then promise secrecy, and
desired to know who the robbers were & after what manner the same was
done, whereupon Jackson did then affirm that himself did creep through
a window into the house, then opened the door for and to William
Smorthwait, Edward Bainbridge and William Manning who came in to
the house and took away the money, & that a parson in the house,
intimating Mr Lodge the tenant of Robinson, had his share of the money
and that Edward Bainbridge had a pair of shoes that was taken at the
same time from Robert Robinson. And did further say to this informant
that he had several times had Lodge's horse to ride into Yorkshire upon
suchlike business. And did then offer to this informant that if he would
any time tell Jackson of any man that had a good purse they could

(intimating his companions) take it from him & this informant should have his share, as well as if this informant were there at the taking of it, and without danger, for that they could put things upon their faces that their nearest neighbours could not know them.

Meanwhile, Jackson himself utterly denied being involved in the burglary. He admitted that the Smorthwaits and Bainbridge had tried to bribe him to take part, but claimed he had refused to accept the bribe. Jackson's account of the events of the night placed him safely in bed in a house about sixty yards from the scene of the burglary. He described how

The very night of the robbery he and William Manning junior going towards the house of Robert Robinson, Manning told him that William Smorthwait, Henry Smorthwait and Edward Bainbridge were that night to meet to break the house. And soon after they three did overtake Manning and him, and they were earnest to persuade him to enter the house. But upon his refusal, Manning and Bainbridge agreed to enter the house. And upon their going thither, he did go home unto his father's house, which was within sixty yards of Robert Robinson's house, and did go to bed. And about two hours after, he was called up by Mr Lodge and Thomas Robinson, son of Robert Robinson, who acquainted him that the house was lately broken and that above £40 and other goods were taken away from Robert Robinson. And within a week afterwards William Smorthwait, Henry Smorthwait and William Manning did acquaint him with the robbery and that Manning and Bainbridge did enter by a window into the house, and that one of them did open the out-door and let in William Smorthwait and Henry Smorthwait and that William Smorthwait did swear Robert Robinson whether he had any more gold or silver than they had found. And he also saith, that William Smorthwait and Henry Smorthwait told him that the spoons which were taken from Robert Robinson were cut in sunder by William Smorthwait and sold with clippings and other bullion unto a goldsmith at York. And he also saith, that Mr Lodge told that hearing one of the persons who came in at the window get a fall, he could not hold from laughing thereat. And about a fortnight after the robbery Henry Smorthwait delivered forty shillings unto this examinate, desiring him to give it privately to Mr Lodge, which he did accordingly and which he believes to be sent him concerning the robbery.

This, then, is what lay behind a single indictment. Yet even to obtain that one indictment in court required a great effort on the part of the legal officers. The way in which the robbers were caught and charged is revealed by Fleming's manuscripts. The formal prosecution for this burglary only started two years later, in January 1683. In the intervening two years it became clear that the Smorthwaits were involved in another activity, which the law regarded as even more serious, namely clipping and coining. It was for counterfeiting that warrants would first be issued against them.

3
Clippers and Coiners

Silver was being drained out of England during the second half of the seventeenth century. It was immensely profitable to melt coins down and sell them as bullion in Europe, where they would then be attracted towards the East.[1] There was thus an acute shortage of silver coinage. Furthermore, a good many of the coins in circulation had been hammer-struck and were consequently irregular in shape, with no raised rim or clear cut edge. Since the design was frequently struck off the centre, part of the design was often missing. All this meant that it was relatively easy to clip pieces of metal from the edges of coins.[2] This situation made it economically rational for people not only to produce large quantities of local trade tokens, (in our region such tokens were produced in Sedbergh, Dent, Kendal and numerous other places)[3] but also to engage in more illicit activities. There were two major activities, making new coins from base metals, or 'coining', and cutting pieces off the edges of coins, termed 'clipping.'

The powerful pressure of market forces thus pushed people towards tampering with the coinage. It could even be argued that to do so was to provide a service which would help trade in general. It must have seemed only a short step away from many legal activities. If one could issue trade tokens or get a licence to mint money, why should one not clip and coin? Yet the very ease with which this could be done and its attractiveness as a rational economic activity may have been among the reasons that it was, along with an attempted attack on the government, the most serious of all offences — high treason, punishable by hanging and quartering for men, burning for women. Acts of Parliament in the reigns of Edward III and Henry V had dealt with this offence, but the statute which Fleming and the

[1] For the reasons for the movement of silver, see Joyce Oldham Appleby, 'Locke, Liberalism and the Natural Law of Money', *Past and Present*, 71 (May 1976), pp. 45–6.
[2] John Craig, *The Mint: a History of the London Mint from 287 to 1948* (Cambridge, 1953), p. 27.
[3] Rev. W. Thompson, *Sedbergh, Garsdale and Dent* (Leeds, 1910), pp. 178–9; Cornelius Nicholson, *The Annals of Kendal* (1861), pp. 130–35.

other Justices worked was passed in 1562.[4] As summarized in the abbreviated *Statutes of the Peace* which Fleming so carefully annotated, the law stated 'It shall be high treason, to clip, wash, round or file current money, whether English or Foreign; for which the offender shall suffer, as in the case of high treason, and also shall forfeit his goods and chattels for ever, and his lands also during life.' To this Fleming added, after the word treason, 'for lucre sake' and, after 'offender', the words 'his counsellors, consentors, and aiders'. A further statute of Elizabeth repeated the punishment,[5] but stressed that there 'shall be no corruption of blood, or loss of dower.' The savagery of the punishment may also have been related to the fact that, in the highly monetized economy present in England from at least the time of the first statute in the mid-fourteenth century, to tamper with the coinage undermined the whole economic and social system. If money could not be trusted and could be manipulated, the state was indeed threatened. Symbolically, too, these activities were treason, for the king's portrait was on the coin, and to deface it was to attack the king.

Out of the conflict between law and economic self-interest there grew a particularly acute problem for the Justices, for in the 1660s they found a growing number of otherwise law-abiding citizens were becoming involved in counterfeiting coins.[6] The ambivalence of attitude might even affect the judicial machinery. A sermon preached in 1694 was explicitly to 'wean' people[7]

> from that soft pernicious tenderness, that sometimes, certainly, restrains the hand of justice, slackens the care and vigilance of magistrates, keeps back the under officers, corrupts the juries (for passions and affections bribe as well as gifts) and with-holds the evidence, both from appearing, and from speaking out, when they appear.

The author explained that the reason why 'more pity usually attends these criminals and others', was that the harm they did was not directed against any specific individual: 'our pity arises from hence, that we see men going to suffer death for a crime, by which we know of none that are undone, or greatly injured; the evil is unfixed, and undetermined, and we cannot put ourselves into their condition who are hurt by these offenders.' In the case of

---

[4] Statutes of the Realm, 5 Elizabeth, cap. XI.
[5] Statutes of the Realm, 18 Elizabeth, cap. I.
[6] This is not to imply that it was a new problem. For examples from earlier periods and literary sources, see Burton Milligan, 'Counterfeiters and Coin-Clippers in the Sixteenth and Seventeenth Centuries', *Notes and Queries*, 182 (February, 1942), pp. 100–105.
[7] W. Fleetwood, *A Sermon against clipping, preached before the Right Honourable the Lord Mayor and the Court of Aldermen, at the Guild-Hall Chapel* (printed 1694, Keynes Library, King's College, Cambridge). The quotations come from pp. 11, 17, 21–4. For the sympathy of at least one judge, though it did not soften his sentence, see G. W. Keeton, *Lord Chancellor Jeffreys and the Stuart Cause* (1965), p. 123.

theft, we identify with the victim, with his fright and injury. But with clipping, 'we think immediately only of a damage to the Treasury, which we esteem above our pity.' The author then proceeds to try to show that the laws were just, for 'every one is injured more or less by clipping.' If the argument is understood,

> The common people then will see and feel the injury and mischief that is done by clipping, which now they cannot understand, or will not well consider. They will find that the little money they then have, will not go for more than its just weight; and be convinced by hunger and thirst, that clippers are as truly thieves and robbers, as those they find upon the highways, or breaking up their house, and so as well deserve their chains and halters.

Not only were the 'common people' sympathetic, but it is likely that many individuals, who might otherwise not have become involved in crime, first entered the illegal world through an offence which many considered trivial, but the law considered very severely.

This may help to explain how it was, for example, that William Smorthwait first started down a road which would lead on to burglary, highway robbery and assault. Smorthwait appears to be have begun to tamper with coins in the early 1670s, well before he became High Constable of the Lonsdale ward. In 1684 he told Bainbridge that 'he was nimbler in clipping, coining and dressing of his Majesty's money twelve years ago than he was when this examinate did see him clip the shillings.' Smorthwait does not seem to have been able to conceal his activities from the servants in the house. Recalling events in 1676, John Harrison remembered that 'whilst he was a servant to William Smorthwait, he found a clipping of silver in the corner of the house of William Smorthwait, which clipping he did show unto Thomas Inman now of Sedbergh, hatter, and then his fellow-servant, who said it was a clipping of silver, and bid him lay it down upon the table and he would speak with some of the house about it.' Inman confirmed that Harrison had brought him 'a clipping of silver, with some letters on it, which he said he had found in a loft or chamber of the house, which he left upon the table, and which was afterwards taken away by Alice Dixon mother of William and Henry Smorthwait.' He also recalled how on another occasion 'Dorothy Swainson (an old woman who lived in William Smorthwait's house) did another time show unto him another clipping of silver, which was thicker than that showed by John Harrison.' Bainbridge remembered that in about 1678 he saw Smorthwait 'clip two half crowns with a pair of great shears near Hawkingford, and did also see him to have there a great deal of other clipped moneys and clippings which he believes was of William Smorthwait's clipping' (see illustration 6). Bainbridge further alleged that Smorthwait told him that 'Bryan Thompson late of

6 Hawkin or Hawking Ford in Middleton, over the river Lune; the crossing between the houses of the Smorthwaits and the Bainbridges and the scene of alleged coin clipping.

Kirkby Lonsdale, alehouse keeper, did several times exchange thirty or forty or fifty shillings of broad money for clipped money', which he believed Smorthwait had clipped. It was through counterfeiting that Smorthwait became linked to a network of clippers and coiners throughout the northern province and even down to London. Several of those involved were, like Smorthwait, men of respectable position, wealthy yeomen, minor gentry, clergymen, attorneys at law. The attractiveness of easy money encouraged them into activities which seemed different from normal crimes of theft.

The size of the counterfeiting network seems to have become fully apparent to the Justices in 1681. The chain which would finally lead to the trials of numerous clippers, including Smorthwait, may have started in the following way. Oliver Heywood, a Nonconformist minister, described how[8]

> One J in Lautherdale in Craven (who was a confederate with clippers and coiners) being apprehended for debt and carried to Lancaster gaol, sent to his companions to help him with £30 to pay his debts, they refusing he resolved to be avenged of them, acquainted some persons at Lancaster that if some persons would go to a place called Stock, three

[8] J. Horsfall Turner (ed.), *The Diary of the Rev. Oliver Heywood, 1630–1702* (Brighouse, 1882) II, p. 287.

miles above Skipton such a day, they should find them at their work, where they might apprehend them together, and they should find their coining irons in the bellows, &c. Intelligence begin given to the Justices in these parts, and no noise being made of it, they went at the day appointed, came to the place which was a retired house in the country, they opened the doors, found them close at work in their drawers and shirts, apprehended thirteen which was their number, with thirty or forty £ of clipped silver, their vices, coining irons and implements, as was described, sent them with their instruments to York where they are to be tried this Assizes which begins Monday March 13, 1682.

The region where this capture was made was the same as that where one of the major informers was living. On 5 August 1681, William Kirkby, a Lancashire Justice, wrote the following letter to his cousin, Daniel Fleming.[9]

Sir,   Lancaster
    At my being here, some days since this informer Woodworth came to visit a friend of his in the castle here. A few days before it seems one Foster had accused this Woodworth for coining etc. And he being then a prisoner in the castle when Woodworth came there, he acquainted the under gaoler, who by some friends of his acquainted me. Upon which I took Foster's information and committed Woodworth, who soon after gave me information against sundry persons for coining etc. Amongst which he gave this enclosed. And being within your county I request your care about it. This Foster and Woodworth are the two great masters in this faculty for making stamps in steel and iron or making moulds of all sorts of coin, clipping, coining and melting down all sorts of metals. They have accused about 140 persons in this county and Yorkshire, several of which are lately apprehended. And indeed I think they may do great service on this account. I have not to add save that I am, sir, your affectionate kinsman and humble servant William Kirkby.

Sadly, the enclosed information has not survived among Fleming's papers. But fortunately, informations by Woodworth and Foster have been found among the miscellaneous depositions of the Palatinate of Lancaster. We are therefore able to see the relations of these 'two great masters' to the Smorthwaits.
    We may look first at the two informations given by Woodworth. Through his references to clipping in Lotherdale, we are able to link these activities to the events described by Heywood. The first information was given at Lancaster on the 26 July 1681.[10]

[9] Fleming Letters, 2439. This is in Lancaster City Library, ms. 6571.
[10] All the examinations of Woodward and Foster are to be found in P.L. 27/1 (PRO).

Stephen Woodworth of Little Newton in Yorks, freemason, informeth upon oath that Thomas Atkinson late of Dent some years since came to him at Newton and desired him to make a coining iron and directed him how to make it, and that he according to Thomas Atkinson's directions did make him a coining iron of iron & steel to coin a thirty pence piece with three XXXs upon. And further saith that soon after one John Atkinson late of Dent came to him at Long Preston to the best of his remembrance and desired him to make him a pair of coining irons of another sort than his brother's if he could and if he could not to make him as good a pair as his brother's were. He did make John Atkinson a pair of coining irons of the same sort as his brother Thomas Atkinson's were with three XXXs upon, being that he could make no other sort at that time. And also saith that one Jeremiah Nealson of Garsdale in the county of York to the best of this informant's remembrance not long after the time aforesaid sent for him to one Thomas Clark's house a tanner in Long Preston and showed him the horse side of a half crown stamp which was rusty, and desired him to make him another of the same likeness, which he accordingly did. And Nealson did say that it was very well done. And also saith that one Thomas Winster of Dent came to him at Newton shortly after and either brought or sent him two lumps of iron and desired him to cut him a pair of coining irons, which he accordingly did with three XXXs upon, and delivered them to Thomas Winster. And he saith that one Peter Scarber near Lotherdale in the parish of Carleton near about the same time brought to him at Newton two lumps of iron and steel, and desired him to cut them into a half crown stamp, which he did with a horse on the one side. And after his making thereof he saw Scarber stamp some half crowns with the stamp, and one of the half crowns coined with the stamping iron this informer showed to one William Foster late of Barley Bank in Tatham in the county of Lancaster. And he further saith that one William Hewett of Lotherdale near about the time aforesaid showed this informant at his house in Lotherdale a piece of white metal like unto silver which he said was transmuted copper, and which he had done by his own art, and showed him some crucibles, of which he gave this informant one.[11] And at the same time or near thenabouts he did see in Hewett's workhouse, being a clockmaker, two lumps, which to the best of his knowledge was two stamps for coining. And he said that about the same time at the request of one Roger Preston of Mearbeck in the parish of Giggleswick he made him the said Preston a pair of coining irons for half crowns with a horse on the one

[11] It is difficult to follow these technical processes without knowing the secret method used by the coiners to transmute baser metals into something resembling pure silver. By chance, a stray document describing the process survives among the examinations. It is published as appendix C.

side, which coining irons he sent to Preston by his brother John Preston of Mearbeck. And further saith that sundry times Roger Preston brought clippings and other lumps of metal, one parcel whereof he said he had for a horse of one William Smorthwait in the parish of Clapham and desired him to melt it down and coin it for him, which he did, but afterwards Roger Preston told him it was not well done, and that he had got it run down again. And he further saith that about a month since one Thomas Dickonson of Nappaw in the parish of Gisburne brought to his house several pieces of metal and put it himself into the pot on the fire. And this informer melted it down for him and afterwards coined the metal into shillings and six pences, which being done they appeared very black. But Dickonson told him he could rub the rust off himself or dress them to try if he could make anything of them.

Smorthwait was already implicated, as were others in Dent and elsewhere. The following day Woodworth gave another information which further implicated people from Dent and the parish of Kirkby Lonsdale.

Daniel Parker of Pembecke in Long Preston, a coverlet weaver about a year and a half since, brought him a small quantity of silver clippings and offered them to him to sell. This informer did agree with him to give him four shillings or thereabouts an ounce, and allowed him the value out of the price of wool this informer sold to Parker. That about three or four years since he being all night at Thomas Winster's house in Dent there came that night to Winster's house a person whose name he was told was Thomas Claughton of Keateholme, and Claughton together with Winster and this informer did melt down some metals. And afterwards Winster put the metal in some moulds and lay it by till it was cold. Then Winster and Claughton took out what was in the moulds and carried it into a chamber and presently after brought out certain half crowns with sand and water and desired him to help to rub and dress them, and those half crowns this informer believes were the same metal cast in the moulds aforesaid. And further saith that about five or six years since, one Samuel Mawson of Firbank in Westmorland was in company with him at New Inns in Craven and there Mawson telling some money showed him a parcel of bad money, being most of them shillings, and asked him what he thought of them, who answered he thought they would pass. And Mawson told him he had them of one John Medcalfe of Healey towards the head of Netherdale. And he further saith that Mawson about four or five years since brought to him several pieces of silver made ready for coining, which he requested him to coin for him. And he having no instrument to coin them with, he carried and delivered them to Peter Scarber to coin. And Scarber delivered to him the same silver metal coined into half crowns, which he delivered again to

Mawson. And Mawson told him they were not well done, and therefore he wàs forced to get sundry of them melted down again. And further saith that Mawson told him that he, Mawson, had the silver metal from Thomas Atkinson who had made the sum ready for coining.

The location of the clippers and coiners allegedly discovered by Woodworth can be seen on maps 1–3. They stretched down from Firbank to Skipton, mainly concentrated in Wharfedale and Ribblesdale. As we have seen, Smorthwait was one of those connected to the network, and Atkinson and other Dent clippers were prominent. Both Smorthwait and Atkinson were again implicated by another set of examinations taken in the same month of July 1681, but this time centred on individuals living in north Lancashire, a few miles south of Kirkby Lonsdale. The central figure here was the gentleman mentioned by Woodworth named William Foster of Crossdale Grains. Foster gave a long information on the 22nd, in which he confessed to various clipping activities. He said

that one John Bond and Christopher Bond both of Lythebank in the county of Lancashire, yeomen, within ten years last past have come several times to his house and brought great quantities of money with them which he saith he clipped for them. And likewise saith John Bond did several times sit by him while he clipped his money, and did file the said money as he clipped it. And he also saith that about nine or ten years ago John Bond brought at one time to his house £80 which he clipped for him and that John helped to file it on the edges. And he also said that John had of him about two years ago six counterfeit guineas which the informant saith he charged him not to vend and that John was very importunate several times to have him make guinea stamps for him. And he further upon oath saith that within seven year last past one John Dobson of Ellers in Caton in the county of Lancashire, attorney at law, together with one Thomas Beetham of Tatham husbandman, came several times to his house. And brought several quantities of bullion, which they did make into shillings and stamp the same with a pair of shilling stamps which stamps John Dobson bought of him, for which he gave him a new silver watch to the value of £3. And also saith that Thomas Beetham came several times himself to his house and brought great quantities of clippings with him which he, together with this informant, made into half crowns and shillings. And he likewise upon oath saith that about three years ago one Richard Beetham of Tatham, tailor, came to him and brought a pair of stamps of him for making and counterfeiting of half crowns, for which stamps he saith that Thomas Beetham, brother to Richard, did pay him for the stamps. And likewise saith that Richard Beetham did at one particular time buy either one half crown or two of counterfeit money of him, for which he gave him five groats apiece. And further saith that Thomas Beetham did give him a cow for a pair of shilling stamps. He further on oath saith that one James Robinson of Tatham, blacksmith, did several times within this twenty years help him to stamp several quantities of counterfeit money and did at one particular time bring about £40 to him, all clipped, together with a great quantity of clippings which he made into money. And he further upon oath saith that within this seven or eight years last past one John Lawrence of Warton, husbandman, has several times come to him with several quantities of clippings and desired him to make the clippings into money, who accordingly did, and also saith that he made £6 of counterfeit money thereabouts at two several times for John Lawrence. And he further on oath saith that about eight years ago he light in company with one John Osliffe of Yealand, husbandman, who showed unto him 1s which he said was his own making. And afterwards he saith he went to John Osliffe's house, at which time John showed unto him a pair of moulds and told him that he made counterfeit money in them and also showed him dust or spall which he also said he did cast counterfeit money into. And he further saith not.

On 26 July, William Foster gave a second information:

That Stephen Woodworth of Newton, about five years since to the best of his remembrance, was at one William Hewett's in Lotherdale in the parish of Carleton where this informer met with him. And Stephen Woodworth, William Hewett and he did go to the house of one Peter Scarber a neighbour of William Hewett's at which time and place they did show to him a pair of half crown stamps which Peter Scarber bought of Stephen Woodworth and gave him fifty five shillings for them and Stephen did confess that he did cut and make the aforesaid stamps. And Stephen did then show to this informer a half crown, which he said was stamped with the said coining stamp and asked him how he did like it. And he further saith that one Jeremiah Nealson of Garsdale showed to him about five years since at his own house at Garsdale a pair of half crown stamps, one side whereof he, Jeremiah, told this informer was cut by Stephen Woodworth and asked him if he knew Stephen Woodworth. And further saith that about six years since one Thomas Atkinson of Dent came to his house in Tatham and showed him there a pair of half crown stamps of that sort which have three XXXs upon and told him that they were cut by Stephen Woodworth.

This was not the end of Foster's evidence, for he was still in prison the following April, when he informed

that one Thomas Bullock of Rantree Fold in the parish of Tatham, drover, a very near neighbour to this informant, did about seven years ago frequently bring several sums of large money to him to be clipped, for Bullock had a lame hand and could not clip it himself. And for such silver clippings he had from the informant commonly an allowance of 2s in the pound. And Thomas Bullock well knew that this informant did usually then make false and counterfeit money of mixed matter. And Bullock did about that time frequently buy of this informant several parcels thereof, giving 20s of good money for 30s of false money. And this informant saith that Thomas Bullock then told him that one Richard Trotter of the same parish of Tatham and divers others had helped him to utter and put off his false money. And he further saith that one Thomas Hobkin of Yealand Redmayne in the parish of Warton, yeoman, who likewise used to buy and sell cattle, as he thinketh, corresponded with Thomas Bullock. And about seven years ago came to him at his house in the parish of Tatham and told this informant that he had seen money of this informant's handiwork and that he had bought for the said Thomas Bullock and had given 20s of good money for 25s of that false money.[12] And understanding that Bullock had received 30s of such false money from the informant for 20s of good money, he thought better to go for it to the fountain head, to him this informant for it. But at that time this informant was not provided to let him have any. And then and several other times Thomas Hobkin did desire of him to sell him on the terms aforesaid such false money, but he doth not remember that he did ever let him have any. And he further saith that since that time Thomas Hobkin came to him and asked if he could make counterfeit guineas, saying he had a friend in London who could put a great deal of them off. And this informant told him he had not a guinea but would try to make a guinea stamp. And thereupon Hobkin shortly after brought his informant a guinea. And this informant did essay [i.e. try] at his instance to make such a stamp, about which time, before this informant had finished the stamp, some persons in Yorkshire or Lancashire were taken and prosecuted for coining false money and Hobkin out of fear desired him to let the matter rest till further time.

Thus it appears that Foster had learnt his skill from Woodworth and had then become the centre of a further network of clippers and coiners. Map 3 shows the distribution of these suspects, who came mostly from north Lancashire. William Smorthwait was not directly implicated in these informations, but he was clearly accused in another information which has been lost. The accusation led to a warrant for his and Henry Smorthwait's arrest. In February 1683 Henry Bouch, a Yorkshire Justice, wrote to Fleming that

[12] Earlier evidence about the exchange rate for 'broad' or good coins is given, along with an interesting fictitious account of clipping operations, in Richard Head and Francis Kirkman, *The English Rogue*. . . (1665; Routledge edn, 1928), pp. 106–10.

'our High Constable had warrants against him and his brother Harry Smorthwait almost twelve months in his hands for apprehending them upon an information given against them by one Foster for clipping and coining, but could not take them, as several times he informed us.' Foster must have visited Smorthwait at his previous home at Middleton, for a servant later deposed that 'the two Fosters [brothers] were at his master's house, the younger brother two nights, and the elder brother part of one night.' Smorthwait himself was examined as to whether he knew William Foster and replied 'that he knows the said Foster and that he had sold him several goods at several times, but never clipped any pieces of his Majesty's coin in the company of Foster or any other time.' The mystery of the other Foster brother may be partially solved by a remark made by Edward Bradrick, a suspected highwayman, who said that he

> doth know one Richard Tatham of Ireby did at one time the last March sell unto Foster a great parcel of clippings, Tatham being to furnish him with a great many ounces more. This same Foster is a man that hath done several injuries in the country, he doth frequent a house at the end of Kidda Lane between York and Leeds with another house at the sight of York in the road between Kirkby Moreside and Fountains Abbey in York, he sometimes goeth by the name of Dawson.

As to the others accused by Foster, a note in the depositions stated that John Bond, Thomas Beetham and Richard Beetham were fled and John Lawrence was dead. James Robinson, Christopher Bond and John Osliffe were all in custody and we have their examinations.[13] They denied any involvement in clipping, and Thomas Hobkin of Yealand Redmayne also denied all the accusations of clipping. The only thing he admitted was lending Foster a guinea, though his account of the reason is somewhat different. He said that

> about eight or nine years since Foster being in company with him, he showed Foster a guinea and asked his judgement of it whether it was a good one or not, it having a ridge or crack in. And Foster answered, it was a good one, and told him that he was going to his friends and desired him to lend it him for it would be a credit to his pocket, whereupon he lent it to him but denies that he lent it to the end to make any guinea stamp by.

A large number of other suspected clippers were also in York gaol. Petitions from a number of them have survived and we may quote just one of these. Thomas Atkinson, probably the notorious Thomas Atkinson of Dent mentioned so many times in the confessions, wrote

[13] A petition from Osliffe, who was a prisoner in irons, asking to be released on bail until the next Assizes is QSP/540/5 (LRO). The examinations are in P.L. 27/1 (PRO).

That your petitioner was comit to the said gaol for suspicion of falsifying, clipping and filing his Majesty's coin and hath remained there ever since the 1st August last past, to the great damage and disgrace of your petitioner, being very innocent of the accusations laid to his charge. To the end therefore that your petitioner's innocency may appear and to show himself a loyal subject, your petitioner humbly prays that he may be admitted to come to trial this present Assizes or else to be let out of gaol upon bail to appear at another Assizes.

And your petitioner shall pray etc.

Thomas Atkinson [signature]

A number of petitions from Woodworth and Foster have also survived, which show that they hoped to be released, having turned evidence for the king. In late 1681 Foster wrote to the Justices saying that one of those he had accused had conspired with another prisoner to assault him. At Easter 1682 both of them wrote asking that the allowances of 6*d* a week which they were receiving in prison be increased. Woodworth wrote further petitions to the Justices at the end of 1683 and early in 1684. He stated that he had been pardoned at the Assizes in August 1683, but had been unable to pay his fees and therefore had been kept in prison by the keeper of the castle. He was therefore in prison for over two and a half years.[14]

Thus by the end of 1682, as the time approached for the first formal prosecutions of the masked robbers, Fleming and other Justices must have had a very clear idea that the Smorthwaits were involved in clipping. What they obviously did not expect was that when Smorthwait and his accomplices broke into Robinson's house, they should have chosen the very dwelling where a suspected clipper lived, and that this clipper should be no other than the village clergyman and schoolmaster of Old Hutton, Edmund Lodge. The investigations into the Robinson burglary had by chance thrown up evidence which enables us to see into a supposed clipper's study and to see the blackmail pressures put upon him when he was discovered. All this needs to be treated with caution, since there are numerous suggestions that the witnesses were accusing Lodge out of malice. But the evidence is interesting, whether true or invented. We have four detailed and overlapping accounts of what is supposed to have occurred. Robert Robinson, the elderly gentleman who was a lodger in his own house, described how

in Lent gone a twelve month one Esther Craven then servant to Mr Lodge acquainted him that she had seen some clippings and melted

---

[14]QSP/540–8, 572–5, 576–8 (LRO). William Foster was one of the thirteen named persons who were accused of clipping and coining in the counties of Lancashire, Stafford and Derby in 1683, and deserving pardons. Justice Jones reported that 'they ought first to do effective service towards a legal conviction of some of their complices.' *Calendar of Treasury Books* VII, pt. 2, p. 854.

silver in her master's press; and that upon the sixth day of April 1682 Esther Craven did show unto him some clippings wrapped up in a paper, as she said they were; and she did also then deliver unto him three clippings of silver (viz: one of an half crown, another of a shilling & the third of a six pence, as this informant believes) which clippings he did keep and hath showed to divers persons, and still hath ready to produce. And Esther Craven did also acquaint him that she meddled not with the melted silver, but that she did take away the clippings, which, lest her Master (as she said) should take from her, she did bind under her stockings, and did keep them there, until she left her service upon Easter Tuesday then next following.

Thomas Cowperthwaite of Bleaze in Old Hutton, shepherd, said that he had been told by Esther Craven that she had found some clippings and had also informed Robert Robinson, and George Holme, of Old Hutton. He confirmed the story of the clippings under the stockings, 'which clippings she permitted this examinate to lay his hand on.' He then continued that

being with Esther Craven at Whaitbrigg in Wensleydale about the third week in April last past, she did show unto him a parcel of silver clippings of half-crowns, shillings and sixpences in a paper; and another parcel of filings of silver in another paper, both which she said she found in Mr Lodge's press. This examinate having given notice thereof unto his late master Henry Bateman of Bleaze, gentleman, deceased,[15] he and Mr Lodge came unto Whaitbrigg about the beginning of May last. And Henry Bateman did order this examinate to go unto, and agree with Esther Craven about the clippings and filings, and that she should not discover them, upon which she demanded ten pounds, But this examinate agreed with her for forty shillings: twenty shillings whereof he then paid her in Wensleydale, having received it from his master, and the other twenty shillings this examinate received about Whitsuntide last of Margaret Rowlandson then servant unto Mr Lodge. And Margaret then said that her master Mr Lodge had left word with her to acquaint this examinate to get as much abated thereof as he could. And this examinate prevailed with Esther Craven to abate three shillings of the latter twenty shillings, which three shillings he still hath in his hand. He further said that Esther Craven delivered the clippings and filings unto him, and he delivered the same unto Mr Bateman his master, who told him that he had delivered the same, without looking upon them, unto Mr Lodge.

[15] This is the same Henry Bateman who had been among those who raised the first alarm, according to Fleming. His house, Bleaze Hall, was built with the profits of cloth manufacturing and the family owned a great train of pack horses, which 'travelled regularly between London, York and the north. . . . During some repairs a curious old dagger and several ancient coins were found behind the wainscotting in the withdrawing room.' J. H. Palmer, *Historic Farmhouses in and around Westmorland* (Kendal, 1946), p. 18.

Further information about the minor blackmailing, as well as the location of the clippings, is given by the other man in Old Hutton in whom Esther Craven had confided. George Holme stated that he had been shown some clippings by Robinson. Afterwards Craven came and

> asked him what he thought of those things which Robert Robinson had showed him; upon which he enquired of her where she had them, who answered that she had them in her master's press where he lay his books, and she said she would show him more of them, and that she knew where he had the shears that clipped them. A day or two after, Esther Craven came unto him and showed him in a paper a deal of silver clippings and filings, which she also said she found in her master's press. She likewise then told him that her master had enquired of her for them, and that she had told him she had them, who asking her what she would do with them, she said that she would be satisfied before she parted with them, upon which he demanded what she would have. She said she would have ten pounds, to which he said that ten pounds was a great deal, but he would give her part in hand and give her bond for the rest, and let no more be said, they too would have a convenient time to talk of it. And this examinate also saith, that the very day when Esther Craven left her master's service she acquainted this examinate, that he had not satisfied her, and she knew not what to do. But if this examinate would permit her to leave her clothes with him she would go & acquaint Mr Bateman therewith, which this examinate yielded unto, and she afterwards said that she had acquainted Mr Bateman with it.

Clearly the whole story of the clipping and possible coining by Lodge depended heavily on the testimony of Esther Craven. Although she had moved to Wensleydale, her examination was sought and was taken by a Yorkshire Justice.

> Who being asked whether she lived with one Mr Lodge the minister of Old Hutton in Westmorland, saith that she lived with him most part of one whole year. And being asked how long it is since she came from him, saith April last past was a twelvemonth since. But withal saith that during the time being with him, upon a time, her master sent her into a press, that had drawers in, and fetched something there which she wanted, and going accordingly, and pulling out one of the drawers, she found in it a little pot, and within it there was several clippings of moneys, at that time she looked at it and left it where it was. About three days after took an occasion to go into the same press again, and found the same pot, where she left it. And seeking further she found a piece of parchment with clippings in, almost the bigness of her hand, whereupon she acquainted one Robert Robinson, that lived in the same house and he went with her

to look at them, and further saith that they both looked at them several times after. One of which times he took some of them away and said he would show them to some other person. At another time this informant saith she took the whole paper and those that was in it and tied them betwixt her stockings and her legs. And shortly after Mr Lodge her master complained that he wanted something that was gone out of his press, whereupon she asked her master what he wanted, he replied again, doth not thou know what I want, then she answered maybe I do, is it not clippings you want, then he said, hath thou them, and she replied I have. Then he asked her what she would do with them. She replied that she would show them to better persons than had seen them before and know whether it was lawful for him to use such doings or not. He desired to know what she would ask to let him have them again and not discover the same to anybody. She saith she asked him ten pounds, and he being not willing to gratify her according to her desire, she forthwith went and showed them to Mr Bateman of High Bleaze, he wished her to forbear to say anything of it and he would speak to her master about it. Whereupon she came to Whaitbrigg in Wensleydale to Thomas Cowperthwaite, servant to Mr Bateman, and gave him the clippings to keep. And about a fortnight after, Mr Bateman together with Mr Lodge came to Whaitbrigg and sent Cowperthwaite unto her to see what she would take for concealing the business. And she having discovered it, being a woman that was ignorant, thought it was best to take what she could get, whereupon they gave her twenty shillings and promised her twenty more. But got but 17s and never no more of it till she was taken with a warrant and brought before me. Where, upon examination, gave this information, and saith that she never saw the clippings after she gave them to Thomas Cowperthwaite, but doth believe that he gave them to Mr Lodge or Mr Bateman and further saith not.

It was on the basis of this evidence that Lodge was imprisoned and brought to trial at Appleby for clipping.

Lodge was not the only one living in Old Hutton suspected of involvement in counterfeiting. In the following year, further evidence emerged when Bradrick, the highwayman confessed that

He very well knows Alexander Guy of Mallerstang blacksmith & hath been acquainted with him for two years or thereabouts; and hath seen him not only clip his Majesty's coin, but also counterfeit his Majesty's coin, within two months now last past. And also one Henry Bateman of Farleton was present with this examinate & did see Guy clip and diminish his Majesty's coin within the time aforesaid. . . . That Bateman in or about the month of April did clip for this examinate several sums of money, as in particular twenty pounds at one time and eighteen pounds

at another time, which this examinate saw him clip. . . . And also
William Marriner together with Edward Bainbridge of or near Barbon
did clip the sum of sixteen or seventeen pounds of his Majesty's coin at
this examinate's request. . . . That John Tyson of Kirkby Lonsdale . . .
hath confessed to this examinate that he had several times clipped or
diminished his Majesty's coin. And he further saith that he having the
clippings of the several sums of money mentioned to be clipped for the
use of this examinate, did send Henry Bateman to sell the same unto
Thomas Atkinson of Dent, who sold the same accordingly for three
pounds odd money, which Atkinson promised to pay in some short time
then next ensuing, in which he failed. And he sent to him for the money
and Atkinson sent to Henry Bateman twenty four shillings, part thereof
in moneys then newly clipped, without being filed or dressed, & the rest
of the money for the clipping Bateman expended in going for and about
the moneys. And Atkinson hath several other times bought clippings of
money and melted the same down and carried and sold the bullion at
York and hath made a great trade thereof. And the twenty four shillings
newly clipped money being sent by Atkinson's brother to Bateman was
seen and taken notice of by John Wilkinson of Farleton and Thomasine
his wife to be so clipped and undressed as Wilkinson and his wife
confessed to this examinate who also informed him that Bateman had
dressed and filed the twenty four shillings. . . . And he also saith that
Joseph Dawson whitesmith, son of James Dawson of Old Hutton, hath
several times received several quantities of clippings from Bateman by
the order of this examinate which Bateman sold unto him at this examinate's request, Joseph Dawson well knowing the same to be clippings of
his Majesty's coin. And after he had melted the same down into buillion
his correspondent to whom he sold and sent the same was one Mr Leigh,
a silver or goldsmith in the city of York, who also hath driven a great
trade in buying of such wares from him the said Joseph Dawson, as also
from Atkinson. And he further saith that one George Mangy of Wakefield about twelve months ago being tried at York for clipping and
coining and being acquitted, before he was at liberty and after his said
trial did coin several counterfeit half crowns and hath been accustomed
to clip his Majesty's coin and to use the trade of coining and counterfeiting his Majesty's coin.[16] And one George Harrison, late of Bowland in
the county of York (being heretofore found guilty of clipping or coining),
hath since been accustomed to sell clippings unto Mangy, Harrison
being now an inhabitant near Doncaster.

[16] The name Mangy is uncommon and it is therefore tempting to link this man with one of the
very rare surviving pamphlets describing a clipping trial, that of Arthur Mangy of Leeds in
1694. 'Trial at York for Counterfeiting of Mr Arthur Mangy. . . ', Thoresby Society IX,
Miscellanea (Leeds, 1899), pp. 204–27, annotated by C. M. Atkinson.

To this long catalogue of clippers, whose location can be seen on maps 1–3, Bradrick added the following note in an information which is not among the official Assize papers: 'That in November last John Bainbridge of the Gillfoot in Mansergh did clip the sum of £26 and upwards, and that Bainbridge with Edward Bainbridge his brother did in December last clip the sum of £13 or thereabouts as he doth remember.' Edward Bainbridge confirmed the involvement of Bradrick and William Smorthwait in clipping. He informed that 'upon Thursday the seventeenth day of April last he was in the company of William Smorthwait and Edward Bradrick, and did see them clip five or six shillings apiece in the parish of Clapham, and did also see them then and there pull out clippings out of their pockets.' A note in Fleming's manuscripts states that 'Edw. Bainbridge did see Will. Smorthwait clip about £5 upon his own table at Middleton in this county about 3 years ago.'

After these informations, it was clearly necessary to question some of those named. Curiously, Henry Bateman of Farleton is not known to have been examined. Alexander Guy of Mallerstang described in detail his various meetings with Smorthwait and Bradwick, but denied that he had ever done any clipping for them or that he knew Henry Bateman. He admitted that he had made a pair of shears for a William Dockwray of Hardraw, but he stated that he did not know what they would be used for. He denied all clipping activities, or any association with Thomas Atkinson of Dent. But he admitted that he had been born in Dent, had served his apprenticeship there and had known Atkinson for over fourteen years. Joseph Dawson was another suspect, and Fleming has a cryptic note that 'Joseph Dawson often carries bullion to York.' Dawson was examined and described how

> about a year and a quarter since [Bateman] came to him and enquired of him whether he would buy any plate or not, to which he answered that he would not buy any; then Henry Bateman replied, what need you be afraid, it is no bullion. And then he told this examinate it was two silver tumblers which were bruised as he said, but this examinate would neither see them nor buy them: and upon Bateman's pressing this examinate to buy them he said he would call forth for some company to see them & to know how he came by them, upon which he spurred his horse and rid away.

Dawson denied that he had ever had any trading with a Mr Leigh, a silver or goldsmith in York. On another occasion when Bateman had tried to sell him 'a steel seal very finely cut with a coat of arms on the one end and a cypher of a name upon the other,' he refused to buy it 'though he had been formerly this examinate's schoolfellow'.

Joseph Dawson and many others implicated in these informations would appear again in the continuing trials of clippers and coiners, culminating in the very detailed confessions of the Dent clipper, Thomas Atkinson.[17] But this was after the final trial of the Smorthwaits, and so we may end our account of clipping and coining here. We have seen how the international movement of silver impinged on a small area of northern England, leading people into treasonable activities. Once engaged in such crime, it was tempting to turn to other crimes where the rewards might be as great as those from literally making money. Stealing from the crown was not the only way to acquire riches. The numerous houses of neighbours also invited the attention of people who had started as clippers. To combine burglary with clipping was logical, for the thefts of money would provide the coins needed for that trade. The value of the haul, as in the Robinson burglary, would be greatly increased by the fact that the edges of the coins could be cut off and used to make further currency.

Thus by the end of 1682 the two Smorthwaits were under heavy suspicion for both burglary and clipping, and warrants were out for their arrest for the latter offence. It was in January 1683 that the Westmorland Justices made their public attack on the suspected criminals.

---

[17] A large number of further depositions concerning clipping in the 1680s are to be found in both the PRO, ASSI/14/2, and P.L. 27/1, and in the Fleming papers at the WRO, WD/Ry/31.34. The wide extent of clipping and coining in the region is shown by the fact that none of the 67 persons named by a Lancashire informer in April 1683 overlapped with the people described in this chapter, *Calendar of State Papers Domestic*, Charles II, 423, no. 53, see also no. 113.

4
Raising the Hue and Cry

The burglary at Robert Robinson's occurred on 3 November 1680. It is clear that some of the occupants of the house had their suspicions as to who the robbers were. Furthermore, rumours soon circulated in the area as to their identity. Yet it was not until January 1683, over two years later, that the public silence was broken. How are we to account for this delay? One obvious reason was fear, as witnesses noted. In a later deposition Robert Ward recounted how at Christmas 1680 he had met Edward Bainbridge and had informed him 'that it was commonly reported he was one of the robbers.' Bainbridge was alleged to have reacted fiercely, and 'did say and swear a great oath, that he would run through with his sword such persons as had reported it.' William Speight also described how he had been let into the secrets of the affair on 10 January 1681. But when the secret began to leak out, one of the accomplices had said 'if thou tell any more thou will undo us all and thou wilt be cut in pieces.' John Jackson explained why he had taken no action, although he had known for two years who the culprits were. He claimed that Edward Bainbridge had threatened him that 'if he did discover anything which they had told him he would be the first man that would run him through and kill him or procure one to do it, for he had friends both in Westmorland and Lancashire and Yorkshire.'

The pressure against prosecution is further suggested by a letter which was written to Fleming. A number of local inhabitants wrote to him, a month after he first took action on 28 February 1683.[1]

Honoured Sir,
    It is well known to all serious and considerate persons how studious and industrious you have always been for the good of the country and that many worthy deeds have been done by you for the ease and benefit of the barony, and though several persons in this part of it have acted against their own and the public interest thereof, which might justly

[1] Fleming Letters, 2635.

have occasioned your displeasure and have abated your former zeal for its welfare, nevertheless you have of late been pleased to give evident demonstration of your constant and continued paternal care for our peace and safety, in that you have been active and instrumental in order to the bringing to light of one of the horrible and dark deeds of that black and terrible troop of notorious malefactors by which this part of the county (if it may be said with honour to some in authority) hath been intolerably infested and issued out your warrants for apprehending of the ringleaders of that dreadful society, so that we are in great hopes by your favourable assistance to be quit of some of those insolent and formidable felons who were so hardened in their impious actions that they were neither ashamed nor afraid implicitly to glory in their treasonable and felonious feats. And yet few had the courage (although they had done them mischief) to give information thereof, some of them giving dangerous hints what they would do to men's persons or houses if complaint were made. The county likewise hath a vehement suspicion (grounded upon several probable circumstances) of several persons who are thought to be of that impious confederacy which are not yet fully discovered, but if they persist, in time may come under your cognizance, unless they be deterred from abetting such notorious malefactors. Some of the most notorious thereof we take the boldness upon us to insert in a paper herein inclosed and humbly subscribe ourselves.

Your worships most devoted servants.

Tho: Williamson   Tho. Robertson   Jo: Shepherd

A more specific account of what was meant by the 'dangerous hints' was contained in an enclosed letter. This revealed the further repercussions of the affair, other people involved, and the fears of the neighbours.

John Bainbridge of Mansergh, brother of Edward mentioned in your warrants, a great receipter and familiar, and believed by his neighbours to have been a great encouragement of such persons, whose house (as we are informed) is well furnished with men's and women's apparel, such as were never bought by either of them and also several rapiers and pistols and other weapons which upon view may make a further discovery, and that John hath lately gone to Bryan Ward's house his next neighbour wishing him what ever he see to say nothing, for that the confederates cared not if they set his house on fire. And to prove the house so furnished, when search was made for Samuel Otway's beefs, there are John Bland and Tobias Hutchinson both of Mansergh with several others which they will name.

There are also James Harrison of the Fellhouse in Barbon and John Bland his son-in-law can give a very large account concerning the beefs before mentioned and several other material circumstances of the confederate's course of living. Besides, since your warrants were issued out for apprehending the malefactors, John Bainbridge and his sister have given the constables and the persons who went in search very ill language.

Also Henry Dixon, father-in-law [i.e. stepfather] of the two Smorthwaits, against whom your warrant was issued out and he thereupon taken but very slender bail taken for his appearance, is verily believed to be as notorious a malefactor as any in your warrants and of greater antiquity for filching, pilfering and receiving, and presumed to be guilty of breaking widow Bainbridge's house in Middleton near Smorthwait's. He, Dixon, living then with William Smorthwait which the persons above named can give a very full account of besides a great many persons more in the Barony. We humbly offer it to your worship's consideration whether it were not fit that search should be made by strangers because we fear neighbours would be negligent therein.

That threats were really issued is made clear by the information of one of Bainbridge's neighbours, Robert Benson, who said that he,

(living by the high way side, and about a quarter of a mile from the house where Edward Bainbridge did dwell in) did divers times see Edward Bainbridge ride very early in the morning and very late in the night, as he did go from home and returned thither generally in a great riding-coat, with a sword or rapier; and he having acquainted some of his neighbours therewith, some of them told him the same, whereupon Edward Bainbridge did threaten this examinate for taking notice of this riding from home and returning thither, saying that if he did but hold up his finger he could have these persons who would speak with this examinate, and who would drive this examinate's goods unto Whiten-dale cross.[2]

These fears are further indicated by the attitude of Robert Robinson, the victim of the major theft. He had been an acquaintance of Fleming since at least 1664, when he had been High Constable and corresponded concerning administrative matters to do with the payments for maimed soliders.[3] Yet he seems to have held back from going to the Justice or any other with a complaint for about two years. One reason may have been his physical decrepitude, as described in a letter written on 1st January to Fleming, shortly after the affair became public.[4] We may quote the second half of the letter.

---

[2] No explanation for this curious phrase or reference to 'Whiten-dale cross' has yet been discovered.

[3] Detailed accounts, kept by Robinson when he was High Constable, concerning disbursements for maimed soldiers in 1664 and 1665, are to be found in WD/Ry/33. Other letters between the two can be found for the 1670s on the same subject in WD/Ry/34 and in Fleming Letters, 1262.

[4] Fleming Letters, 2623. For reproductions of this and another letter, see illustrations 7, 13.

7 *The letter from Robert Robinson, the victim of a burglary, to Sir Daniel Fleming, asking for Fleming's assistance.*

Sir, I make bold humbly to intreat your good worship, that as for many years I have found your love and favour and good respects towards me, that now in my old age you will be pleased to do me that lawful favour you can as to the trouble and charge of prosecution of the thieves concerned in this robbery. I shall be willing to the best power I can for their discovery and to give what evidence I can against any of them. I am near 80 years of age, and very dim of my eyes, and lame of one of my legs having two holes in it, and have been under surgeon's hands eleven or twelve years and have suffered much already both by loss and affrighten-ing and I never look to get any of it again. Good Sir, I humbly beseech you pardon my boldness in this my trouble, having no other friend but you to desire this favour upon. I pray God to bless you with health and life to your comfort.

Resting your good worship's friend and humble servant to his power.

Robert Robinson.

As far as we can see, the public silence was broken on Friday 12 January 1683. The Quarter Sessions took place on that day and there is no formal record that anything happened. But Fleming noted that 'Henry Yeats gave information first to Mr Fisher, afterwards to the rest of the JP Jan 12 1682 — upon which Jo. Jackson was taken and examined and committed Jan. 1682. Other witnesses being first examined that day.' It appears from Yeats's examination that he himself was first suspected of the burglary, and that to clear himself he started to implicate others. The following day the examinations of William Speight, Robert Robinson and James Dawson, were taken by the Justices. All the depositions were taken before the full complement of the six Justices. It is clear that the suspects knew what was happening. In a later deposition James Dawson described how 'upon Sunday morning the fourteenth of January William Smorthwait late High Constable of Lonsdale ward, Henry Smorthwait, his brother, Edward Bainbridge and the wife of Henry Smorthwait called at his house in Old Hutton and stayed there a while.' William Smorthwait had been waiting for a barrister, but left before he arrived. Dawson added that 'some of the persons enquiring of him what was done before the Justices of Peace at Kendal the day before concerning the robbery of Robert Robinson, he answered that he believed there would be further enquiry into the matter.'

John Jackson had been committed to gaol upon Yeats's information. But he was not prepared to take the blame for what he alleged were the offences of others. Fleming notes 'J. Jackson having writ Febr.2 to Mr Jo. Fisher, made a confession before Mr Ed. Musgrave Febr. 12.83.' Jackson's letter, in his own hand, was later passed on to Fleming by Justice Fisher.[5]

[5] Fleming Letters, 2626.

Dear Sir,

According to your desires at the last sessions at Kendal I am now willing to give information upon oath of what I know against some persons that I do now stand committed for. And good sir appoint when you will take it and I shall make it my endeavour to let you know the truth that both you and I may live in safety with our friends. Desiring you to do what you can for my liberty, I rest, sir, your humble servant. John Jackson.

From the common gaol of the county at Appleby.

Justice Fisher wrote a covering note with this letter, when he sent it to Fleming.[6]

Worshipful sir,

I intended to have waited on you myself, but must defer it to another opportunity: William Speight of Hutton told me that you would have had a copy of the information against Jackson which I have here enclosed sent you with the letter I had from him. . . .

I am your very much obliged and humble servant John Fisher, at Stainebank Green, 13 February.

The examination itself was taken before Edward Musgrave, and he duly sent a copy of it to Fleming, with another covering note, on 12 February.[7]

Sir,

According to your desire I have done my endeavour to sift out of this John Jackson the truth of this concern as far as I can, which you may see by the enclosed examination. And to the rest he has discovered and made out against, I leave the prosecution to you and the rest you confer with to your discretions. So wherein I may be serviceable you may command, sir, your humble servant, Edward Musgrave, Asby Grange.

To this was added a curious note, as follows:

The gaoler tells us that he had one John Bland of Barbon a prisoner, and swore often to him that he could hang William Smorthwait for clipping or coining or suchlike thing.[8]

John Jackson's main value to the Justices was to implicate a new figure, Edmund Lodge. Jackson's motives for this are partly revealed by one of his neighbours, Giles Helme, who later testified that when he went to visit him in prison, Jackson said 'that if Mr Edmund Lodge would have come in and

[6] Fleming Letters, 2633A.
[7] Fleming Letters, 2629.
[8] Fleming noted that John Bland of Barbon 'came July 26.83. Denies what the gaoler said.' He also noted, 'offered me moneys to favour him', the only hint of attempted bribery in the case.

spoken the truth, he needed not to have continued a prisoner half an hour', but that 'Mr Lodge could not do it and clear himself.' Giving information against Lodge did not lead to Jackson's release, as he had hoped . He was still in Appleby gaol on 17 April when he wrote to Fleming direct, addressing it to 'the right worshipful Sir Dan Fleming'.[9]

Worthy Sir ,

May it please your worship. I humbly desire you will take it into your serious consideration and grant that I may have liberty to go under bail till the Assizes, or that I may once come to speak to your worship and I will faithfully disclose unto you all that I any way can what I know that is truth. I am afraid some wrong information against me hath altered your worship's opinion of me, otherwise I expected to have had some favour from you before this time. But I doubt not to give your worship good satisfaction if you please to let me come anywhere to your worship. I humbly and earnestly desire so, hoping to receive what lawfully your worship. I am your worship's humble and faithful servant. John Jackson.

This letter, also, seems to have been of no avail, for Jackson wrote another from Appleby gaol on 31 July, which reached Fleming on 10 August, a few days before the Assizes.[10]

Honoured Sir,

My father coming to Appleby I have informed him before my landlord the gaoler viz that what as I did inform to the Justice of the Peace I will never whilst there is life in me deny. It is a perfect truth and that I shall never be ashamed to speak. Only god knows it was my ill fortune to be often in a glass of ale in their company when I heard all but never no actor with them. And sir, as for Mr Lodge, Henry Smorthwait told me that there was a prize to be got and that if I would be one, he would never discover and he would be one to keep counsel. And I am certain if Lodge would have spoke truth I need never have been kept in prison, and I wish it with all my heart that he may discharge a good conscience and I am certain to be clear. As I say before Lodge did inform Henry Smorthwait where it was to be had, and told him that he would have had me but durst not tell me. So that I really believe Lodge was the main contriver but as for other things I know nothing of him. This is all from your humble servant John Jackson.

The letter was accompanied by a short note from the gaoler, William Dargue, confirming that he had heard Jackson say that 'whoever was the actors of that robbery Lodge was the contriver.'

[9] Fleming Letters, 2648.
[10] Fleming Letters, 2703.

Jackson's examination on 12 February constituted strong evidence against the major suspects. Fleming consequently wrote that 'warrants were issued out Febr.15.83. by 4 JP for the apprehending of Will. Smorthwait, Hen. Sm. Edw. Bainb. & Will Manning; and because of their riding well armed together, the Trainbands were required to be aiding and assisting upon which Henry Smor. was taken, examined and committed by Sir C[hristopher] P[hilipson].' There is no trace of these warrants in the Sessions papers, but fortunately Fleming kept rough copies, which are in his own hand. Two warrants were made out, one for those named above, and another, as Fleming also noted, against 'Henry Dixon (father-in-law [i.e. stepfather] to the 2 Smorthwait), and their great companion'.

The first ran:

> Sir Daniel Fleming and Sir Christopher Philipson Knights, William Fleming and John Fisher Esquires four of the king's Majesty's Justices of the Peace for the county of Westmorland, to the Sheriff of the said county, and to all constables, bayliffs, and other his Majesty's officers and subjects within the county aforesaid, greeting.
>
> Forasmuch as we are informed by the proofs of credible persons, that Henry Dixon late of Middleton yeoman is a person of ill name and fame, and a common companion of thieves: These are therefore in the King's Majesty's name to command you, and every of you, that you or some of you, do forthwith cause Henry Dixon to come, and in case of refusal to bring him before us, or some of us, or some other of his Majesty's Justices of the Peace for this county, to find sufficient sureties, as well for his personal appearance at the next Quarter Sessions of the peace to be holden at Kendal for the county, as also in the meantime for his being of good behaviour towards his Majesty and all his liege people. And if he shall refuse so to do, that then you or some of you convey him to his Majesty's gaol at Appleby for the county, and deliver him to the keeper thereof, who is hereby commanded to receive him and keep him a prisoner until he shall be discharged by due course of Law. And hereof fail not at your peril. Given under our hands and seals the fifteenth day of February, 1683.

The second had the same heading and continued:

> Being informed of divers burglaries and other felonies that have been lately committed within the county, and having received an information upon oath against William Smorthwait . . . Henry Smorthwait . . . Edward Bainbridge . . . William Manning . . . for felonious taking the money goods and chattels of Robert Robinson of Old Hutton. . . : These are in the King's Majesty's name to command you and every of you, that you, or some of you, do forthwith attach the bodies of William Smorth-

wait, Henry Smorthwait, Edward Bainbridge and William Manning, and them bring before us, or any of us, or some other of his Majesty's Justices of the Peace for this county of Westmorland, to be examined touching the premises; and to be further dealt withall according to law. And since we are informed, that the offenders do usually ride well armed together, the trainband soldiers and all other within the said country are hereby required to be aiding and assisting in the apprehending and disarming of them. Hereof fail not at your peril. Given under our hands and seals, the fifteenth day of February 1683.

As Fleming noted, Henry Smorthwait was immediately caught, but the rest of the suspects were less easily apprehended. William Smorthwait, for example, lived across the border in Yorkshire. The local Justice, Henry Bouch, wrote eight days later to Fleming from Ingleton.

Honoured Sir,
    Yours I have received and shall do to the utmost of my endeavour to answer the desires of yourself and the rest of the Justices of the Peace of your county. As for William Smorthwait, I hear he is from home at present and there will be some difficulty in the apprehending of him; for our High Constable had warrants against him and his brother Harry Smorthwait almost twelve months in his hands for apprehending them upon an information given against them by one Foster for clipping and coining, but could not take them, as several times he informed us. Sir, wherein I can serve you in this or any other affair, you may be always assured to find me, sir, yours in any service Henry Bouch.

Consequently the search was intensified. Fleming noted that Henry Smorthwait having been apprehended, but 'the rest of them flying, hue and cry was sent after them by the JP at Kendal Quarter Sessions April 20. 1683.' The only copy of this is again in Fleming's hand in his papers.

Sir Daniel Fleming and Sir Christopher Philipson Knights, Edward Wilson, Henry Wilson, William Fleming and John Fisher, Esquires, six of his Majesty's Justices of the Peace for the county of Westmorland. To all constables and others his Majesty's officers and subjects within the said county, or elsewhere within the realm of England, whom the execution hereof may concern, greeting. Whereas we have received information and charge against William Smorthwait . . . Edward Bainbridge . . . and William Manning the younger . . . who are persons of evil fame and who are charged before us with the felonious taking away of the money, goods and chattels of Robert Robinson of Old Hutton. . . . And they William Smorthwait, Edward Bainbridge and William Manning are very much suspected to have committed divers burglaries, robberies and other felonies; and notwithstanding several endeavours for the apprehension of them, they have not as yet been apprehended, but have withdrawn themselves, and are fled. These are therefore in the King's Majesty's name strictly to charge and command you, and every of you, to make diligent search within your several and respective precincts for William Smorthwait, Edward Bainbridge and William Manning, and to make hue and cry after them from town to town and from country to country, and that as well by horsemen as footmen, according to law. And if you shall find William Smorthwait, Edward Bainbridge and William Manning, or any of them, that then you do forthwith apprehend and convey them and every of them before some one of his Majesty's Justices of the Peace within the county, or place where they or any of them shall be taken, to be dealt withall according to law. Hereof fail not at your utmost peril. Given under our hands and seals at Kendal, within the county of Westmorland, the twentieth day of April, 1683.

These warrants were made out at the Sessions. During the preceding days Fleming had been busy. Between 10 and 16 April he examined or received information from another eight persons (see illustration 8). Several of these had been summoned by a writ to the constables:

Sir Daniel Fleming and William Fleming . . . to the constables of Old Hutton and Homescales . . . greeting.
    . . . to summon James Dawson of Old Hutton, yeoman, George Holme of Old Hutton, webster, Robert Scott of Bleaze, husbandman, and Richard Rigg of Old Hutton, waller, personally to appear before us upon Monday next at Rydal Hall . . . 10th day of April 1683.

In the Quarter Sessions papers themselves, the only indications of the affair were recognizances binding six people to appear at the Assizes. One example of this type of document may be given: 'Henry Dixon of Bentham in Yorks, bound £40, John Walker of Kendal in £20 and James Taylor of the same £20 for Henry to appear at the next sessions.' Clearly the Smorthwaits' stepfather had been apprehended. The very brief documents recorded in the court only partially reflect much fuller recognizances, a draft of which, heavily annotated by Fleming, has survived. This draft ended with a note by Fleming to the clerk: 'Pray do these carefully; and send me what is to be returned into court under your teste, and return me this paper, so soon as you can.'

The difficulty of catching Edward Bainbridge was compounded by the attitude of his brother John. We have seen that the local worthies had warned Fleming to search John's house for weapons and clothes, and this had obviously been attempted. But there had been resistance. So, according to another note by Fleming, 'a warrant of search and of good behaviour against Jo. Bainbridge (brother of the said Ed. B. with whom he lived) for

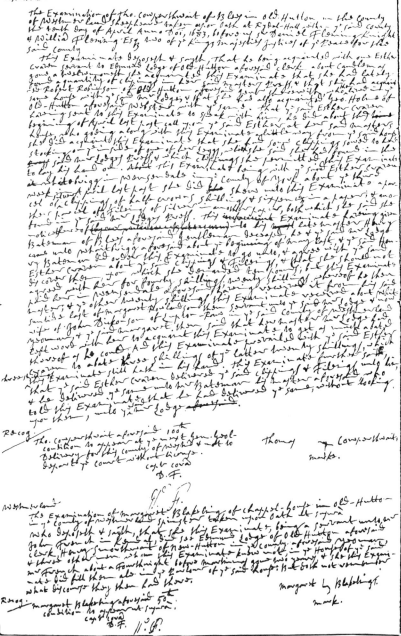

8 A rough draft by Fleming of examinations of Thomas Cowperthwaite and Margaret Blakeling, taken on 10 April 1683, with recognizances for their appearance.

threatening the officers for searching for the said Edward B.' was duly made. A copy of this warrant in Fleming's hand survives, dated 5 May.[11]

> Westmorland. For as much as we are informed by the proofs of credible persons, that divers felonies have been lately committed within this county of Westmorland; that John Bainbridge of Mansergh, yeoman, is a person of ill name and fame, is a common companion of thieves, hath divers guns, pistols and other arms (although he is not qualified by law to keep them) and divers suspicious goods, in his possession; and that he hath lately threatened the constables and other persons for the due execution of their office: these are therefore in his Majesty's name to command you forthwith to make diligent search for the arms and goods in all suspected houses and places within your constablewick and bring John Bainbridge, and such of the said arms and goods as you shall find, before us, or some of us, that he may be examined, and the arms and goods may be secured, according to law. And hereof fail not at your peril. Given under our hands and seals at Kendal.

Fleming continued to gather evidence from other quarters. On the day after the meeting of the Justices at Kendal, he examined a minor accomplice. George Scaif, re-examining him on 4 June. On 13 June he examined Simon Mount, a carrier, from whom a valuable pack of cloth had been stolen. On the 24th, Mount wrote a letter in his own hand, not only confirming a detail concerning the robbery, but giving information about William Smorthwait's whereabouts.[12]

> Sir,
>   Mr Daniel Fleming. These are to let you understand that the cloth was gone 12th December 1682. And as for William Smorthwait, he was drinking wine the last Tuesday night in Settle being 19 day of this instant June. So I rest your loving friend, Simon Mount.

The circumstances of Smorthwait's capture suggest that it was accidental. He was examined on 11 July by Henry, Lord Fairfax and four other Yorkshire Justices. Smorthwait denied all the charges, but admitted that 'about a quarter of a year ago he heard that a hue and cry came out of Westmorland against him and others for the breaking of the said [i.e. Robinson's] house.' One of the Justices was Fleming's relative, Henry Bouch, who sent an account of the capture to Fleming, dated from Ingleton on 14 July. The first line implies that Fleming had written to him, perhaps mentioning the wine-drinking in Settle.[13]

---

[11] Fleming Letters, 2657.
[12] Fleming Letters, 2671.
[13] Fleming Letters, 2689.

Worthy Sir,

I could not before this time return an answer to your letter concerning William Smorthwait which might be satisfactory to you, so I have sent my servant with this to acquaint you concerning the apprehending of him. Sir, on Tuesday last [i.e. 10 July] going towards our Sessions at Skipton I met with him upon the road and did secure him and ordered him that day to be brought to Skipton, which was done accordingly and after examination he was committed and sent to the gaol at York where he is now in custody. Our mittimus was grounded upon two informations we had received, the one was for clipping and diminishing his Majesty's coin upon an information we have from one William Foster who is now in Lancaster gaol and the other for burglary upon the information I received from you concerning the breaking of Mr Edmund Lodge's house in Hutton in the night time and taking away several sums of monies. We have another information against Henry Smorthwait his brother (who is now in your gaol at Appleby) given by Foster for clipping and diminishing his Majesty's coins and these informations are lodged with our Clerk of Assize at York. Now I shall leave it to your discretion to consider whether you will remove him from York to Appleby to have him tried there with his brother both for the treason and for the burglary, seeing they are both alike concerned. Which if you resolve upon it; then I conceive it were the best way to move the judges at York at the beginning of the Assize for the removal of him; before they order the Sheriff of Lancashire to bring Foster to York, which will save expenses, being nearer Appleby than York. Besides as I remember that by Foster's information the fact was done in Westmorland. I shall not further enlarge only begging your pardon for the trouble which my humble service presented. I remain your affectionate kinsman and humble servant Hen Bouch.

It is clear that Fleming took Bouch's advice, for William Smorthwait was duly removed from York Castle to Appleby gaol to await trial there with his brother. What Fleming made of another suggestion in Bouch's letter we do not know, for a note added at the bottom read:

Sir, I hear that there are several evil disposed persons has raised bad reports of Mr Lodge of Hutton, and has given some information against him. I do verily believe they are but the effects of a malicious contrivance to lessen his reputation and to invalid his evidence upon the trial at your Assizes at Appleby.

A few days later Fleming summoned a number of other people. A warrant was sent out to bring in people as witnesses, who would then be bound by recognizance to appear at the Assizes, as follows:

Sir Daniel Fleming Knight and William Fleming Esq . . . to the constables of Old Hutton and Holmescales . . . greeting.

These are in the Kings Majesty's name to will and command you, that
you do forthwith summon Henry Yeats of Old Hutton, yeoman, Joseph
Dawson of the same, whitesmith, Thomas Robinson junior of the same,
yeoman, Richard Jackson of the same, miller, William Beck of Bleaze in
Old Hutton, husbandman, and the wife of John Yeats of Holmescales,
carrier, personally to appear before us upon Friday next at Rydal Hall,
then and there to answer to such matters as on his Majesty's behalf shall
be objected against them. Hereof fail not at your peril. Given under our
hands and seals the eighteenth day of July 1683.

Copies of similar warrants sent to the constables of Barbon, Mansergh,
Killington and Middleton also survive among the Fleming papers. Those
who were summoned duly appeared and were examined or bound over.
The Assizes were now drawing close and Fleming was even busier. On 4
August he examined one person, on the 6th two more, one on the 8th, two
more on the 10th and two more on the 12th. Evidence was coming in from
other parts of England as well. A key witness against Edmund Lodge was
Esther Craven, Lodge's former servant, but she had moved into Yorkshire.
She was duly examined on 6th August by Cuthbert Wade, who sent a copy
of the examination with the following covering letter on the same day.

> You will receive here enclosed an information taken by way of examina-
> tion before me touching the business which you have made some en-
> trance into as I am given to understand. The which with those you have
> already taken, may please to deliver to the Clerk of the Assizes. You have
> also herewith a recognizance from the informant, who I verily believe will
> make her appearance accordingly and give her evidence now at your
> Assizes at Appleby publicly, according to what she hath before me done
> privately, this being all that I could do in this case. I shall enlarge no
> further but to subscribe sir your humble servant Cuthbert Wade.

Esther Craven's information was tainted, however. In April Fleming had
received a paper from Thomas Lodge, schoolmaster at Lancaster, possibly
one of Edmund Lodge's relatives, who threw doubt on[14]

> what reputation the woman is able, that she was a light, loose, wavering
> woman. That she would not (he believes) stick to say or swear anything

[14] No kinship link has so far been traced between these two schoolmasters, but the coincidence
of name seems likely to be more than accidental. Thomas Lodge was kinsman and teacher of
William Stout of Lancaster the diarist, who said he was 'then reputed the best. . .master in
these north parts.' *The Autobiography of William Stout of Lancaster, 1665–1752*, ed. J. D. Marshall
(Manchester, 1967), p. 72; see note 27, p. 247, of the same for a brief biography of Thomas
Lodge.

to take away any man's life. That she said her mistress was grown hard with her but she would be revenged of her. That she said she had £10 or £20 proffered as a reward to accuse her master and that Robert Robinson told her she might get £10 out of her master by threatening to swear against him that unless he would give her the said sum she would stir up against him H Yeats W Whitwell and W Speight [blank] Cowperthwaite.

This must be a reference to the supposed blackmailing of Lodge, described in the previous chapter.

Thus when the case came to Appleby Assizes in August, there were thirty-nine separate examinations and informations as evidence. These examinations were taken in accordance with notes which Fleming had made in his annotated *Statutes*.

Of witnesses — set down at large, all material circumstances that they shall declare to prove the offence, or offender guilty of it. *Of the party — set down* every particular answer that he shall make to the question that shall be demanded of him.

The Clerk of Assize had a copy of these examinations, as did Fleming. As for the prisoners awaiting trial, the gaol calendar is missing in the official records, but again Fleming supplies the lost details. The calendar named eight persons as being in gaol. Two of these, a man accused of stealing two heifers and a woman accused of murdering her bastard child, had nothing to do with the Smorthwait case. The other six were:

John Jackson of Old Hutton committed the 13 day of January. . .for the suspicion of felony and murder.

Henry Smorthwait of New Hutton committed the 17 day of February. . . charged with the felonious taking of the moneys, goods and chattels of Robert Robinson.

George Scaif of Hutton Park in New Hutton, committed the 27 day of June. . .for the felonious taking of the moneys of Thomas Aray and. . . other persons.

Edmund Lodge late of Old Hutton clerk committed. . .charged with the suspicion of treason and felony.

William Foster delivered over to the Sheriff of Westmorland by the Sheriff of Lancaster the 17 day of August 1683.

William Smorthwait then delivered by the Sheriff of Yorkshire.

The absence of Edward Bainbridge and William Manning is conspicuous. Foster and William Smorthwait had been brought over at the last minute. Henry Smorthwait's presence had caused Fleming some anxiety, for he had suspected that Smorthwait might be allowed to escape. Fleming wrote to the gaoler on 16 July, keeping a rough copy among his papers.[15]

15 Fleming Letters, 2694.

Mr Gaoler,

Being informed of an extraordinary authority you assume of giving liberty to your prisoners, contrary to law; lest you should transgress too far, let me acquaint you, that I am informed a Justice of the Peace hath an information of high treason against Henry Smorthwait, one of your prisoners; therefore look well to him, lest it prove more penal to you, than would be wished. Your loving friend Daniel Fleming.

To this the gaoler replied four days later.[16]

Yours this day I received for which most humble manner I do give thanks. As for liberty to Henry Smorthwait or any other, I never will give contrary to your worship's order or his Majesty's Justices of Peace in any wise. And good sir, I do humbly beg of you if in any case I have transgressed, I will as in just reason humbly submit and crave your assistance, for I do assure you I never look of them. And all the liberty is only from the gaol to my house to get a little meat, and always with a guard. And if you be pleased to lay your commands upon me no sooner laid but observed, by, sir, your humble servant, Wm Dargue.

Henry Smorthwait's escape would have been irritating too, because conveying him to prison, like all other such acts, had cost the country money and time. Among Fleming's papers is a short account from the constables of New Hutton, dated 17 February, 'for the charges laid down by him for the carriage of Henry Smorthwait to Appleby'. The constable also gave the expenses of 7s 3d for catching Dixon and Scaif, but these are crossed out and deducted by Fleming. The reckoning was stated to be (in pounds, shillings and pence):

Laid down at Mr Sands. . .0-17-9
In our way to Appleby. . .0-2-6
For other things provided for our journey. . .0-1-2
Laid down at Appleby. . .1-19-0
Laid forth in our homecoming. . .0-0-10
For horses shoeing. . .0-0-10
Spent at Margaret Sill. . .0-0-10
Remains. . .3-02-11

There were also difficulties with Lodge. Not only was he a cleric, but the evidence against him came in very late, Esther Craven's information only being taken over in Yorkshire on 6 August. It appears that when he received this, Fleming wrote to Lodge asking him to come and see him. Lodge wrote a prevaricating letter on 8 August from Old Hutton.[17]

[16] Fleming Letters, 2699.
[17] Fleming Letters, 2705.

Honourable Sir,

I had a week ago designed this day and tomorrow for the management of such extraordinary business as nearly concerns me, and which I cannot possibly waive without great prejudice, both to myself and others. And so it is that another day may be too late if this be neglected. Therefore, sir, in all humble submission, I beg your excuse if I presume to look after an emergent occasion, and choose to wait upon you at any other time and at what place you will appoint when your best leisure pleases to command. Sir, your most humble servant. Edmund Lodge.

Fleming summoned him to appear on the 10th and issued out a *mittimus*, a formal order for a person to be committed to gaol, against Lodge.

Westmorland. Sir Daniel Fleming Knight. . .to the keeper of his Majesty's gaol in the said county, his deputy and deputies, greeting. I send you herewithal the body of Edmund Lodge late of Old Hutton, clerk, charged before me with the suspicion of treason and felony, commanding you in his Majesty's name to receive him into the gaol, and him there safely to keep, until he shall be from thence delivered by due order of law. Hereof fail not at your peril. Given under my hand and seal at Rydal Hall, the tenth day of August, 1683.

On the back of this, Fleming noted: 'This and Mr Lodge were then delivered unto the constable of Old Hutton.'

Fleming had thus managed to assemble six persons in gaol. But it was also necessary to gather the accusers and witnesses at Appleby. As well as a copy of all the recognizances taken at the Quarter Sessions, the Assize papers contain a summary of numerous other recognizances, with large penalties for non-appearance, against other persons. In all, twenty-seven persons were bound over to appear to give evidence against specified persons. (See illustration 9) We may therefore assume that most of those who had been examined by Fleming and the other Justices now went up to Appleby for the trial. Fleming himself went up to Carlisle on 13 August and proceeded to travel with the Assize judges on their tour of the northern gaols. In his manuscript account book he noted down the expenses of this tour.

Aug. 13 Delivered to my sons Will. & Dan. when we went to the Assizes. . .00-15-00. Spent out of my own pocket at Carlisle Appleby & Lancaster Assizes (my two sons, cousin Roger Wilson, & Will. Banckes being with me) between August the 13. & 28. AD 1683, besides what my cousin Kirkby paid for me at Lancaster, I and Jo. Banckes being there his witnesses, in all the sum of. . .03 06 00.

There is no reference to this trial, but Fleming may have assisted his cousin William Kirkby with the trials of clippers at Lancaster.

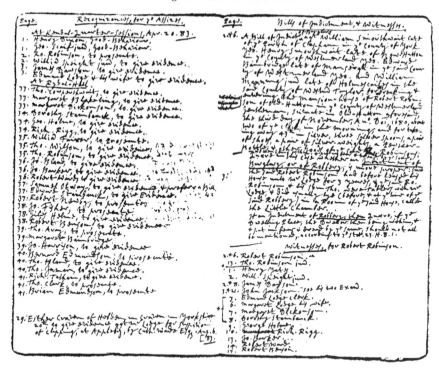

9 Notes by Fleming of recognizances, bills of indictments and witnesses for the Assizes in 1683; page numbers refer to full copies of documents also made by Fleming.

The accusations, or bills of indictment as they were known, were now in the hands of the Clerk of the Assize. Draft copies of these bills have survived, filed alongside the examinations as well as in Fleming's papers. There are sixteen accusations in all. The formal, approved, indictments accord with Fleming's notes in the annotated *Statutes* concerning 'An Order to be observed in the right framing of Indictments.'

> *Quis*, the person with his name, surname, addition of the town, country, art & degree.
> *Quando*, the day and year.
> *Ubi*, the place, town and county.
> *Quid*, the thing taken, the colour, mark, the price, & value.
> *Cujus*, the owner of the thing, and whose it was.

The drafts were abbreviated but included the names of witnesses, with page references to the file of depositions. These latter details will be omitted here. The draft bills were written in English, as follows:

1 A bill of indictment against William Smorthwait late of Clapham in the county of York, yeoman, Henry Smorthwait late of New Hutton, yeoman, Edward Bainbridge late of Mansergh, yeoman, and William Manning junior late of Holmescales, tailor, for robbing of Robert Robinson of Old Hutton, gentleman, and taking from him forty three pounds in silver, three silver spoons, a pair of shoes, a pair of silver weights and a pewter bottle, the third day of November 1680 about two of the clock in the morning in the dwelling place of Robert Robinson at Old Hutton, the said Robert Robinson then being within and put in fear and dread by the same.

This was the most important bill, but Fleming was not quite sure how to get it absolutely correct.

In his personal papers Fleming had sketched out a rough bill along the same lines, and had added this note:

Query in this case whether an indictment of burglary, or of robbery is more proper: since the said Robert Robinson had before leased his house unto Mr Lodge for 3 years and the said Robert Robinson and his son Thomas were tablers with Mr Lodge and did usually lie (before and at the time of the said robbery) in a room of the said house, called the little chamber. If an indictment of robbery, then query, if the dwelling place, the dweller then being within, and put in fear and dread by the same, should not all be mentioned, according to the Stat.23.H.8.1.

Fleming or the Clerk of Assize decided that robbery was a more appropriate charge. '2 Another against William Smorthwait for clipping &c.' This bill is amplified in the surviving indictment to read: 'William Smorthwait of Middleton on 20th October 1676 for clipping twenty shillings of half crowns, twenty shillings of one shillings and twenty of sixpences.' The third was: 'Another against Edmund Lodge late of Old Hutton clerk for clipping.' This is expanded in the surviving indictment, where it was specified that the clipping took place on 1st April and the sums of money exactly as in the Smorthwait bill.

4 Another against Edmund Lodge for being an accessory to the robbing of Robert Robinson as aforesaid. 5 Another against Henry Smorthwait, William Smorthwait, Edward Bainbridge, and George Scaif for stealing Simon Mount's pack &c. 6 Another against William Smorthwait, Henry Smorthwait, Edward Bainbridge for breaking Margaret Bainbridge's house in the night and for stealing three petticoats and a rapier about Candlemas, 1675.

There then follow five draft bills against George Scaif for various minor thefts, after which we find: '12 Another against Edmund Lodge for picking

of the pocket, and taking out of it a purse worth 21*s* 6*d*, a seal, and a key of
Jo. Fisher upon Acension Day gone 2 years. 13 Another against Henry
Smorthwait and Edward Bainbridge for stealing of a heifer or cow, from
Samuel Otway and Anne Gibbonson about October 28 1680.' An indictment for this last offence survives, adding that the cow was black and
valued at 40*s*. '14 Another against Edmund Lodge for stealing John Walton's
silver cup, about three years ago. 15 Another against Edward Bainbridge
aforesaid, for stealing of veal from Bernard Edmundson upon Whitsun Eve
about six years ago. 16 Another against Edward Bainbridge for stealing a
coat worth 24*s* from Bryan Edmundson, upon Whitsun Even about six
years ago.' An indictment which appears to correspond to this has survived,
though it is very badly damaged.

There were thus sixteen bills and a very large number of written depositions. If the defendants were found guilty on these charges, they would be
executed: clipping, robbery in a dwelling house and burglary were all
capital offences, that is to say that there was no 'benefit of clergy'. 'Benefit of
clergy' was an ancient right which, by this period, had been extended to
mean that a person convicted of a felony might escape the death penalty for
a first offence by reading a portion of the Bible or another text.

We can only partially reconstruct what happened in the court room,
largely from what we know of the form of process in general. The bills would
first be examined by the Grand Jury, a group of gentry who were to inquire
whether the bills were technically sound or not. The oath this jury had to
take is copied in Fleming's annotated Statutes:

> You shall truly inquire and due presentment make of all such things as
> you are charged withall on the Kings behalf, his Majesty's council, your
> own, & your fellows, you shall well and truly keep. And in all other
> things the truth present, so help you God, & by the contents of this book.

The prosecutors and witnesses would be called and sworn and examined in
secret, so that if the charge were found to be false, or *ignoramus*, the accused
could not prosecute them. In this case it is possible to gain some idea of
what happened from a sheet retained by Fleming: 'This I had from Sir
C[hristopher] P[hilipson] being sent unto the Grand Jury.' On it are
thirteen questions to be addressed to witnesses and prosecutors. Three of
the questions were clearly attempting to see whether there were false
accusations out of malice, particularly in relation to Jackson.

> To ask Jackson if he was not tampered withall by W[illiam] S[morth-
> wait], H[enry] Y[eats] &c to accuse Mr L[odge]. That Jackson said in
> the hearing of [blank] that if ever he had said or ever should say anything
> against Lodge concerning the robbery, he wronged him and was the
> veriest rogue in nature, and that he knew nothing against him, but that

he was an honest man in that business, and this he repeated several times. That Yeats said that he would bring Mr Lodge's neck into the halter, or his wife's, or both.

There were also a number of specific questions concerning the burglary at Robinson's house.

To ask Margaret Dickonson, whether ever she saw Smorthwait at Mr Lodge's or in company with him.

To ask her what locked rooms they had or chest etc.

Whether she heard any sound of shoe feet upon the loft when they were supposed to come in.

The first words she heard, Sirrah house is surrounded.

The maids being up and stirring might rather prevent the mischief.

And whether the robbers threatened Mr Lodge or no, and how.

Whether they sought through and threw down all his pewter and struck twice into a tankard to try whether 'twas silver as is imagined and left it thrown under the table.

Whether Mr Lodge called to R. Robinson and his son to make help or no.

That the window which they tell of was always open unless it was a great wind, and was open when she went to bed.

That Mr Lodge would have had R. Robinson to go to a Justice the next morning and would have gone with him for a warrant or otherwise as should be directed, but Robert Robinson would not because he durst not venture on his own mare, thereupon Mr Lodge proffered him his own horse but could not prevail with him.

That the nurse having not been in bed for five nights before was gone to bed and the maid rose to spare her and to wait on her mistress.

That Mr Lodge moved R. Robinson to pursue the rogues after they were gone and proffered to be one to pursue but 'twas disapproved by Robert Robinson.

Before answering these questions, the witnesses upon bills of indictment had to take the following oath:

The evidence that you shall give to the inquest upon this bill shall be the truth, and the whole truth, and nothing but the truth; and you shall not let so to do for malice, hatred, nor evil will, not for favour or affection. So help you God, and by the contents of this book.

After examining the sixteen bills, the Grand Jury endorsed those it supported as 'true bills'. In this case we only know that the Jury passed eight bills, namely numbers 1, 2, 3, 13, 15, 16 and two of the five bills against Scaif for pickpocketing. What happened to the other eight we do not know. It was often the practice to destroy rejected bills, but since the surviving indictments are black with dirt and were placed in the wrong box, it is possible that others have been lost rather than rejected. What is certain is that at least eight very serious indictments now stood against the main offenders.

The form of the trial before the second jury was standardized and we can reconstruct it from other trials of the period which have been reported verbatim.[18]

Clerk of Arraignment	Crier make proclamation.
Crier	All manner of persons that have anything more after adjournment to do at this general Assize of Nisi prius Oyer and Terminer and general gaol delivery, draw near and give your attendance.[19]
Cl. of Arr.	Set Mr William Smorthwait to the Bar (which was done). William Smorthwait hold up thy hand (which was done). William Smorthwait thou standest indicted in the county of Westmorland by the name of William Smorthwait late of Middleton in the county of Westmorland, yeoman, for that thou, the fear of God in thy heart not having, nor weighing the duty of allegiance to the King, but being instigated by the Devil treasonably, traitorously, and against the known laws of this realm, our Sovereign Lord the King his crown and dignity, didst on 20th October 1676 clip twenty shillings of half crowns, twenty shillings of one shillings and twenty of six pences. [The other indictments against Smorthwait also read out.] How sayst thou William Smorthwait, art thou guilty of this high treason and felony whereof thou stand indicted or not guilty?
Smorthwait	Not guilty.
Cl. of Arr.	How wilt thou be tried?

[18] Obviously a few words might vary in their spelling: for instance, some trial accounts give the cry as 'O Yes', others as 'Oyez'. But the various verbatim reports, whether of trials in King's Bench or the Assizes, whether in treason or non-treason, whether for the home circuit or northern circuit are extraordinarily similar. The main trials used for this reconstruction are: the trial at the northern Assizes at York for counterfeiting of Arthur Mangy, reprinted in Thoresby Society, IX, *Miscellanea* (1899), pp. 207–27; 'The Trial of Edward Coleman, Gent. for conspiring the death of the King. . .1678', King's College, Cambridge, E.27.1(2); 'The Trial of Sir Miles Stapleton, bart. at York Assizes, for High Treason, 1681', reprinted in T. B. Howell (ed.), *A Complete Collection of State Trials* (1816–31) VIII, pp. 502ff. More standard formularies for the seventeenth century are cited by Dr J. Baker in J. S. Cockburn (ed.), *Crime in England 1500–1800* (1977), pp. 299–309. I am most grateful to Dr Baker for checking and improving the reconstructed trial.

[19] The judges at Assizes sat by virtue of five separate commissions; that of Assize allowed them to deal with ejectments, that of Nisi Prius with civil matters, of Oyer and Terminer with treasons, felonies and trespasses, and of General Gaol Delivery with the prisoners in gaol. They also sat as Justices of the Peace.

Smorthwait	By God and the country.
Cl. of Arr.	God send thee a good deliverance. Crier make proclamation.
Crier	Oyez, Oyez, Oyez. All manner of persons that can inform his Majesty's Justices of Nisi prius, Oyer and Terminer and general gaol delivery, the King's Counsel, the King's Attorney, or the King's Solicitor of any treasons, felonies, misdemeanours or breach of peace against William Smorthwait prisoner at the Bar let them come forth and they shall be heard, for now the prisoner stands upon his deliverance.

The prisoner was then freed of all his shackles, so as not to be under duress or to appear in a humiliating posture during the trial. The other defendants associated with Smorthwait would then be arraigned in a similar fashion and the trial would continue.

Cl. of Arr.	Call the Jury. You the prisoner at the Bar, these good men that you shall hear called and personally appear are to pass betwixt our Sovereign Lord the King and you upon trial of your life and death, if therefore you will challenge them or any of them, your time is to challenge them as they come to the book to be sworn.

The names of the jury of twelve men were then called out, and the prisoner in a capital trial was allowed up to thirty-five challenges without giving any cause for the challenge. There are several names on the jury list which probably relates to the Smorthwait trial where the juryman was not, finally, sworn.[20] Two of these were from the Smorthwait's native chapelry of Middleton and may therefore represent challenges. But one Middleton man, James Bouskell was among those sworn, the rest being from parishes other than Kirkby Lonsdale. The jurors were men of yeomanry level, of roughly the same social position as the Smorthwaits and Bainbridge. After they were accepted they were required to take the following oath (according to Fleming):

> You shall true deliverance make between our Sovereign Lord the King and the prisoner at the Bar as you shall have in charge, according to your evidence, as near as God shall give you grace, so help you God, and by the contents of this book.

The formal business would then proceed.

Cl. of Arr.	Cryer, make an Oyez.
Crier	Oyez. Our Sovereign Lord the King does strictly charge and

---

[20] It is impossible to be certain since there are *two* surviving jury lists in the Westmorland bundle for this date. One of them, however, is attached to a separate indictment and it therefore seems likely that the jury for the Smorthwaits and associates is that headed '1st jury'.

command all manners of persons to keep silent upon pain of imprisonment.

Cl. or Arr.   William Smorthwait hold up thy hand (which he did). You gentlemen of the Jury look upon the prisoner and hearken to his cause. He stands indicted in the county of Westmorland by the name of William Smorthwait aforesaid, in the indictment and against the form of the statutes in that case made and provided. [Here the substance of the charge should be read again in the third person.] Upon this indictment he hath been arraigned and thereunto hath pleaded not guilty and for his trial hath put himself upon God and his Country, which country you are. You are to enquire whether he be guilty of the high treason and felony whereof he stands indicted (in manner and form as he stands indicted) or not guilty. If you find him guilty you are to enquire what goods and chattels, lands and tenements he was possessed of at the time when the high treason was committed or at any other time since. If you find him not guilty you are to enquire whether he fled for it. If you find he fled for it, you are to enquire of his goods and chattels as if you had found him guilty, if that you find him not guilty nor that he fled for it you are to say so and no more and hearken to the evidence.

Crier   If anyone will give evidence on the behalf of our Sovereign Lord the King against William Smorthwait the prisoner at the Bar, let him come forth and he shall be heard, for the prisoner now stands at the Bar upon his deliverance.

At this point the Counsel for the King would summon witnesses and produce evidence, namely the persons and examinations which Fleming had assembled. They would be cross-questioned by both the Judge and also the prisoner, who acted as his own counsel. Smorthwait could also call unsworn witnesses in his defence. This was the longest part of the trial. At the end of the giving of evidence for both sides, the Judge would make a speech summarizing what had been heard and attempting to guide the Jury as to some of the legal niceties of the case. The same process would then occur with Henry Smorthwait, Lodge and Scaif. The Jury would choose a bailiff or 'keeper'. This man would be given the following oath: 'You shall well and truly keep this inquest from meat and drink, fire and candle; you shall not suffer any man to speak with them, more than to ask them, if they be agreed, until such time as they be agreed. So help you God, and by the contents of this book.' The Jury would retire to consider their verdict, and then return to the court.

Cl. of Arr.   Gentlemen are you agreed of your verdict?

Jury	Yes.
Cl. of Arr.	Who shall say for you?
Jury	Our foreman.
Cl. of Arr.	William Smorthwait hold up thy hand. How say you, is William Smorthwait guilty of the high treason and felony whereof he stands indicted or not guilty?
Foreman	Not guilty.

When they returned, the jury found the two Smorthwaits and Lodge 'not guilty' on every indictment. There is only one verdict of 'guilty', against George Scaif for one of his pickpocketings. No verdict is recorded against Manning or Bainbridge although above Bainbridge's name it is noted that he pleaded the benefit of a general pardon. No indictments against Jackson have survived. The Jury then enquired as to whether those not guilty had fled, and it was answered that they had not done so and therefore their goods were not forfeit.[21] The accused were then released.

If the verdict had been guilty, the prisoner would have been returned to prison to await sentence the next day. Before passing sentence, the Judge would have asked: 'What canst thou say for thy self, whereof judgement of death should not be given against thee, and an execution awarded according to law?' The Judge would then make a summary speech outlining the seriousness of the offence and give sentence. After this the prisoner might make another speech, repeating his innocence or confessing his guilt.

After all the evidence had been collected, it is not surprising that Fleming should have been irritated. He believed that the jury of life and death had been over-favourable. Almost a year later he wrote to the Clerk of Assizes that 'William Smorthwait and Henry Smorthwait escaped their being convicted (by the help of a very favourable jury) at last Appleby Assizes.' He advised that any future trial should be at Carlisle where the juries 'will not probably be so favourable, or so afraid of, these offenders, as they have been in Westmorland.' It is probable that if the Smorthwaits had desisted at this point, the whole matter would have been dropped. Edmund Lodge, for example, disappears from Old Hutton and was buried in July 1696 at Clapham, where he had been vicar since 1684, leaving personal property inventoried as worth £58, including £5 worth of books.[22] But the Smorthwaits were less easily deterred.

---

[21] The jury was to inquire whether those found not guilty had fled, for to flee was an offence in itself, even if a person was subsequently proved to be innocent.

[22] Lodge's will and inventory are among the Archdeaconry of Richmond probate materials in the Lancashire Record Office, Preston. For the dating of Lodge's stay at Clapham, and other details concerning Lodge, I am most grateful to the Rev. Peter Winstone, vicar of Clapham.

5

'Insolent and Formidable Felons'

For the historian the acquittal is useful. Instead of withdrawing from the brink, the Smorthwaits allegedly proceeded to expand their activities. What happened is described in a general way in a letter from Fleming to the Clerk of the northern Assizes. Having pointed out their lucky escape, he proceeds:

> Not withstanding they then run the risk of losing their lives there, yet it wrought no reformation upon either of them. For since that time they have committed divers great offences (as the enclosed copies of examinations will inform you) and they became so bold, as they played their pranks in the very county where they were well known, and in the day time; and they did grow so numerous, and vapoured at so great a rate, as many in the country were much afraid of them; and our tradesmen durst not travel without being well accompanied and armed.

During the autumn and winter of 1683 and the following spring, the Smorthwaits and their accomplices undertook a number of further robberies and an attempted burglary.

As it became apparent that nothing had changed, Fleming and other Justices started to gather evidence once again. The first recorded official action of which we know started in April 1684. The 'vapourings' Fleming complained of were now reaching a high level. Although we have to treat the evidence with caution, Edward Bainbridge later informed that during a quarrel with William Smorthwait he had given Smorthwait 'ill words' about a stolen horse, 'and William Smorthwait did then say that he did not fear Sir Daniel Fleming for he could raise as many men as either Sir Daniel or any other Justice of them all could do.' Furthermore, the exploits of Smorthwait were attracting the attention of others, who were starting to imitate his 'vapourings' and deride the law. Fleming received a letter written on 25 April, which he marked on the outside, 'concerning Henry Holme's personating William Smorthwait'. His correspondent wrote:

Sir

On Monday last I went down to the Endmoor and Crooklands and Heversham to enquire if William Smorthwait had been of late amongst them. But I find that Henry Holme of Sedburgh was drinking at James Burrow's house in Heversham, and being got merry as he came from it hence called at Crooklands for one or two quarts of ale and called himself by the name of William Smorthwait and did ride up and down madling [sic] and said he cared for no man and no man could take him or words to this purpose. And Thomas Sill, servant to James Burrow, did drink to him and called him Mr Smorthwait. And then Henry Holme came up to the Endmoor to John Preston's house where he stayed all night and gave no evil words towards any man. And this is all that I find touching in this matter, not else but that I am your humble servant George Scaif, Kendal.

But Smorthwait was not content merely to boast and be imitated. In the same month there occurred the event — a particularly violent attempted burglary — which would set off the proceedings leading to another trial. Then 'Henry Preston of Farleton in the county of Westm. yeo. was Apr.15.84. in the night–time cruelly wounded and robbed of a fawchion [sword] by William Smorthwait, Henry Smorthwait, Bryan Thompson and 3 persons unknown.' Preston had resisted the robbers and when he ventured out to call the neighbours he had been set upon. He was ill for some time, but on 12 May he gave a detailed information concerning the affair to two Justices. Four days later one of the Justices examined a blacksmith from a neighbouring village who had his forge broken into on the night of the Preston affair and had two hammers and some horseshoes taken away. These were found at the scene of the crime. Two days after this the same Justices called Preston's wife, also a woman who had nursed the injured Preston, and a neighbour, to an inn at Lupton, just near the place where the affair had occurred. They all corroborated the story. A suspected accomplice, and two of the suspected assailants, Henry Smorthwait and Bryan Thompson, were all examined, but denied any involvement. The evidence was strong enough, however, for the Justices to send Smorthwait and Thompson off to Appleby gaol, under a *mittimus* dated, like the examinations, 20 May. But Preston and his wife had spoken of six assailants, so there were still four to be found.

The following day, the five Justices of the Peace for Westmorland signed an order addressed 'to the High Constables, petty constables, surveyors of the highways, churchwardens, & overseers of the poor, within Kendal & Lonsdale wards'. The second part of this concerned various matters such as bridges and highways and absentees from church. But the first half was related to the violence, and the additions to the draft in Fleming's hand (in italics) are especially revealing.

These are in the Kings Majesty's name to command you, High Constables of Kendal & Lonsdale wards, forthwith to issue out your warrants to the petty constables within your several wards respectively, requiring them that they be *very* diligent in the making of privy searches within their respective constablewicks for the discovering, *disarming* and apprehending of all robbers, *highwaymen*, felons, rioters, such persons as shall presume to go or ride armed against the King's Peace to the disturbance of his Majesty's people; and all rogues, vagabonds, sturdy beggars, & suspicious persons; and that the petty constables be *very* careful in causing to be kept in their constablewicks respectively, from henceforth until Michaelmas next, an active and strong watch and ward, every night and day, by able and well armed men, for the apprehending of the said offenders; and such of them as shall be so arrested, are forthwith to be conveyed unto some of his Majesty's Justices of the Peace, to be examined and further dealt withall according to law. And all persons whatsoever are hereby commanded to be aiding, assisting & obedient herein unto the petty constables and watchers; and if any suspicious person will not obey their arrest, then they shall levy hue and cry upon him, and fresh suit shall be made after him (and all felons) from town to town, and from country to country, and that as well by horsemen as footmen, according to law. . . . And hereof neither of you, nor any of them, are to fair at your *and their* peril. . . (See illustration 10)

It is possible that this and the earlier warrants would have finally led to Smorthwait's arrest. But, ironically, in the same way as he had happened to meet a Justice on the road to the Quarter Sessions in 1683 and had been arrested, so again in 1684 his arrest was an accident.

Ten days after the issue of this order, in a small village called Padiham near Burnley in Lancashire, a constable received a 'warrant of hue and cry' for the arrest of the suspected highwayman Edward Bradrick. One of those accompanying Bradrick was John Lyley, who later wrote two petitions to the juries describing the capture. One of these, written in early November 1684, may be quoted.

The humble petition of John Lyley, a poor prisoner in the gaol at Lancaster Castle and in double irons. Humbly showeth whereas your poor petitioner being unhappily in the company of one Edw. Bradrick and one William Smorthwait at Padiham and a warrant of hue and cry issued out to take the same Bradrick and all his company was by virtue of the same taken with them and brought too before his Majesty's Justice of the Peace at Clitheroe. And was committed to this gaol amongst the parties aforesaid. And was committed to this gaol amongst the parties aforesaid. And continued here prisoner since before midsummer last and not guilty of any misdemeanour upon any account excepting his unhappiness to be in that evil company. And by reason of his

10 A copy of an order from the Justices to the High Constables on 21 May 1684,
ordering them to send out further warrants for the apprehension of robbers, highwaymen,
burglars and other felons.

confinement so far distant from his friends and relations (being very
poor) is not able to procure bail for his appearance next Assizes, hath
nothing to relieve himself withal but his bare 6d a week allowance but is
forced to complain to your worshipful bench for your charitable
consultation of his miserable and distressed condition. Therein may it
therefore please your worships to take his sad and miserable condition
into your pious and charitable consideration and grant that your poor

petitioner may upon his own bail for his appearance next Assizes be
released from his miserable imprisonment and have his liberty to labour
for an honest livelihood and not perish under afflictions for want of relief.
Your poor petitioner as in duty bound will ever pray etc.

Lyley failed to mention that he had been in York prison the year before for
some other offence; yet he clearly felt that he had been unfortunate to be
apprehended alongside Bradrick. William Smorthwait may have felt
equally unfortunate that he was accidentally arrested.

The circumstances of the capture are more fully described in the examinations taken at Clitheroe. It appears that Lyley and Bradrick were
travelling south from Kendal and stopped for the night at Smorthwait's
home town of Clapham on the night of Friday 30 May. Lyley went to see
Smorthwait, 'having acquaintance with him when they were prisoners in
York Castle together'. The next day he and Bradrick set off by themselves,
but were soon joined by Smorthwait and a man called Tennant, who were
also journeying south. On the Sunday night they were staying in Padiham,
and were 'apprehended together upon the suspicion of highway robbers.'
Tennant described how he had several times sold wheat to Smorthwait and
so agreed to accompany him on a journey to Manchester. On the road they
overtook Bradrick and Lyley and travelled on to Padiham where they were
apprehended. The relationship between Bradrick and Smorthwait was
indicated when 'after a little discourse between them Bradrick called
Smorthwait father and Smorthwait called Bradrick son.' The scene of the
capture was described by several witnesses. The constable of Padiham said
that he 'received a warrant of hue and cry under the hand and seal of
Ambrose Pudsey Esq. one of his Majesty's JP for the West Riding of York
on 31st May last for the apprehending of one Edward Bradrick and three
other men, persons very suspicious to be highway robbers in observance
whereof he apprehended four men. . . and their horses, searched them but
found nothing about them except 19s in Smorthwait's pocket.' He then
went on to describe how he had sold the horse Smorthwait was riding to pay
for the expenses of taking them to prison; later a man from Appleby came
and claimed that the mare had been stolen from him. It is not clear whether
the constable arrested all four men by himself. A Padiham shoemaker was
certainly present at the searching of the suspects and said that he had found
vizards in the pockets of Tennant and Smorthwait and a pistol hidden in the
house; but he may have come in later, as did Thomas Hartley, a
blacksmith. Hartley, 'hearing a noise' in a neighbouring house at about ten
o'clock at night, 'went to see what the matter was and coming thither found
the constable of the town and certain men whom he had apprehended as
suspected persons for highway robbers quarrelling and they endeavouring
to make their escapes whereupon the constable charged him to assist him.'

Hartley then started to talk to the apprehended persons, 'and discoursing with one of the persons called Edward Bradrick, he [i.e. Bradrick] told him there was gold money and clippings of silver hid in the house if they would find them.' Hartley searched round and found 'two bags of clippings of silver hid between a pair of bindings weighing 41 oz or thereabouts'. Another weaver was also present. The prisoners were captured late on the night of Sunday 1st June. On 2nd June they and some of their apprehenders were examined at Clitheroe. They were then taken on to Lancaster gaol. The gaol calendar includes under 'committed as highway men' the three names of Bradrick, Smorthwait and Lyley; under 'committed as alesellers harbouring of highway men' is Tennant. Significantly, of the thirty men listed in the calendar, the only two with the honorific 'Mr' against them were Smorthwait and Bradrick.

By 1st June, the Smorthwaits, Bradrick and Thompson were all in custody. The effect was probably too much for Edward Bainbridge, who was still at liberty. If the man who had boasted that he did not fear Sir Daniel Fleming or any other Justice could be arrested by an alehouse keeper, there was obviously little safety for him. Furthermore, he had already fallen out with Bradrick and Smorthwait. He had picked Bradrick's pocket and Bradrick in retaliation had stolen Bainbridge's brother's horse. When Bainbridge had traced it down to Clapham and was about to retrieve it, Bradrick and Smorthwait had come out and attacked him. Bainbridge decided to inform on his accomplices, possibly motivated by other reasons as well. Fleming later wrote to the Clerk of Assize that Bainbridge had informed because, 'being of late very sickly, and repenting him of his former unlawful action', he had 'come unto Sir Christopher Philipson and my brother Wilson, and (upon their promising to use their endeavours with the Judge that he might be made use of as a witness) gave them information of divers offences.' This was on 6 June. Bainbridge made a much fuller confession before Fleming and three other Justices on the 23rd. We have a list of eleven questions which Fleming wished to put to Bainbridge. The questions related to all the supposed offences; for example question 4 was: 'His, Will.Smor. & Hen. Smor. breaking Marg.Bainbridges house in the night & stealing three petticoats and a rapier about Candlemas 1675.' Meanwhile, the matters discussed on the 23rd and in a later confession in July had been expanded by a very detailed confession of another accomplice.

We left Edward Bradrick and William Smorthwait in Lancaster gaol. Bradrick may have heard of Bainbridge's first confession, for four days later, in the presence of the gaoler, two Justices and another witness, he poured out a very long confession describing in intimate detail what he had heard and what he had done. Bradrick, a small red-faced man as he was later described, had been a principal actor in the events since the first trial.

The circumstances of the examination were explained in a covering letter containing the examinations, which was sent by one of the Justices, Fleming's cousin William Kirkby, written on 14 June from Lancaster.

> Sir,
>
> My occasions having obliged my residence some days here I had opportunity to discourse one Edw. Bradrick a prisoner in this castle an eminent highwayman and a great rogue as you may perceive by the enclosed examination. It is true he is a condemned person, but it seems made his escape from York before his execution. Upon some discourse with him I prevailed with him to make the enclosed discovery which is all that concerns Cumberland and Westmorland. What concerns Yorkshire I have sent of cousin Bouch and what is in this county I have taken care of myself. And though it is true this is the information of a condemned person it bears such strong circumstances of truth that for my part I cannot doubt the truth of it and I cannot think that but a very good cause to make those persons find sureties for their good behaviour and do appear at the Assizes. Which proceeding they probably raise and bring in direct evidence against the malefactors. . . . The judges that come this circuit when you meet them at Carlisle you will have an opportunity to discourse them about it. In the meantime, I should be glad of any opportunity to see you. I purpose to go homewards tomorrow where I hope I may be some time. And if I can make any further discovery you shall have an account. In the mean, desire you will esteem me, sir, your most affectionate kinsman and most humble servant William Kirkby.

It is worth noting that even before they left London, the Assize judges would be receiving informations concerning the Smorthwait affair. Bradrick's very detailed confession implicated many others, for he had operated over a wide area, between his home in Leeds and Carlisle in the north. His evidence was supplemented by that of his wife, who was examined on 23 June by Fleming. Bradrick himself was soon afterwards taken over to the prison at York Castle to await trial there. But not before he had given a further confession to Kirkby. Kirkby wrote again on 8 July to Fleming.

> Sir,
>
> Since the last account I gave you of Bradrick's information, I have received this further enclosed information from him which I thought necessary to transmit to you, not doubting your care about it. I shall be glad if any opportunity offer to see you before the Assizes, especially if any occasion draw you our way. And then upon least notice I will wait upon you. I purpose, God willing, homewards tomorrow. I remain sir your most affectionate kinsman and humble servant William Kirkby.

This later information appears nowhere in the official Assize papers, but survives among the Fleming papers, implicating a number of hitherto unsuspected persons.

The first informations of Bradrick and Bainbridge were enough to propel Fleming and Philipson into action. On 18 June, according to copies which Fleming made, warrants for summoning various witnesses were made out. They were sent out to the constables of Farleton, New Hutton, Old Hutton, Kirkby Lonsdale, Mallerstang and Mansergh. The form was identical, so that we may give just one instance, the last of these.

> Sir Daniel and Sir Christopher Philipson Knights. . . to the constables of Mansergh, greetings.
> These are in his Majesty's name to command you forthwith to apprehend Edward Bainbridge of Mansergh yeoman and to bring him before us upon Monday next at Mistress Forth's house in Kendal then and there to answer to such matters as on his Majesty's behalf shall be objected against him. And hereof fail not at your peril. Given under our hands and seals the 18th day of June 1684.
> Signatures & seals of D. Fleming & C. Philipson

Those summoned by these warrants duly appeared. On the Monday specified, Bainbridge, Joseph Dawson and John Tyson were duly examined. The following day at Rydal Hall, Alexander Guy was examined. On 23 June Tyson and Cartmel were also bound under the sum of £50 to appear at the next Assizes to answer such matters as should be objected against them. The collection of evidence continued through July. During that month a further ten people, some of them living north of Penrith, came down to Kendal and Rydal Hall to give evidence. Most of them were then bound to appear at the following Assizes. The Assizes were to meet on the 6 August and the final preparations included a recognizance on 2nd August for both John Bainbridge and Edward Bainbridge to be present, under pain of penal bonds of £50 and £100 respectively.

One problem for Fleming was what to do with all the new evidence concerning offences which had already been tried in 1683. He now had confessions which immensely strengthened the case, but he realized that a man could not be tried for the same offence twice. He raised this problem with the Clerk of the northern Assize when he wrote to him about the impending trial.

> Edward Bainbridge hath cleared that burglary of Robert Robinson in this account; and although the two Smorthwaits were found not guilty thereof at the last Assizes; yet having now more evidence, I submit it to your consideration whether they may not be indicted for the robbing of

him, and whether they may plead in Barr Auterfoits Acquit.[1] If you intend that they shall be indicted for robbing of Robert Robinson, then let me know, that notice may be given to the witnesses to appear at the next assizes at Appleby. Bainbridge speaks also very fully as to the stealing of Simon Mount's pack of cloth, and I do not remember that they were tried for that at our last Assizes. I wish you would let me know upon what indictments the two Smorthwaits were tried at the last Assizes at Appleby, and then I should the better know what witnesses to summon to appear at the next.

The Clerk answered only one of these questions directly. Concerning the re–trial for the same offence, even though there was more evidence, he was in no doubt: 'The two Smorthwaits were indicted for burglary in the house of Robert Robinson and acquitted. We cannot try them again for the same burglary.' But the Clerk also advised Fleming in general to 'provide what evidence you can against them in Westmorland that we may be ready for their trials there in case they scape in Cumberland.' This slight ambiguity may have led Fleming to consider the possibilty of trying to get the previous offences tried again under a different guise. In a 'memoirs' he noted: 'For breaking of Mr Lodge's house (vide supra Rob. Robinson) cutting and bruising a new pewter tankard, Robert Robinson query if all his goods were mentioned in the former indictment.'

The preparations for the trial were complicated by the fact that the offences had been committed in four different counties, Yorkshire, Lancashire, Westmorland and Cumberland, and the accused lived in the first three counties. Where were they to be tried, where were they to be gaoled pending trial, where should the witnesses be assembled? The position less than a month before the Assizes was a muddled one. A gaol calendar in Fleming's papers for Lancaster Castle on 14 July mentions among the prisoners: 'Mr Edward Bradrick, William Smorthwait, John Lyley, committed as highway men'. It was noted that Bradrick was 'removed to York'. A 'calendar of prisoners that now is or hath been since the last Assizes in the gaol at Appleby' for 1684, also in the Fleming papers, mentioned only five persons as having been imprisoned during the year at Appleby. Three were for theft, the fourth was Henry Smorthwait and the fifth Bryan Thompson. These two had been 'committed by Edward Wilson and Henry Wilson Esq. . . for the felonious endeavouring to break into the house of Henry Preston at Farleton in Westmorland and for grievously beating and wound-

---

[1] A 'bar' is a plea or peremptory exception of a defendant sufficient to destroy the plaintiff's action, or, in this instance, the crown's; in this case it was on the grounds that he had elsewhere been acquitted for the same offence.

ing Henry Preston'. It was also noted that Smorthwait had been committed by a *mittimus* from Fleming and two other Justices, 'charged by an information to the said Justices for committing of burglary and robbery'. We have a copy of the original document in the Fleming archive, dated 20 May.

> Edward Wilson and Henry Wilson Esq., two of his Majesty's Justices of the Peace for the said country [Westmorland] to the keeper of his Majesty's gaol at Appleby, his deputy or deputies, greeting. We send you herewithal the bodies of Henry Smorthwait of New Hutton and Bryan Thompson of Kirkby Lonsdale, being this day brought before us and charged with the felonious endeavouring to break the dwelling house of Henry Preston of Farleton in the said county in the night time on the 15th April last and putting the people in the house in great fear and grievously beating and wounding the said Henry in coming forth of his house to defend the same. Therefore we command you that you receive the said H.S. and Bryan Thompson unto your custody and safely to keep in the said gaol until they shall from thenceforth be delivered by due order of his Majesty's laws.

This was reinforced by a further letter to the keeper of Appleby gaol:

> Sir D. Fleming and Sir Christopher Philipson & William Fleming Esq. 3 of &c. to the keeper of his Majesty's gaol at Appleby in the county aforesaid greeting.
> Having lately received an information, that Henry Smorthwait now a prisoner in the gaol aforesaid hath committed burglary and robbery, these command you to keep him safely discharged by due course of law. And hereof fail not at your peril. Given under our hands and seals at Kendal within the said county the 18th day of June 1684.

The main problem was that one of the best documented of the offences committed by the Smorthwaits had occurred near Penrith. Because of this, as well as the likely impartiality of the jury there, Fleming felt it advisable that the Smorthwaits should be tried at the Cumberland sessions at Carlisle in the first instance. If that failed, the prisoners could then be taken down to Appleby for a second trial. But Fleming needed advice and permission to shift prisoners from gaol to gaol. It was mainly on this problem that he wrote to the Clerk of Assize at York on 10 July. He gave a full outline of the legal difficulties of the case. Making the point that the juries might be less favourable in Cumberland, Fleming also pointed out that the evidence for the Cumberland offences was stronger: 'I hear, that the persons who attempted to break the house of Henry Preston of Farleton are of the opinion, that the offence will not reach them, the house being not broke by them, and he not being killed.' Fleming was not convinced by this, pointing out that, 'besides the heinousness of the riot and battery, I should think the robbing him of his fauchion should make it a robbery in them all.' But there were doubts, whereas 'Andrew Bell's examination gives a good account of the Cumberland burglary aforesaid; and I believe ere long I shall have more examinations concerning the robbery.'

For all these reasons, Fleming thought that a trial at Carlisle would be best. He explained the location of the prisoners at that date, 'and if you'll send orders, by this bearer, for removal of the two Smorthwaits unto Carlisle, and Bradrick unto Appleby; I shall take care to get them safely delivered, as you shall direct.' This request was sent to 'his much honoured friend the Clerk of Assize'.

> Having not the honour to be known unto my Lord Chief justice [i.e. Jeffreys], nor unto Mr Justice Holloway; and having had experience of your ability and willingness to serve King and country in these kind of affairs; I adventure to give you the trouble of this paper, and to send you copies of the most considerable examinations that I know of in this country; to the end you may acquaint the Judges herewith, if you shall judge it convenient; and you may know what tricks have been played in this, and some other countries.

Ten days later the Clerk wrote a brief reply:

> Sir, Yours I received by Mr James Walker and showed your letter and the information to the Judge who has given order for writs to remove William Smorthwait and Henry Smorthwait to Carlisle which writs I herewith send you. I desire you to take care to get them delivered in time that they may be at Carlisle before the Judges be there and to provide what evidence you can against them for that county.

As for the removal of Bradrick, 'Bradrick is here and has execution awarded against him and will be hanged.'

'The Judge' who was shown the informations was Judge Jeffreys: copies of four writs for removing William and Henry Smorthwait have survived, dated 14 July at York, only four days after Fleming's original letter was sent. All were from 'G. Jeffreys, Knight and baron'. They are in Latin, the first directing that William Smorthwait be removed from Lancaster and be taken to Carlisle before 6 August next, and the second directed to the custodian at Carlisle to receive and guard Smorthwait. The other two do the same for Henry Smorthwait from Appleby gaol. Within five days of the Clerk's letter being written in York, Fleming was writing covering letters for the writs to those who would have to execute them. We have rough copies of the following letters.

Mr Sheriff,   Rydal July 25.84

You being authorized for the breaking up of writs[2] in this part of the county; and I having lately received from the Lord Chief Justice of England two writs concerning removing of Henry Smorthwait now a prisoner in Appleby gaol, unto the city of Carlisle. I have therefore sent them unto you by this bearer, not doubting but that you will forthwith acquaint the Earl of Thanet and Mr Gabettes therewith;[3] and that some will be ordered to remove this prisoner according to the writs here sent you. Our Clerk of Assize would have the prisoner to be at Carlisle before the Judges shall be there. Pray give my humble service unto my good Lord of Thanet when you shall see him, with my hearty thanks for his Lordships very noble and kind entertainment. I shall be glad to hear from you by this bearer, and shall remain your affectionate friend and servant.

Dan. Fleming.

For Mr Robert Nelson Deputy Sheriff hast these, at Kendal.

The following day the Deputy Sheriff replied

Honoured Sir,

I received your letter this day with the two writs enclosed, the one for removing the body of Henry Smorthwait from Appleby to Carlisle, the other for receiving him there. I shall take care to deliver them carefully to Mr Sheriff with all speed, and shall not fail to present your due respects to my Lord of Thanet. I am very glad you are well come home from Appleby and subscribe myself,

Sir, your obliged humble servant   Ro: Nelson.

Kendal 26th July 1684.

As regards William Smorthwait at Lancaster gaol, Fleming wrote to the keeper of the gaol there, keeping a rough copy of the letter:

Mr Foxcroft   Rydal, July 25 .84

Your High Sheriff living (as I am informed) out of your county, and not knowing certainly who is now his under–sheriff: I have therefore sent the two writs here enclosed unto you, hoping that you will forthwith acquaint your sheriff therewith, that William Smorthwait now in your gaol may be removed unto Carlisle, according as the Lord Chief Justice of England hath ordered. Our Clerk of the Assize would have your prisoner to be at Carlisle before the Judges shall be there. I shall not doubt of your special care in this affair, and I shall be glad to hear from you (by the next post) of your receiving these writs.

---

[2]   Possibly the breaking open of a sealed document.
[3]   The Earl of Thanet owned Appleby Castle where the gaol for Westmorland was located. I have not been able to find Mr Gabettes.

I am your affectionate friend and servant D.F.
For Mr George Foxcroft keeper of his Majesty's gaol at Lancaster haste
these at Lancaster.

It was also necessary to summon all the witnesses to the trials, especially
those who had not been previously bound to appear. One example may be
given.

> Sir Daniel Fleming Knight one of the King's Majesty's Justices of the
> Peace for the county of Westmorland to the constables of Old Hutton
> and New Hutton, within the said county, greeting.
> These are in the King's Majesty's name to will and command you, and
> every of you, forthwith to summon Edmund Lodge, clerk, Robert
> Robinson, gentleman, and Thomas Robinson, his son, all of Old Hutton
> aforesaid, and Thomas Wilson of New Hutton aforementioned, yeoman,
> personally to appear at the next general gaol delivery to be holden in the
> said county of Westmorland, before the Judges there, and then and there
> to give the best evidence they can on his Majesty's behalf, and not to
> depart without licence of the said court. And hereof fail not at your peril.
> Given under my hand and seal at Rydal Hall within the said county, the
> first day of August, 1684.
> (signature, seal, of Dan: Fleming).

This is, incidentally, further evidence that Fleming was considering using
the Robinson break–in as a pretext for another indictment in Westmorland,
if the Cumberland trials went badly.

As well as getting the prisoners moved and ensuring that sufficient
examinations would be ready, Fleming was also engaged in correspondence
with various others about the affair. A few of these letters survive. From his
fellow Justice Sir Christopher Philipson, Fleming heard of further informations by Edward Bainbridge. Unfortunately the first part of the document is
torn, but it ends with a curiously ambiguous reference to the theft of either
'bees' or 'beasts'.

> The informant further saith that Rich. Tatham of Ireby did help to steal
> Sam Otway's 'beas' and took 10s of William and Henry Smorthwait for
> two parts in one of the 'beas' within a week after the heifer was stolen.
> And afterwards he swore against Smorthwait. [at the bottom of the
> page] Sir Dan. Bainbridge last Saturday came to me and informed me of
> this above, so if you think it fit to send a warrant before the sessions I
> shall willingly join in it. I have however ordered him to come again then.
> My service to yourself and all yours I rest yours whilst, Christopher
> Philipson.

Fleming also received letters from Cumberland, concerning the exam-

inations taken in that county about the burglary near Penrith. From Justice
Henry Browham, he heard in a letter dated 12 July:

> Sir, I have sent you a copy of the examinations of those persons you writ
> to me. If there be anything amiss or that I have omitted anything that
> should have been inserted in them pray let me know wherein that they
> may be corrected before the Assizes though I look upon their evidence
> insignificant unless the felons own confession be their conviction. . . .
> My service to your self and all my cousins I rest your most affectionate
> cousin and humble servant Henry Browham.

The burglary had occurred very close to Hutton Hall, the house of
Fleming's brother-in-law, Sir George Fletcher. Fletcher was absent in
France in July, but one of his servants wrote with further information on 15
July.

> Sir, this enclosed came to my hand from my Lady yesterday and the
> other from Mr Browham. . . . I have likewise sent you the examination of
> Andrew Bell touching the robbery of Richard Hindson's house at Ling
> near Hutton, which is all the papers I have concerning that. I hear there
> is one Bradrick in Lancaster gaol one of these robbers last taken, who
> was at Hutton two or three times when Mrs Sandford was here, pretend-
> ing to court her maid. And he was at Carlisle since and made use of my
> name there as I hear. And he gives a particular account of Hutton at
> Lancaster and tells what servants are now living in the house. I believe
> we have missed their intentions as I hear by several circumstances which
> I shall give you a further account of when I see your worship. I have not
> else at present but am your faithful servant Edward Dobinson.

Fleming would receive further material when he met Dobinson and
Browham and others at the Carlisle Assizes.

As the final preparations were made for the Cumberland trial, various
pressures were brought to bear to avoid execution. Fleming had written to
the Clerk: 'it is reported that some of them are endeavouring to get their
pardons; but it is hoped by many that his Majesty will not pardon such
grand offenders.' The crucial witness was Edward Bainbridge, and his
evidence was conditional on favour being shown to him. Fleming also wrote
about the matter to the clerk of Assize. Having explained how Bainbridge
had repented in his sickness and come forward to give evidence, Fleming
continued by describing how all the Justices had then together examined
him.

> We have all (upon his frank confession) promised to move the Judges on
> his behalf, & that he may be made use of as a witness; and we believe it
> will be much safer for the country to save him, than any of the rest. For he

is not so bold and desperate as Bradrick and the two Smorthwaits are, and he is much more penitent. Unless we may have him for an evidence little will be made of the burglary and robbery near Sir George Fletcher's house in Cumberland.

As far as Fleming was concerned, anything could go wrong — witnesses fail to appear, the jury be too 'favourable' again, the bills be thrown out on the grounds of technical inaccuracy. Fleming rode up to Carlisle on 5 August. He accompanied the Assize judges over the next fortnight, and in his account book we find a description of his movements and of the political favours he performed for the Judges. For this was not just a judicial tour. Charles II had decided to revoke the old city and borough charters and to issue new ones based on some recently issued for London. But with corporations so jealous of their rights, the handing over of a charter on the mere promise of a new one was difficult to negotiate. Fleming's account book entries for this period read:

Aug. 5   Memo. I persuaded Andrew Huddleston Esq. High Sheriff of Cumberland and his company to meet Henry Duke of Norfolk about 2 miles from Carlisle, and to wait upon his Grace thither this day 00 00 00

6   This day Sir Christo. Musgrave and I with many gentlemen met Sir Geo. Jeffreys Lord Chief Justice of England about 3 miles from Carlisle, and Sir C.M. as lieutenant of the ordinance ordered him 15 guns at his coming into Carlisle and going out, although the Lord Morpeth ordered but 9 for the Duke of Norfolk 00 00 00

7   Given to my Lord Chief Justice's crier (Carlisle charter was now surrendered [crossed through] 00 02 00

9   This day Sir Christo. Musgrave and I, with many other gentlemen, did go along with the Lord Chief Justice unto Allison's Bank in Scotland 00 00 00

11   This day my son and I did go along with the Judges from Carlisle to Appleby, who stayed a while at Penrith; and given to Judge Holloway's crier 00 02 00

12   I prevailed this day with the Earl of Derby and my 3 cousin Layburnes of Witherslack, to refer their differences unto my Lord Chief Justice's arbitration 00 00 00

13   This day I prevailed with the corporation of Kendal to surrender their charter and they appointed Sir John Otway to be their attorney. The Judges were made Freemen thereof the same day 00 00 00

14   Going this day along with the Judges from Kendal to Lancaster I prevailed with the corporation of Lancaster to

surrender their charter, which they did & appointed Sir John Otway to be their attorney. The Judges were made Freemen thereof the same day 00 00 00

[15 omitted]

19   Spent at the Assizes at Carlisle, Appleby & Lancaster between Aug.5th and 19 inclusive the sum of 01 14 00

Another of those present at the Assizes was William Nicholson, later bishop of Carlisle. His diary of the same few days corroborates some of Fleming's details, but perhaps because he was writing a diary rather than an account book, he did not fail to mention the Smorthwaits. Furthermore he did so in a manner which suggested that the case was a notorious one, though what his allusion to a reprimand for Mr Nichols, the lecturer at St Mary's, Carlisle, refers to, it has been impossible to establish.

Aug.   4   I went to Carlisle to wait on Sir Ch. Musgrave who was welcomed into the town with nine guns.

Aug.   6   the Judges (my Ld Ch. Jeffreys and Mr Just. Holloway) were received with 15 guns: by Sr Ch. M's order.

Aug.   7   Charge given by my Ld Ch. J. principally against such called Trimmers & Whig–Justices. Sermon preached (length and stuff intolerable) by Mr Nicols. Mr Nelson pleased to quarrel me for placing Mr Monpesson in the bishop's seat.

Aug.   8   Trials of the two Smorthwaits which gave occasion to a severe reprimand to Mr Nicols. Witch of Ainstable cleared. . . .

Aug.   9   . . . After Dinner my Ld Ch. Justice went to Scotland: desiring *to see something as bad as his own country.*

Aug.   10   . . . Neither of the Judges at church in the afternoon.

Aug.   11   . . .The Judges went to Appleby.

Fleming gives no clue in his accounts as to the fate of the Smorthwaits, but Nicholson does give their sentence in a brief line which has been omitted from the passage above. Before we look at that sentence and at other facts about their fate and the legends that grew around them (in chapter 10), we may examine in more detail the nature of the evidence upon which they were tried.

6
Burglars and Assailants

Clipping and coining were held to be treason since they directly affected the state. For the theft of the goods of another person, various intricate distinctions were made, depending on the time, place, amount stolen and degree of force used. A theft occurring after the entry of another's premises, when the owner or his wife or his children or his servants were present, was termed housebreaking (in the daytime) or burglary (at night). A theft from another's person was robbery, and if it took place in or near the king's highway it was highway robbery. Goods stolen from either houses or fields, in the absence of the owner, his family or servants, was termed larceny. Robbery of a person without his knowledge was pickpocketing. If the value of the object taken in larceny was one shilling or less, then it was petty larceny, if over that sum, grand larceny. Although all these offences were clergiable by common law, benefit of clergy had been removed by parliamentary statutes from housebreaking, burglary and highway robbery.[1] The penalty for all these offences, except petty larceny and pickpocketing of sums under one shilling, was death by hanging, unless a person successfully pleaded benefit of clergy.

Daniel Fleming's copy of the *Statutes of the Peace* recorded a number of laws against burglary, starting in 1275. The major legislative change in the numerous acts was that if the house was occupied by the owner, his children or servants at the time, whether they were aware of what was happening or not, the principal or accessories were not to be allowed to plead benefit of clergy. In other words, the full rigour of the law was to be exacted and they were to be hanged. By an act of Elizabeth, this applied

---

[1] Benefit of clergy, which enabled a person convicted of felony to escape the death penalty for a first offence by reading a portion of the Bible or a similar work, has already been explained. The position in relation to robbery has kindly been summarized for me by Dr J. Baker. Robbery was always a felony; at common law it was clergiable; by a statute of 23 H.8. c.1. clergy was taken away if (a) the robbery was done in a house, the owner, wife, children or servants being within and put in fear or (b) it was done in or near a highway. This statute was modified by 5 & 6 Edward 6, c.9.

equally to an offence committed in the daytime or at night. In the margin of the *Statutes*, Fleming added some further notes, extracted from various law books, concerning the definition of the offence. He suggested that 'burglar is from burgh an house & laron a thief.' Night he defined as 'when by the light of day one cannot discern the countenance of a man'. A burglar he said 'is by the common law a felon, that in the night breaketh and entereth into a mansion house (or church) of another of intent to kill some reasonable creature or to commit some other felony within the same, whether his felonious intent be executed or not'. Thus it was the actual act of breaking in that was the burglary; after that there might be all kinds of other felonies. But there had to be forcible entry. Fleming continued: 'It must be an actual breaking of the house; for if the door or window be open and a thief enter to steal, or with a hook or other engine draweth out some goods, no burglary; but if he breaketh the glass of the window and hook out any goods contra' — in other words it was a burglary. He commented: 'There must be also an entry of the thief, or of some part of his body or of a gun, or hook, of intent to kill or steal within and of the house.' But what, exactly, was a house? The statute of 5 & 6 Edward 6 (cap. 9) said that the owner or his servants and children merely had to be within the 'precincts' of a house, which included 'booths, or tents' and a later act spoke of 'any dwelling house or outhouse'. Fleming added: 'Mansion house extends to hall, parlour, &c, and to barns, stables, cowhouses, &c, to a chamber or room. Also to churches, shops.' On the question of the presence of the owner, Fleming stated: 'It's burglary, though all be some part of the night out of the house when it's committed.' He finally confirmed that 'clergy taken away in all cases of burglary', and ended by cross-referring to the standard legal text, Edward Coke's *Institutes*, part 3, p. 63 etc.

Of all the activities which the Smorthwaits and their accomplices engaged in, the burglaries are the most minutely described. As in the description of the Robinson burglary, we have an unusual opportunity of witnessing events first-hand, as seen through the eyes both of those who made the break-in and of those who were within the house. Before embarking on further accounts, it is perhaps as well to remind ourselves that only a minute proportion of the houses in the region were so attacked. There were many shops in Kirkby Lonsdale, Kendal, Penrith and elsewhere, but none of them was visited by the gang, as far as we know, and the only recorded break-in to a shop, about which we learn little, occurred at Keasden Head in Yorkshire. There were within the area covered by the robbers many thousands of isolated farms and homesteads, yet we hear of the breaking and entering of only six of them. What happened in the other five cases we may now recount, as described at the time.

Four of the burglaries occurred after the Robinson break-in, but one had occurred well before it. In about January or February 1676, there was a burglary at Hawkin Hall, Middleton. This house still stands about one hundred yards from Abbey Farm, where William Smorthwait, soon to be High Constable for Lonsdale ward, was living. It was occupied by a recently widowed woman, Margaret Bainbridge. Her husband's elder brother was an eminent scholar, sometime Milton's tutor and Master of Christ's College, Cambridge.[2] No one seems to have been apprehended or charged with the burglary, for it was impossible to be certain as to the culprits. Yet some seven years later, when the activities of the Smorthwait brothers became known, Margaret Bainbridge described what had happened 'about Candlemas gone seven years (as this examinate remembereth)'. The reader, already aware of the activities of Edward Bainbridge, who lived just across the river, and of Smorthwait, living next door, will appreciate some of the ironies of the account. Margaret said:

> She did see George Shuttleworth (commonly called Red-head) and William Smorthwait then of Middleton standing together and dis-coursing very friendly near the dwelling house of William Smorthwait; whereupon she being afraid of having some mischief done her, and finding Edward Bainbridge at her house, she acquainted Edward Bainbridge (being a kinsman of her late husband's) that she had twenty pounds in the house and desired him to stay with her, which he said he would do awhile. Soon after which George Shuttleworth came to her house and promised her that he would never wrong her nor any other widow, or fatherless children. And she further saith that, about a week after, William Smorthwait came along with one Lathat unto her house to pay her some money; which as soon as she had received, she carried the same up into her study, and then William Smorthwait and Lathat did go away. Soon after which the mother of William Smorth-wait came about bed-time unto her house, where staying a little, she returned unto William Smorthwait's, the next house to this examinate's, and then she and her maid did go to bed. And she being asleep that night was awaked by the noise of some breaking open her study door, upon which she got up, and called up her maid, and would have gone into the chamber where her study was and where she did see a light and hear some persons therein. But the door of the chamber being made fast, she cried out, whereupon the robbers did blow out their candle, and did go out at the chamber window where they came in. After they were gone she bid her maid go out and call in some neighbours, which she could not then do, the out doors all being made

[2] Rev. R. Percival Brown, 'Bainbridge of Hawkin in Middleton, Westmorland', *TCWAAS*, n.s., XXIV (1924).

fast on the outside with new cording, whereupon she was forced with her maid and children to stay in the house until it was daylight. And then she bid her son Christopher go out at the hall window, which he did, and opened the kitchen door. And then her maid did go forth to acquaint some neighbours with what had happened. She did then also bid her son climb up the ladder, which the robbers had set to the chamber windows, and go in at the window (out of which they went) and open the chamber door where her study was, which he did, and she then looking what was gone, she and her maid only missed three of her petticoats and her late husband's rapier, one of which petticoats (with a cloak-bag) was found near the foot of the ladder. But to whom the cloak-bag belonged she knew not, which she hath still in her custody. She also saith that when as William Smorthwait came into her house (after other neighbours) in the morning after the robbery, he came buttoning of his buttons as if he were newly got out of bed, and seemed as if he were much troubled. She also saith that she believeth that the robbers had climbed up the ladder and broken a pane of the glass, had opened the casement, and had cast a wooden stanchion and so got into the chamber. And that the robbers had taken away her money and other things if they had not been affrighted by her crying out. She also saith that the mother of William Smorthwait, a little before the robbery, enquired of her how late she usually did sit up at night: and she also saith, the mother of William Smorthwait did not use to come to visit her so late at night.

The details are supported by other witnesses. John Harrison of Middleton, who had been a servant of Smorthwait's at the time, said that the night after Hawkin Hall was burgled,

> going out of his master's house early next morning he did see the back door of her house tied with a cord or rope, before he saw any of the house, and hearing some of them cry out that thieves had been there, he did go to the house, where he did see a ladder standing to the chamber window, where they said the thieves got in; upon which he went home and told some of the family.

Further details concerning the stolen petticoats were provided by Thomas Bland, who said

> that about four years ago he being with one Mary Lamb (then servant to Henry Bland) in Sedbergh, widow Bainbridge came unto Mary Lamb, and challenged a red petticoat that she then had on; and enquired of her where she got it, upon which Mary Lamb answered that Edward Bainbridge did give it her. Afterwards Mary did go home, and this examinate did never see her wear the said petticoat again.

Finally, we have the examination of another of Smorthwait's servants, Thomas Inman, whom we have previously encountered witnessing to Smorthwait's clipping. He said he had been a servant to William Smorthwait for over seven years, and had left him about five years previously. On the night of the break-in to widow Bainbridge's house he

> did go to bed about eleven or twelve of the clock, and left his master up, but he thinks he was making ready to go to bed. That Henry Smorthwait, brother of William Smorthwait, did then live with his master; but the night of the house being broke this examinate did not see (to his remembrance) Henry Smorthwait in his master's house. That William and Henry did lie a good way distant from the place where he and his fellow journeymen did lie. He also saith, that the next morning after the breaking of widow Bainbridge's house, having notice thereof from John Harrison his fellow-servant, he did go to the house, and did see two of the doors thereof tied on the outside with new cording.

This concludes the facts about the Hawkin Hall break-in. The evidence was circumstantial, though Margaret Bainbridge clearly had her suspicions about Edward Bainbridge and Smorthwait. In passing, it is interesting to note the tying of the doors to prevent a chase, a device employed in the Robinson burglary. It is remarkable, too, that several ruffians should flee precipitately at a widow's cry, and that they should feel it worth taking petticoats, which were relatively easily traced.

It was over four years until the accomplices attempted another major burglary — the attack on Robert Robinson's house already described. They had clearly grown much bolder in the meantime. A feature of both the burglaries described so far was the fact that, either through living next door to the victim, or having accomplices on the spot, the burglars were able to tell that there was a 'prize' worth obtaining. Their second burglary was far more violent and brazen than the first, and their success in terms of booty was greater. We do not hear of any more such burglaries for another two years, and then in October 1682 some of the gang travelled on a much longer expedition up into Cumberland to burgle a house there. Again, as we shall see, they had a local accomplice, and again they used threats and violence. Their actions were observed by the neighbours.

A general overview of what happened is provided in the confession of Edward Bainbridge. He confessed that he, William Smorthwait and Henry Smorthwait

> being accompanied with a Cumberland butcher or miller. . .did go all together about two years ago to Shap in this county by daylight. Where drinking at an alehouse, they afterwards did go all together to Penrith

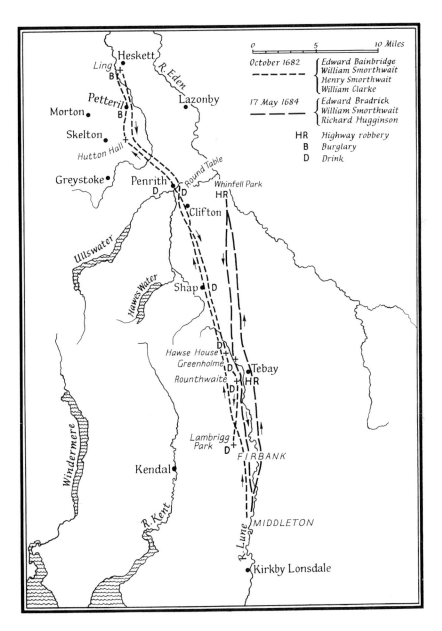

Map 4 *Journeys of the burglars and highway robbers.*

in the county of Cumberland in the night time, and there calling did buy some white candles, and then rid on by Sir George Fletcher's house at Hutton, and the butcher and Henry Smorthwait calling at a stone-getters house one of them lighted a peat and the other of them stole a gavelock. And then coming to an old man's house not far from Hutton. . .the butcher, William Smorthwait and Henry Smorthwait did each of them light their white candle at the peat, and then the butcher did break open the out door of the house with the gavelock, and William Smorthwait going in with a pistol in his hand did look for a young man called Bell in the house and found him amongst the beasts. And William Smorthwait watched him whilst the butcher and Henry Smorthwait did take about eight pounds in silver and a piece of gold, and did take away a bundle of bonds (to the value of threescore pounds or thereabouts) and two pair of sheets; and during the time the persons were robbing of the house, this examinate did hold their horses near the door of the house. After the robbery was committed William Smorthwait, Henry Smorthwait and the butcher or miller and he did that night turn back again unto Shap before it was day, not calling therein because the butcher was there well known, and the people were not up. But this examinate and the butcher did drink at a house at Rounthwaite, & William Smorthwait and Henry Smorthwait did drink at the Hawse House, and then this examinate and the other three went all together to Lambrigg park and there drunk at the house of Richard Walker where they stayed and refreshed themselves an hour or two. And then this examinate and Henry Smorthwait did go to their several homes, and William Smorthwait and the butcher did go unto Austwick. And he also saith that William Smorthwait having all the money which was gotten in the robbery, he said he would clip the same before he did divide it amongst them.

Bainbridge added a few more details in a further examination in July:

that the name of the Cumberland butcher, or miller, mentioned in his former examination was William Clarke, and this examinate forgot in his former examination to give an account of the said William Clarke and William Smorthwait and Henry Smorthwait and this examinate's calling at an alehouse in Clifton near the Round Table in this county the evening before they robbed the house of the old man near Hutton in Cumberland whose name was Hindson as this examinate doth now remember.

A Penrith chandler, Edward Huetson, confirmed that the night before the robbery, William Clarke and three other men came on horseback to his shop in Penrith and Clarke 'called for a gill of brandy, which they did drink at the shops door, and then he alighted and got half a pound of white candles.' He had also heard that the robbers had stopped the next morning at an alehouse in Clifton. The events on either side of the robbery were corroborated by a chief witness, Andrew Bell, who confirmed the story of the candles, the stolen gavelock and borrowed peat, and added that one of the robbers had fallen into a 'clay-hole' near the house of Richard Bunting of Petteril, waller, the man from whom they took the gavelock. But Andrew Bell's main description was of the actual break-in. Again we have a graphic account of what went on inside the house. Bell stated that he

> lived with Richard Hindson of Ling husbandman, for above nineteen years last past, who is a kinsman. And that about three weeks before Martinmas gone a twelvemonth Richard Hindson, his wife, Jane Scot his servant, a little boy, and he, being all in bed (this examinate and the little boy lying together in a bed behind the back door of Richard Hindson's house) late in the night he heard the door shake, upon which sitting up in bed and seeing a light and three men at the door, he asked who was there, to which one of them replied, Thou shalt know full soon. And then they broke open the door, upon which he leapt out of bed in his shirt and went into a cow-house and stood on the far side of a cow. So soon as the robbers got into the house, one of them came unto this examinate's bed-side and demanded of the boy where this examinate was, threatening to pistol the boy if he would not forthwith discover him; upon which he desired the robber not to hurt the boy for this examinate was there. Then the robber spoke to him saying that the King of France was come in, and all the beacons were on fire; that they were to search all the houses betwixt and Carlisle [sic], and that they were there to begin, it being an house thought on more than ordinary. The robber then enquired of him whether they could get fourteen pounds in that house, or not. And he answered, that he believed they could not get ten pounds in silver, and also desired the robbers that they would not hurt Richard Hindson, he being a good old man and that none there durst hinder them from taking what there was. Thereupon the robber charged the rest to spill no blood at their perils. Then the robber demanded how much money he had and where it was. And then he told him that he had only eighteen pence and a plack which was in his breeches lying upon the bed, which the robber searching he took away the money, and held it in his hand, shewing the same to another of the robbers, and acquainting him that he had said this examinate had more money, but that in his hand was all he found, which the robber afterwards put into his pocket. He also saith that the robber which watched him was a very big man of body, had brown hair, a

11 Fair copy of the deposition of Andrew Bell on 14 July 1684, concerning the burglary at Ling in Cumberland, with Fleming's signature.

white hat on, a horeseman's coat girded about him with a leather belt, holding a rapier or a sword with a lanthorn and a candle in the one hand and a pistol in the other hand. After the other two robbers had taken away what they had a mind to, then all three went out of the house, the last of them bidding the other blow out their candles, and he who watched him having charged him not to stir out, he said he would watch this examinate until within an hour of daylight. He also saith, that not long after, he did go into the other end of the house, where he found Richard Hindson lying bleeding in his bed, one of the robbers having wounded him upon his nose and one of his fingers, as he told this examinate. And he further then acquainted him that the robbers had taken from him a bundle of bills and bonds and about eight pounds in silver and a guinea of gold, and that they did take part of the money out of his chest, which one of the robbers broke open with a gavelock, and the rest of the money out of his hand. Jane Scot did also then acquaint this examinate, that she did see one of the robbers take away his coat and put a great many clothes into a sack, and they having taken some clothes belonging to herself, upon her desiring of them, they were left. The wife of Richard Hindson did also acquaint him that the robbers had taken away two pair of sheets and other clothes, with some linen and yarn. [See illustration 11]

This is the only examination of the persons actually in the house which has survived among the Assize depositions. But Fleming's manuscripts contain three further examinations. One of these was of Richard Hindson himself who said on oath:

that on Thursday about midnight three weeks before the feast of St Martin 1682, there came two unknown men which broke open his doors with a gavelock, and entered therein with each of them a lighted candle in their hands, and came to his bed-side, and told him that the King of France was come into England, and that all was broke loose, and that they were commanded to search every house betwixt this informant's house and Carlisle; and forthwith they went and broke open this informant's chest with a gavelock, it being in the chamber where he and his wife lay, and took out of the same chest fifty six shillings, and then went to his bed-side, and took out of his hand both gold and money which was in a purse, but the certain sum he does not know, and then went to his breeches and took out of his pocket fifteen shillings, or more, and told him that seeing they could get no more money, they would take away his writings, and did accordingly, and further saith not.

Some further details of the affair are contained in the deposition of Hindson's wife, Elizabeth:

On Thursday about midnight, when they were all in bed, three weeks before the feast of St Martin 1682, there came two unknown men into the chamber where she and her husband lay, with drawn swords and lighted candles in their hands, and took out of the same chamber three hanks of yarn, and as much flax, as would have been about a hank and a half of yarn, with three pair of linen sheets, two linen pillow coverings, two linen aprons, a table cloth, a petticoat of shop stuff, a broad cloth waist coat, and two new coats of her husband's, and several other pieces of small linen. And she saith that the yarn, woollen, and linen cloths, that was at that time taken from her by these two unknown men she valued at three pounds at the least. And further she saith that one of these two men said to her husband, that if he would give them no more moneys, he would cut his nose, and did accordingly.

We are also able to see the affair through the eyes of the servant, Jane Scot, now married with the surname Arey, who said:

that on Thursday about midnight, when they were all in bed, about three weeks before the feast of St Martin, 1682, there came two unknown men into the chamber where this informant and her master and dame lay, with drawn swords and lighted candles in their hands, and said to her master, Old rogue give us thy money, and then straightway went to a chest which was standing by this informant's bedside, and broke it open with a gavelock, but what was taken out of it this informant knows not; and further she saith that out of another chest standing close by the other chest these two unknown men took linen and woollen cloths, but of the particulars and value of them she can give no account.

It is worth noting that though the event took place in October 1682, it was only in July 1684 that these witnesses gave their depositions. In the meantime, members of the gang had been tried and acquitted once.

Within a few months of their release, some associates of the Smorthwaits were engaged, so it was said, in further burglaries. We only have passing allusions to two of these. In November 1683 someone broke into the house of a widow in Killington near Bainbridge's home township of Mansergh, and stole 40s. Bradrick suggested that the culprits included John Bainbridge, Edward's brother: 'The informant knoweth one Thomas Skafe of the Ashes near Hutton in the county of Westmorland, who with Benson and with John Bainbridge of the Gillfoot did break a widow's house in Killington or some place there adjacent and took away from the house the sum of forty shillings or upwards.' But when Robert Benson was examined he told a different story and provided a partial alibi:

Who saith that he being fishing in the river Lune about Martinmas last, with John Jackson of Mansergh, husbandman, late one night with low and lister,[3] when they returned home from fishing that night they did see a light in the house of Isabel Bradley of Mansergh, widow (aunt to this examinate) and he hearing at home that his aunt's house was broken, went thither, and he was there told that Peter Burrough (his aunt's servant) had 40*s* taken from him that night, but by whom he knows not.

His story was substantiated by John Jackson of Mansergh, who claimed to have gone fishing with him.

A second reputed burglary took place in March 1684. Bradrick confessed that he himself 'with William Smorthwait and one John Taylor of Eldroth Lane in Yorks and William Taylor his brother with Richard Mitton did in or about the month of March last in the night time break the shop of one John Stout of Keasden Head in Yorkshire and thereout took some flax, hemp, brandy, and about five horse loads of iron.' There is a good deal of evidence, as we shall see, concerning the efforts to get rid of the stolen objects from the only reported shop burglary, but no deposition describing the actual break-in has been found.

Then in April 1684 another burglary was attempted, at Farleton, only about seven miles south of the break-in at Old Hutton. This was the most violent of all the actions, for the owner, Henry Preston, put up a struggle. The confession of Edward Bradrick shows that again there was probably an accomplice on the spot. He alleged that the attackers were the two Smorthwaits, George Scaif, Richard Mitton of Arkwright in Yorkshire, and Edward Bainbridge. To this 'was privy one Joseph Cartmel of Farleton, who informed this examinate and William Smorthwait that there was a good sum of money to be had at the house, whereof Cartmel was to be a sharer if the same was to be gotten.' Both Bainbridge and Henry Smorthwait afterwards denied being involved. Bainbridge admitted that William Smorthwait and Edward Bradrick had been wounded in the attempt, while Henry Smorthwait insisted that he did not even know where Preston lived. One of the major descriptions came from Henry Preston himself:

On Tuesday the fifteenth day of April last about ten of the clock of the night, six persons came armed with swords and pistols to his house at Farleton, he and his family being gone to bed. And hearing the dogs barking, his wife wished him to rise. And he looking out of the casement did see three persons with each of them rapiers in their

---

[3] 'Low and lister' was a method of catching salmon. 'Low' is a light and 'lister' a pronged fork for spearing fish, according to the Oxford English Dictionary.

hands, with pistols cocked and white candles in their hands lighted, whereupon he called his wife out of bed and said to her, I fear we shall have a cold storm this night, and said to his wife, I will go and call for help of my neighbours, and bid her bolt the door after him. And upon his going forth of the house, six persons set upon him and gave fire upon him and did wound him with hail-shot, he having a falchion in his hand did wound two of the persons as he conceived. After that the persons all of them gave fire upon him again, he getting hold of one of them pulled of his vizard whom he very well knew to be William Smorthwait. And two other persons he did know very well to be Henry Smorthwait, brother of William Smorthwait, and one Bryan Thompson of Kirkby Lonsdale. And for the other three persons, one had a vizard on, and the other two, he believes one of them was a woman in man's apparel, and thinks he could know them if he did see their faces again. Upon the last firing upon him, they took his falchion from him and knocked him down and trailed him to a dunghill side. And he shouting and crying out Murder, they stopped his mouth with straw and dung mixed together. And he heard them say, he is murdered. And lying in a swound for some time, and coming out of it, he sees them beating with a great smith's hammer and puncheons at his dwelling house door, which door being a double door they could make no entrance so soon. But that he arose and got away from them and did raise the town, whereat the persons got away and did leave eleven horse-shoes where they had tied their horse near unto his house. He also saith that one Joseph Cartmel of Farleton his neighbour about three nights before came to his house and sitting down beside him said, Henry, thou has money and I will sell thee as much ground to the value as the money thou hast received. His wife replied we have no more money than we have occasion for, then Joseph told them that he had been at a horse race at Connygarth in Lancashire. And as he came home he called at Bryan Thompson's at Kirkby Lonsdale and met with William Smorthwait and Henry Smorthwait his brother, who asked Joseph Cartmel if he could guide them to a purchase of money. And if he would guide them to it, in case they got it, he should have all the narrow and clipped money that was in it for informing them. And Joseph said to him, Had not thou better buy land than have thy money taken from thee, for they will come shortly with hammers and puncheons and break thy door open to spelders. And Joseph Cartmel about three days after the intended robbery, meeting with one Elizabeth Gibson, who usually wrought at Henry Preston's, asked her what became of Henry Preston and wife's money. This informant further saith that all the men of the town of Farleton (excepting Joseph Cartmel) did arise upon his crying out murder, and were ready to assist him all that night, he Henry Preston having received several wounds in his head, in his neck, in his arms, in his body, and in his legs.

This is the only deposition which survives in the Assize records at the Public Record Office. But Fleming's manuscripts contain six further examinations concerning the affair. The reason for this is partially explained by a sentence in Fleming's letter to the Clerk of the Assize: 'I have sent you only the copy of Henry Preston's information; and the rest relating to that business and to their breaking of a smithy a little before in the same night, you will receive at the same Assizes at Appleby.'

One of these depositions was a brief one by Bryan Thompson, denying all complicity. He said 'that he was about his lawful occasions of ploughing and sowing the 15th April last and that he was never at the said Henry Preston's, nor doth he know where he dwells.'

Joseph Cartmel also tried to deny all involvement, though he admitted having met Bryan Thompson. He said

> that he was at a horse race at Connygarth in Lancashire after Easter and that he was at Kirkby Lonsdale in his coming back and called at Bryan Thompson's house, where Bryan was sitting in a chair, but he did not drink with him nor had any conference with him, neither did he see William Smorthwait nor Henry Smorthwait but came straight home. And that night that the robbery should have been committed at Henry Preston's house he was in his bed sick in a shaking ague and further saith not.

But the evidence against them was supported by several others. A local woman, Mary Saule, who was sent to nurse Henry Preston, witnessed to the gravity of the wounds:

> The same night Henry's house was reported to have been like to be broken, she was sent to view the wounds of Henry at his house in Farleton, which she did accordingly. And, after search, found he was wounded in his head and sore bruised and grievously wounded in his left hand, stabbed in the right arm and a small touch like it had been of a rapier on his throat with hail-shot in his forehead. And further saith that it was about a fortnight she was forced to go to dress his wounds, and since he hath come to this informant to be dressed about two or three miles distance.

A neighbour, Thomas Thexton, described the intimacy between Cartmel, Thompson and Smorthwait in graphic detail. He said

> that after the intended or supposed robbery Joseph Cartmel came unto one Joseph Thexton's at Farleton. Where this examinate was present and heard Joseph say that after the horse race at Connygarth he came

to one Bryan Thompson's of Kirkby Lonsdale where in a chamber he espied William Smorthwait and went to him, and Smorthwait hugged Cartmel and asked him if he could guide him of a purchase of money and Cartmel then replied (as he said and confessed at Farleton) that Henry Preston had money for he had sold a horse lately and received money. And Cartmel said he then told Smorthwait that he would have all the broad money and Smorthwait should have all the clipped in regard he, Smorthwait, knew better how to get it off.

Finally there is a further detailed account of the affair as seen through the eyes of Henry Preston's wife, Elizabeth. Again this implicates Joseph Cartmel and again shows the lack of care in planning these affairs.

On Tuesday the fifteenth day of April last, about ten of the clock in the night, she, her husband and family being all in bed, she heard a noise about the house and looking out at the window saw some persons about the house with which she acquainting her husband, her husband opened the door and went out, this informant and her son and her maid and others being in the house. And thereupon she heard the persons struggle with her husband and that her husband cried out still lamentably: and after some small time she did believe they had murdered her husband hearing him to be silent. And saith that then they came to the house door of her husband and violently fell upon the same and endeavoured to break open the same by lying on great knocks which seemed to be hammers as she believes. And soon after they heard the knocking cease, then came a great deal of the neighbours of Henry together with her husband, who was most grievously wounded. And further saith that by reason of that disturbance she and all the family that were in the house were put in great fear. And she also saith that Joseph Cartmel of Farleton, a near neighbour to this informant, came (about four or five days before the said time the persons came about her husband's dwelling house) and said he would sell her husband half an acre of land and that he had spoke to one Robinson a clerk to draw a deed. She replied, they had no money but what they had occasion for. And thereupon Cartmel replied to her and her husband that he had been at a horse race and calling at one Bryan Thompson's at Kirkby Lonsdale and was with William Smorthwait and another man and that William Smorthwait asked him if he could guide him where he could get a purchase of money. Joseph then replied, Yes he could. And then William Smorthwait promised Joseph that he should have all the clipped money and Smorthwait should have all the broad.

A final information, concerning the 'breaking of a smithy' to which

Fleming had referred, explains the presence of the mysterious horse-shoes. Robert Cragg, blacksmith, said

> that on Tuesday the fifteenth day of April last past in the evening after
> he left work, having two doors in his smithy, he bolted the one and
> locked the other, and lodging at his mother's house being distant from
> his smithy one quarter of a mile or thereabouts, one Jervaice Sill came
> to him the next morning and told him that his smithy was broken. One
> John Thompson who lives at the next house to Henry Preston's came
> to him immediately before and told him that he might go mend Henry
> Preston's house door, and going up to his smithy for some tools found
> his smithy door broken open, and the door cheeks displaced, and that
> one great hammer about eight pound weight to the value of two
> shillings and another little hammer and eleven new horse shoes were
> taken away out of his smithy. And thereupon he came down to Henry
> Prestons's to mend his house door which was broken, being less than a
> mile from the smithy. And John Thompson brought this informant
> eleven new horse shoes from the place they supposed the horses were
> tied, which shoes this informant knew to be of his own making and the
> same shoes to be taken out of his smithy as he believes.

This ends the description of the last and most serious case. Although
only six achieved or attempted burglaries in all are mentioned, and two of
these were outside Westmorland, they clearly caused a great stir. If
inhabitants could not be safe in their homes at night, the law was no
protection, and it is obvious from the bills lodged and the relative amount
of information gathered that this was the most grave of all offences. The
wearing of disguises so that near neighbours could be attacked made the
activities even more of a threat.[4] To their offence of corrupting the
coinage, the life-blood of a market-economy, the accused had added the
heinous violation of private space and private property. If an Englishman
could not treat his home as his castle, where could he retreat? Certainly
there was no safety in public places, for here too the Smorthwaits were
active.

---

[4] Some interesting comparative material on the importance of disguises, and particularly
'blacking' of the face, is given in E. P. Thompson, *Whigs and Hunters; the Origins of the Black Act*
(Peregrine, 1977), especially p. 247.

7
Highway Robbers

The element of force was central to burglary. It was also one of the distinguishing features of robbery on the highway. Under 'Robbery' in his version of the *Statutes of the Peace,* Fleming merely had a reference to an act of Elizabeth I about cut-purses and pickpockets, to which he made various annotations. But he added a general definition of robbery as follows: 'Robbery is a felony by the common law, committed by a violent assault upon the person of another, by putting him in fear and taking from his person his money or other goods of any value whatsoever.' This was based on Coke's *Institutes*, and we may expand the legal position a little more, from Coke and Jacob's *Law Dictionary*. Although robbery in a general sense could mean 'any wrongful taking away of goods', in a specific sense it was confined to that act done with threat and violence. Done on the king's highway, it was punishable by death, even though the amount taken might be only one penny or less. But something had to be taken, and the element of fear had to be involved. There was much further definition of what constituted a real threat or a real taking, of whether a horse taken while tethered in a person's presence was really taken from his person, and of the guilt of accomplices. The seriousness of the offence is clear, for in a strict robbery there was no pleading benefit of clergy, and the value of the object taken was immaterial. If the offence was committed on private premises, then it was possible to claim benefit of clergy. Once more, highway robbery was a particularly grave crime because it was a threat to peaceful communications, to the king's highway, and thus to the state and the crown. If people could not proceed along such highways in a peaceful manner without threat of fear and robbery, the arteries of a highly developed commercial society would be blocked.

Again, in considering the following few cases, we must remember that there was an enormous amount of movement in seventeenth-century Westmorland and Yorkshire. People were constantly travelling around with small and large sums of money and other goods. On most days the roads through the Lune valley would have been well peopled with drovers, carriers, farmers and others taking their produce or rewards for produce to the various markets. A flow of goods came from Scotland and Cumberland, particularly cattle down the old drove roads through Kirkby Lonsdale, while corn and cloth were transported along the numerous green lanes that lay from east to west. It is clear that many of the small alehouses mentioned in the depositions helped to provide shelter for the numerous travellers. Among these thousands of people on the move, only a very few were destined to encounter the Smorthwaits and their accomplices, though fear of their activities, as Fleming noted, could cause a general anxiety.

Robbery on the highway does not seem to have been favoured by the Smorthwaits as a method of extracting money, though they contemplated robbing Robinson on the fells and then missed him by sitting in an ale-house. No highway robberies are reported until after the first trials at the Assizes. The major highway robber was not one of the regular Westmorland gang, but the Yorkshireman, Edward Bradrick, who seems to have been far more active and who now came into his own. He confessed that

> Henry Bateman and he did in the month of April now last past [i.e. 1684] rob one Michael Flitcroft of this county (Yorks) upon the high-road about three miles and an half from Rochdale and took from him the sum of eight pounds in money and a silver tobacco box; and Bateman and this examinate about the same time, viz. in April last did rob above or near thirty several persons in Yorkshire between the towns of Bradford & Otley, or towns near thereto adjacent, and took from them several sums of money; and Bateman and he did also in April last rob one Roger Camm of Settle chapman, near Long Preston, and there took from him near or about fourteen pounds.

Bradrick had other accomplices and was not above house theft as well. The galloping around the countryside and manner of sleeping is revealed in an examination of Robert Taylor of Leeds, taken on 9 November 1682. Taylor said

> that upon Saturday the fourth of November 1682, about one o'clock in the morning he and Edward Bradrick and William Crossland did take out of a close called Cappleton Close one gelding of Richard Lumley's of Leeds. And also afterwards the same night he and Bradrick and Crossland took out of another close near Leeds one gelding belonging to Joseph Sykes of Leeds merchant and a mare of one Robert Gowlands of Leeds with intent to sell the same. He saith that immediately they rid towards Harewood and from then to Masham upon the geldings and mare this examinate saith that Bradrick rid upon the mare which was Gowland's. . . . He further saith they were at Masham about noon the

Sabbath Day which was about twenty seven miles from Leeds and
continued together there until Monday noon and came to Leeds on
Tuesday night after and turned the two geldings and mare into a close of
one Mr Thomas Foster's near Leeds and took them up the same night.
And he and Bradrick and Crossland lay under a stack of hay. And about
ten o'clock on Wednesday forenoon he, Bradrick and Crossland went
with the geldings and mare to a place called Scotch Wood near Leeds
and continued there till it was almost night and then went to a place
called Black Moor where they stayed for about an hour where the other
two, to wit Bradrick and Crossland parted from him and told him they
would go towards Skipton. This examinant returned back to Leeds and
lay under the same hay stack where they had lain on Tuesday night
before and continued there till about five o'clock on Thursday morning
keeping Gowland's mare in the close by him and about five o'clock in the
morning he turned her into the same close whence she was taken out and
the bridle and saddle he lay under a stack of hay of one George
Hargreaves.[1]

Bradrick's highway robberies took him all over the north. The distances
he travelled from his house in Leeds, as well as the casual manner of
deciding on a victim, are illustrated in the examination of another suspected
highwayman. John Lyley of Huddersfield confessed that he had been up to
Carlisle on 26 May 1684, where he had stayed for three days and that
'Bradrick had drunk with him.' They then met again near Kendal 'and as
they were coming on the road Bradrick advised him that they might rob the
first man they met' but Lyley claimed 'he would not consent to it.' By the
31st they were down near Clapham and on the night of 1st June were both
arrested as highway robbers at Padiham, just outside Burnley.

In November 1683 Bradrick had joined William Smorthwait to undertake a highway robbery in Killington. Bradrick confessed that he and
Smorthwait had taken nineteen or twenty pounds from a Cumberland
carrier, and Bainbridge confirmed that he had been shown the money by
Smorthwait and that Smorthwait had boasted that 'Bradrick could not
have taken the money from him but by his assistance.' The victim was
Richard Myles of Lazonby in Cumberland, a drover. Myles said that he,
being at Kirkby Lonsdale the twenty-ninth of

> November last past, and having there received eighteen pounds, fifteen
> shillings and two pence for cattle, he returning homeward he was robbed
> by two men of all the money, about two of the clock in the afternoon of the
> same day, near Stone Park in Killington. . . . One of the robbers was a tall

---

[1] ASSI/45/13/2 (PRO).

man and the other a little man with a red face, and that the tall man was William Smorthwait.

Myles added that 'one Eskrigg was pulling ling, and did see the two persons who robbed him.' He also believed that Bryan Thompson 'did acquaint the robbers or one of them with his receiving of money'. Again there was a local accomplice, the same alehouse keeper who was suspected to be involved in clipping, in the break-in at Farleton, and other offences. The place where the robbery took place is a remote spot on the old drove road on the top of Killington fell.

The following month Bradrick moved further north and carried out one or more robberies near Shap.[2] Bradrick himself described how, along with a certain William Marriner, an 'alehouse keeper (and by trade a webster)', he did 'rob on the highway about a mile and a half from Shap one George Huck of Shap, and took from him about twelve pounds fifteen shillings.' None of the original central actors was involved in the actual robbery, but Edward Bainbridge had heard from William Smorthwait that 'Henry Smorthwait did give them notice of the money, and that Henry Smorthwait being a cowardly fellow they had given him no part of the money.'

The most audacious of the ventures occurred on Whitsun Eve 1684, that is on Saturday 17 May. Bradrick told how he, William Smorthwait and a certain Richard Hugginson of Burton in Lonsdale, went up to a place just south of Penrith and 'did on the highway by Whinfell Park Side rob a certain drover, living near Ireby in Cumberland. . .and took from him threescore pounds or thereabouts, and at that time stabbed and killed the drover's horse, and also stabbed or pricked another of the horses belonging to the same company, which he believes afterwards died.' This attack on the horses was presumably to prevent pursuit, but it does not seem to have been entirely successful. Another witness, Edward Huetson, described how, coming from Appleby Fair at about five o'clock in the afternoon by the side of Whinfell Park he 'did meet three men on horseback riding as fast as they could, one upon a black, another upon a grey, and the third upon a bay-horse or mare'. He continued that 'he who rid upon the bay was a proper tall man with a vizard on, and the other two rid bare-faced.' Shortly afterwards he met William Beeby, a Cumberland drover, 'with some other persons following the three horsemen who had robbed the drover as he said'. The horsemen meanwhile had ridden into the park and disappeared. But not from our view: some six hours later, and fifteen miles further south we encounter them on a back road at Greenholme, refreshing themselves and their horses. The local alehouse keeper Lancelot Dennison described how

---

[2] A map of this expedition (map 4) is given on p. 125 above.

about eleven of the clock at night, he going to bed, heard some call at the door, and going thither he did see three men on horseback, two of their horses drinking ale which had been delivered unto them by his servant. They continued at the door about an hour, where they and their horses did drink one shilling and eight-pence in ale and they had four penny-worth of oats for their horses. He also saith, that he called for a candle to the door. But one of them said there should come none thither. When the reckoning was paid he questioned the goodness of a shilling which one of them said they had coined that day. He also saith that one of them was a little man, who had a greyish horse or mare, another of them was a proper tall man with a bay horse or mare, and the third man was of middle stature and had a grey horse or mare. He told them that he believed they were highwaymen, to which one of them answered, that they were in the highway.

Refreshed, the men (and horses) proceeded south, apparently undismayed by the suspicions of the alehousekeeper, for they then attempted a final robbery. Bradrick admitted that the three of them 'did rob one Lancelot Aray of Rounthwaite within the town of Rounthwaite, butcher, and took from him about six shillings.' Rounthwaite is a couple of miles south of Greenholme, so the robbery probably took place at about one o'clock in the morning. It seems to have been an accidental meeting, to judge from the examination of Lancelot Aray. He described how he

having been at Kendal upon Whitsun Eve last and returning homeward, together with Thomas Crosby his wife's son, late that night, they met with three men on horseback within a stone-cast of his dwelling house, which three men came riding furiously on the highway, and two of them seizing upon him, one of them held his hand, whilst the other of them put his hand into his pocket and did take forth all his money (excepting six pence) and did carry the same away, being between thirty and forty shillings. He also saith that the third of the robbers did follow Thomas Crosby, who alighting from off his horse and leaping over a wall got into the house, the said robber pursuing him to the very door, and then falling short of him. The robber killed the horse on which Thomas Crosby rid upon.

This concludes our description of the highway robberies; but it is not the end of the activities of the Smorthwaits and their associates.

8
Pickpockets and Thieves

As in all systems of classification, there are anomalies and picking a pocket in the king's highway fell between major types. It was like robbery in that it was taking from a person's body, and it occurred on a public highway. Yet it was not done with an element of open violence, neither did it cause fear. The fact that it was not possible to plead benefit of clergy in this case suggests that it was closer to robbery than to larceny. The residual nature of certain types of larceny, which were defined more in terms of what they were not than what they were, is shown in Fleming's note under his own heading 'Theft or Larceny' in his annotated *Statutes:* 'Larceny by the common law is the felonious and fraudulent taking and carrying away by any man or woman, of the mere personal goods of another neither from the person, nor by night in the house of the owner. If the personal goods amount to above the value of 12*d* then it is grand larceny, but 12*d* or under it is petty larceny for which one shall forfeit all his goods and be whipped &c.' Thus larceny was a theft of goods in a man's absence; the goods must be personal goods, not real estate such as land or housing. By definition the offence occurred on private ground, and if there is no trespass there is no larceny.

We may deal very briefly with pickpocketing. Despite the widespread carrying of small sums of money, only three of those accused in these depositions were suspected of taking from purses and pockets. Bainbridge, we have seen, picked Bradrick's pocket. The schoolmaster and curate Edmund Lodge was accused of picking the pocket of a certain John Fisher of Old Hutton, carrier, who deposed that he was with Lodge, Lodge's wife and other people in the house of Elinor Moor of Kirkby Lonsdale.[1] They all travelled home together and he had his purse, with twenty-one shillings and six pence in it, taken out of his pocket, as well as an 'alchemy seal and a little key'. When asked the next day about this, Lodge and his wife denied all guilt.

[1] A further note by Fleming states, on the contrary, that the theft had actually occurred at Miles Hodgson's house in Kirkby Lonsdale.

Most of the pickpocketing was undertaken by a minor figure, George Scaif. His deposition gives some insight into petty crime and into the informal settlement of minor thefts. A number of the offences were technically not 'pickpocketing' in the true sense, but another form of larceny, for the owners were not wearing the garments at the time. Scaif confessed that

> he being working as a tailor, about two years ago in the house of Thomas Aray of Blakethwait, husbandman, did steal one shilling out of the pocket of Thomas Aray when as he was out of the house, and his breeches lay in his chamber; which he confessed afterwards unto him upon examinations, and gave Thomas Aray another shilling for it. Soon after, he did also steal four shillings out of the pocket of Thomas Blakeling of the Drawell in Bland, husbandman, when he was out of the house and his breeches lay in his chamber; which he confessed afterwards unto him upon examination, and gave the said Thomas Blakeling other four shillings for them. And he also saith that about two years since, he being working as à tailor in the house of William Fairer of Graygrigg in Westmorland, yeoman, did there steal five shillings out of the pocket of William Fairer, when he was out of the house, and his breeches lay in his chamber; which he afterwards upon examination confessed unto William Fairer, and delivered unto him other five shillings for them.

His lack of success and subsequent discovery is further shown by two other depositions of those whose pockets he had picked. Robert Newby of Little Hutton testified that he,

> together with Michael Beck of New Hutton, husbandman, Richard Harrison of New Hutton, tailor, and George Scaif, late of Hutton Park, tailor, was in the house of Margaret Sill of New Hutton, widow, about Lammas last, where they did drink a while together, and about eleven of the clock in the night he left them and laid him down upon a bed in another room, where he slept until it was daylight, and the next day he telling over his money he wanted three shillings and enquired afterwards of George Scaif for the same, he at first denied that he had the same three shillings; but afterwards he said he would deliver this examinate the same, which he did accordingly.

The final information against Scaif was by Thomas Clark of Holme in Westmorland, yeoman, who said:

> that about the twenty eighth day of October last, meeting with George Scaif at Robert Walker's in Holmescales and George Scaif having seen this examinate (as he believes) receive some money, he travelled with this examinate unto Lambrigg Park, where they stayed together in an

alehouse until late in the night, when George Scaif desired to have a bed showed him, which was done. But he coming out of his chamber came again to this examinate and said he would not go to bed unless this examinate would go to bed with him; upon which this examinate sit up until he was sleepy. And then this examinate desired to know where he might lay him down upon a bed which some of the house showing to him he laid down and slept an hour; and at his awaking he found George Scaif lying upon the same bed beyond him and then he looking for his money in his pocket, he wanted fourteen shillings and sixpence which he had in his pocket at his lying down; upon which he enquired of them in the house for it, who denied it, and then he enquired of George Scaif for the money, who would not confess with it, and would not stay any longer there, but did go away presently.

Scaif was obviously an occasional pickpocket, stealing money when people were out of the house or asleep, but very frequently being the obvious suspect and hence being caught.

We may now turn to the types of larceny or theft in which they were involved. It is clear from the inventories which have survived in this part of the north that many houses were well furnished with ornaments and valuable possessions, that shops were filled with costly goods and that the fells were populated with sheep, cows and horses; the roads moreover, were filled with pack horses.[2] Of this wealth of possessions, the toll taken by the Smorthwaits and their associates was minute — three or four horses (one of them stolen by Bradrick from Edward Bainbridge's brother in revenge), two or three cows, half a dozen sheep, a carrier's pack and three items from shops or private houses. Yet these cases demonstrate how the accused combined larceny with burglary and robbery, and they give considerable insight into the way neighbours tracked down suspected thieves; they also show how very difficult it was to dispose of stolen property. For convenience sake, we may divide the larcenies by the nature of the objects stolen, non-animal and living animals.

The earliest simple larcenies occurred in May 1677. They both took place on the same day in Kendal and involved Edward Bainbridge. Bernard Edmundson, a Kendal butcher, described how

upon Whitsun Eve, having killed a calf in Kendal, a quarter thereof was taken away, and enquiring of Richard Preston (his servant) for the same, he looked about for it, and hearing (of Mr Thomas Fisher's children) that a man with a whitish stuff coat and bright buttons had carried away a quarter of veal, Richard Preston followed him until he met the person

---

[2] One estimate is that by the of middle of the eighteenth century, something like 175 pack-horses would leave Kirkby Lonsdale each week. Alexander Pearson, *Annals of Kirkby Lonsdale*. . . (Kendal, 1930), p.77.

in Stramongate, who going into Bryan Lancaster's house, Richard Preston sent for this examinate. And upon his going thither, the person proved to be Edward Bainbridge of Mansergh. And Edward Bainbridge showing the quarter of veal to this examinate, this examinate knew it to be his. Whereupon (by the persuasion of Mr John Troughton an attorney at law, and of Mr Ralph Wilson of Spittle) this examinate received three shillings of Edward Bainbridge for the same. And he likewise saith, that his brother Bryan Edmundson had a coat taken away the same Whitsun Eve. And he making a great stir about it, William Smorthwait then of Middleton and James Dawson, came upon Whitsunday unto Mr William Potter's house in Kendal and sent for him, upon whose going unto them, William Smorthwait said that if Bryan Edmundson would go over unto Middleton, he should have as much as would buy him another coat, and Bryan and this examinate going the next day unto William Smorthwait's house in Middleton they met (in the way) with Edward Bainbridge, where he agreed to give Bryan above twenty shillings for his coat, and William Smorthwait passed his word for the paying thereof, which William Smorthwait paid unto Bryan Edmundson.

In both these cases the theft was traced to Bainbridge and he was put under pressure to pay for the stolen articles. Fleming stated, however, that the repayment was in 'bad' or clipped money. He also noted that in another, unprosecuted case, Bainbridge had to return the stolen object.

Edward Bainbridge did take a quarter of veal and a coat from Bernard Edmundson a butcher in Kendal and he sealed a bond for satisfaction at Will. Smorthwait and paid in bad money. Item he did take a coat of Joseph Heblethwaites from Jane Wathman's of Kirkby Lonsdale widow, and which he brought again and found hid in her house.

Bainbridge appears to have been a fairly incompetent thief, and his victims tolerant.

Another incompetent suspected thief was Edmund Lodge. The victim of a supposed theft, Margaret Walton, described how

about three years ago Mr Edmund Lodge, together with two or three other persons, did drink at the house of her husband, and soon after they were gone she wanted a little silver cup, which they did drink brandy in. And presuming that Mr Lodge had taken it away in jest, she procured Elizabeth Helme (her sister) to enquire after it , which Mr Lodge sent by her the next day.

Lodge tried to brush off the incident as a 'jest'. for we have the information of Giles Helme, who said that

His wife (as she informed him) was desired to go unto Mr Lodge to enquire of him for a silver cup. . . and his wife then demanding the same of Mr Lodge, he said Oh! Dear Betty, are you come for the cup, I was just ready to saddle my horse to bring it. Then she asking him if he had it in his pocket, he replied no, it is in my closet, whereupon he fetched it and delivered it unto her.

Clearly the Justices did not treat it as either a jest or an oversight, for it formed the basis of one of the indictments against Lodge.

It is naturally impossible to know how many other minor thefts occurred without leading to prosecution. That there were some is shown by various notes of Fleming. In one case, the objects were small quantities of corn: 'James Harrison of Barbon (the farmer of Mr Shuttleworth's estate) can inform against Henry Dixon late of Middleton yeoman that he took some of his corn for an horse. Twas but a little. [above] Will Speight sayeth that.' This is mentioned elsewhere, where reference is made to a man of the same name, William Clarke, as the butcher or miller of Cumberland who helped at the Hindson burglary.

William Clarke of Middleton husbandman. Farmer to Will. Smorthwait, was privy to Henry Dixon's stealing of James Harrison's corn then lying in his house, whether he ever received any corn or sacks unlawfully come by, concerning clipping &c. James Richardson of Barbon deceased had 4 sacks of corn which was probably for [unreadable] Will. Clarke's use at Rich. Bayliffs in Middleton. Denies all upon his oath.

On another occasion, the erstwhile High Constable was believed to have stolen the communion wine. Fleming wrote himself a note to 'enquire of Mr Trotter concerning William Smorthwait's stealing of the wine bought for the communion, whilst the churchwardens were asleep, and filling the bottles up with washings, which was not discovered until they came into the chapel.' 'Mr Trotter' was an attorney, which suggests that the case may well have been taken to court other than the Quarter Sessions and Assizes, and perhaps the ecclesiastical court as well. Other minor thefts and nuisances unspecified are implied by a neighbour of Edward Bainbridge, Robert Benson, who said that 'before the Justices of the Peace sent out their warrants for the apprehending of Edward Bainbridge several things were stolen, and divers gates were thrown down in the night within Mansergh, but since the flying away of Edward Bainbridge this examinate hath not heard of anything stolen there, or of any gates thrown down.'

The thefts described so far were of fairly small items, though even when a coat was stolen , the owner made 'a great stir about it'. But on one occasion the object was cloth worth over £20, extensive search was made and a very large amount of general interest was generated. The case also illustrates the difficulty of disposing of stolen property. The theft was a premeditated act against one of the numerous carriers who serviced the very important cloth trade of the area. Henry Yeats gave information that John Jackson had come to his house and 'desired him to let them [i.e. William Smorthwait and Edward Bainbridge] know when anyone either English or Scottish lodged there, with any charge of money or gold, and this informant should have a share of it, and never be questioned about it, and should lie quietly in his bed, for they would ride out disguised.' Yeats claimed that Jackson had also said 'that there was one Simon Mount a carrier who often brought great parcels of money that way, and that they would have about him ere it was long.' The theft itself was described by the carrier Simon Mount, who had been at Settle in Yorkshire. On 12 December 1682 he brought 'from thence two packs, or fardels, into his own house in Old Hutton, in which packs there were eleven pieces of cloth, called kerseys and half–thicks, of the value of twenty one pounds sixteen shillings and six pence. And the packs this informant laid that night in his stable, and looking for them early the next morning they were gone and stolen as he verily believes.' Simon Mount also claimed that 'six pack sheets, two cheeses, and other things' were also stolen.

The thieves then had the problem of dealing with the merchandise. They tried to persuade Bainbridge to hide most of the cloth in his father's house but, as he confessed, 'he not daring to do, they hid the same in Mr Godsalves wood at Rigmaden where it lay two or three days covered with brackens and then he did see them carry it away upon Bryan Ward's mare into Yorkshire.' Their attempts to hide the rest of the cloth under a pile of vegetation were less successful. Mount described how

> About a week after this he heard that Thomas Wilson of New Hutton, husbandman, found a piece of half–thick of the value of three pounds in a close of his, covered with moss, between a hazel bush and a wall, when he was getting of spelks there, who acquainting the constable therewith, the constable, Thomas Wilson, and some others watched the same in hope that some would come to fetch it away. And that night the wife of Henry Smorthwait, daughter of Thomas Wilson, was seen to come towards that place where the piece of half–thick was found.

The unfortunate Thomas Wilson, who had trapped his own daughter, corroborated the story, stating that he had found the cloth in a close called High Field, covered 'with moss and some dead fog, between a hazel bush and a wall'. He went to the constable, Miles Tarn, and they laid their trap. The woman turned back just before she reached the hidden cloth, and, when asked why, said that 'she came hither to meet her husband and she turned back again because she did see something like a black head, which she thought was of somebody.' Wilson had to admit that when he saw the woman approaching, presumably recognizing her and seeing what was about to happen, 'he coughed or hemmed, upon which she turned back again.' Once again the trail had led to a suspect, as in the case of the petticoats stolen from the widow Bainbridge of Hawkin Hall. The ramifications of the family connections between Henry Smorthwait, his wife and the watcher, as well as Wilson's behaviour is further shown in a note by Fleming:

> Thomas Mansergh of New Hutton husbandman heard when Thomas Wilson of New Hutton told his brother Edmund Wilson of Killington that the wife of Henry Smorthwait coming towards the place where the pieces of half–thick was found, the said Thomas Wilson asked her what she had to do there and bid her get home to her children. Simon Mount told me this June 13.83. Thomas Wilson told the same to William Speight of Bendrigg in Old Hutton yeoman. Enquire of the said Edmund Wilson whether Henry Smorthwait lodged with him or endeavoured to convey away his estate.

At first it looked as if the theft had been carried out by the Smorthwaits, Bainbridge and George Scaif. Consequently, they were named in a draft bill at the Assizes in 1683. This seemed to be partly confirmed by Bainbridge's examination in 1684 when he admitted that 'William Smorthwait did confess that he stole a pack of cloth out of Old Hutton and carried it away upon Bryan Ward's mare which this examinate believes was Simon Mount's pack.' But the situation was confused by the testimony of Edward Bradrick. He confirmed that Bainbridge had received some of the stolen cloth. An undated letter from Simon Mount to Fleming reads

> Honoured Sir,
> John Gathorn acquaints me that when he was at Lancaster with Bradrick then a prisoner there he told him that Bainbridge has a piece of grey cloth of mine that was stolen from me, which I thought good to acquaint you with.
> And am
> > Honourable Sir. Your humble servant Simon Mount.

But at the bottom of this in the same hand is a note: 'Theres an information also about the same against Fisher the carrier.' For Bradrick had named four entirely separate people as responsible. As well as John Jackson, he had mentioned the carrier Fisher and two men who, we have seen, were vaguely suspected of burglary in Killington.

> The informant knows one Robert Benson and one John Barker of Killington with one John Jackson of Hutton with one John Fisher of Hutton some place there adjacent in Westmorland, who did break the

house of one Simon Mount of Hutton in Westmorland and took from him several pieces of cloth to the value of a pack or thereabouts, the cloth was kersey, one of the pieces was brown and another of them was green, and likewise took away two cheeses at the same time from the said Mount.

Obviously Fleming took this seriously, making a note elsewhere: 'Robert Benson of Mansergh husbandman, a great comrade of Edward Bainbridge's who would have had him to have kept something for Edward Bainbridge soon after Simon Mount's packs were stolen, enquire what it was and who hath it. He to appear upon Wednesday or Saturday next.' Yet we do not know, as yet, that these new suspects were brought to court.[3]

Theft of animals was perhaps more difficult to conceal: if a carcase was stolen, it had to be disposed of, and if the animal was alive, it left hoofmarks. Four thefts of horses are mentioned in the depositions. Richard Myles, the carrier who was robbed on Killington fell, seems to have been a favourite victim of the associates, for in March 1684, 'being all night at Rowland Wallas his house in Kirkby Lonsdale, [he] had his horse stolen out of the stable, which was near Bryan Thompson's house.' A note in Fleming's manuscript adds a little detail: it is part of Bradrick's supposed confession. 'This informant doth know one Bryan Thompson of Kirkby Lonsdale with one Thomas Nowell of Wennington who did the last March or thereabouts convey a horse from an alehouse near unto Bryan Thompsons of Kirkby Lonsdale, but the informant doth not know the name of that house but the horse was one Richard Myles of Cumberland.'

Another occurred when John Gathorn of Holmescales, stapler, had a horse stolen from Hutton Park. Gathorn went to see Bradrick in prison and learnt from him that Bradrick had received his horse from the pickpocket George Scaif. Gathorn retrieved the horse from the under-gaoler. William Smorthwait was also riding a horse probably stolen from an Appleby shopkeeper in May 1684, when he was apprehended at Padiham.

The fourth horse theft was not a simple one. The motive for the theft is given in the confession of Bradrick, who alleged that Edward Bainbridge had picked his pocket and taken £8 out of it, 'for which service he did beat Bainbridge and also as a further satisfaction he stole from him a mare.' Having the mare, he excused Bainbridge £6 of the stolen money and was to have another 40s in clippings. Unfortunately for them, the mare was not

[3] Fleming seems to have made enquiries concerning the honesty of the carrier, John Fisher. A letter dated 19 July 1684 from a Mr James Simpson to Fleming reads as follows. 'Worshipful sir, this bearer John Fisher came to me and desired me to write two lines by him. Truly as I have known him several years, he is our carrier for Wakefield, and I never knew nor heard nor indeed in the least suspect anything but honest. However, notwithstanding, it may be otherwise, and therefore I do not go further, only beg you what lawful favour you can do for him, unless it appear to your worship otherwise than I imagine. Pardon this, which neither it nor I will in usual. I am your most humble servant, James Simpson.' Fleming Letters 2785.

Edward Bainbridge's, but belonged to his elder brother John, who told how the mare had been found in the possession of William Smorthwait and Edward Bradrick. What happened is described by Edward Bainbridge. He traced the mare from the stable in Gillfoot, Mansergh, to 'a stone near Lune Bridge, but could trace no further by reason of the highway.' This was possible because the mare had a canker on her back foot. Bainbridge suspected Smorthwait of the theft and went down to an alehouse in Clapham, where he found the mare 'with saddle and bridle on, and her tail docked'. He started to lead her out, when Smorthwait and Bradrick 'fell upon and beat him and took the mare from him.' A short note by Fleming implicated another man in this affair, though nothing more is recorded concerning this: 'Mr Charles Saul of Cowbrow late Mr Lamplughs man had a hand in stealing of John Bainbridge's mare, and Bradrick gave him a pair of boots and a coat.'

There is only one reference to sheep stealing, though these animals must have been a relatively easy target and other associates may have engaged in this type of theft. For instance, Bradrick mentioned a certain Nowell 'hath been guilty of several small thefts as stealing of sheep and other goods at several other times.' In the one case involving central members of the gang, we know of no prosecution and the confession of Edward Bainbridge was gratuitous. He said that 'William Marriner, William Smorthwait and Richard Huggison had stolen six or seven sheep from Barbon and had set up a sheep tail or two upon the hedge where they took them, and that one Gerard Scaif late of Thornton in Yorks had a part of the sheep.'

There were two reputed cattle thefts. In the first, two cows were taken. There was some dispute as to who had done this. Bradrick accused William Smorthwait, Edward Bainbridge, Marriner, Huggison and Gerard Scaif. Bainbridge said it was William Smorthwait, Edward Bradrick and Richard Huggison who 'stole one or two fat beasts from the man who was robbed on Killington fell'. Whoever the culprit was, the unfortunate Richard Myles was again the victim, stating that having 'put eleven cows to grass all night with William Newton late High Constable of Lonsdale ward, that night one of them was stolen, as also another cow belonging to another man.'

In the second theft of cattle, we are given a detailed picture of the attempts to find the thieves. Edward Bainbridge described how William Smorthwait and Marriner had asked him to 'go into Barbon to see if there was any fat beasts there.' He returned and 'told them there was good beasts both in Middleton and Barbon.' Afterwards, Smorthwait and Marriner stole two heifers from Barbon Beckfoot. The animals were jointly owned by Anne Gibbonson and her brother Samuel Otway. Otway described how they were stolen out of a close on 28 October 1681:

And upon the missing of them, he did go into Yorkshire to enquire after them, who hearing not any thing of the said heifers, he returned home again. . . .Whilst he was from home, a boy told Anne Gibbonson that he had seen Edward Bainbridge in the close not long before the heifers were missed. Upon which (as he hath heard) she procured a warrant for a search and the searchers did find in the house where Edward Bainbridge dwelled a side of beef, which Edward Bainbridge said he had brought of Henry Smorthwait of New Hutton.

They found another side of beef in Henry Smorthwait's house. Then Otway

was advised by John Newton his attorney to sue Edward Bainbridge in an action of trover and conversion, but the attorney dying, and no demand being made, Edward Bainbridge got costs against this examinate and then Edward Bainbridge and Henry Smorthwait did both sue him, and brought down two trials against him. And this examinate also sued them and brought down a trial against them both. And at the Assizes at Appleby 1681, before any of the said trials came on, James Dawson of Old Hutton, whitesmith, moved a reference between Edward Bainbridge, Henry Smorthwait, and this examinate. And James Dawson and Joseph Baylif of Middleton, whitesmith, did agree the parties, awarding this examinate eleven pounds to be paid him at Michaelmas following. Which being not paid, he sued Edward Bainbridge for the same, who being arrested, he paid this unto this examinate's attorney, Mr James Knowles of Kirkby Lonsdale.

The use of law, of informal settlement, of various warrants and writs, is well illustrated. A few added details are given in a note by Fleming concerning Samuel Otway of Barbon: 'Edward Bainbridge was to pay him some money, and upon non-payment Edward Bainbridge was imprisoned at Appleby by Samuel Otway. Mr Knowles at Kirkby Lonsdale was his attorney to whom £10 was paid by Mr Joseph Ward of Firbank about this business.' Edward Stainbank of Middleton, butcher, also deposed that he had gone with the constables when they searched Bainbridge's house and saw 'a fine rapier hanging in a room of the house', possibly a reference to the theft from Hawkin Hall. He was present as well at the search of Henry Smorthwait's house, where 'there was also some beef found which Henry Smorthwait's wife said her husband had brought in when she was from home with a sick wife.' The robbers seem to have been unable to keep silent about their theft. Richard Tatham of Ireby reported William Smorthwait as saying that 'he would tell him a business of great concernment if this examinate would not divulge it; whereupon he answered no, if it was not either treason or murder.' Smorthwait then described how flesh had been found in the houses of his brother and Bainbridge. Bainbridge came out of the house and confessed that he had found the heifer at Barbon Beckfoot and that Henry Smorthwait had half of her, which Henry Smorthwait later confessed to Tatham. This one theft had led to several searches, warrants, search parties, various actions and the involvement of two whitesmiths as mediators as well as at least two attorneys. None of this is reflected in the surviving Assize records.

9
Accomplices and Neighbours

So far this history has indicated that, although it would be wrong to speak of a 'sub-culture', there were networks of people who were known to act outside the law, particularly where clippers and coiners were concerned. In order that the Smorthwaits might operate, several different kinds of accomplices were needed. One of these was the messenger. We have already seen that Bainbridge and Dixon were able to escape because they were fore-warned, and that they could make effective robberies because information was brought to them. The messenger about whom we hear most was the journeyman tailor-cum-pickpocket, George Scaif. His account of his activities over these months illustrates the movements that went on behind the scenes.

Scaif lived about half a mile across the fields from Lodge and Robinson at Holmescales. He described how

> The night when Simon Mount had his pack stolen from him, he was at the house of Michael Beck of New Hutton husbandman, working as a tailor until twelve of the clock that night, and that then he hired an horse of William Beck, brother of Michael, and promised to give him a shilling for the loan thereof, unto the house of Henry Smorthwait of New Hutton, about two miles from Michael Beck's house. And when he came to Henry Smorthwait's house, he was in bed and did rise to open the door for this examinate, and Henry Smorthwait did go to bed again. And this examinate did lie in his clothes upon the bed by him, his wife lying in another bed in the same room until the next morning, when this exami-nate returned with the horses (and ten shillings which he borrowed that night of Henry Smorthwait) unto the house of Thomas Beck of Bleaze in Old Hutton, yeoman, and paid the ten shillings unto William Beck, and then returned unto his work at Michael Beck's house.

Clearly Scaif was trying to provide an alibi for himself and Henry Smorth-wait, both of whom were suspected of being involved in the theft of Simon Mount's pack. He also gave evidence of his activities as a messenger:

Hearing of the commitment of John Jackson upon suspicion of robbing Mr Robert Robinson, he did borrow Henry Smorthwait's mare, and did ride unto Kendal to visit John Jackson, with whom he stayed about two hours. And the next day, after Henry Smorthwait was committed for the same offence, he did ride upon the mare by the house of Edward Bainbridge in Mansergh, and unto Henry Dixon's house in Yorkshire, to give him notice of Henry Smorthwait's commitment, and to desire Henry Dixon (who had married the mother of Henry Smorthwait) to come over into Westmorland.

Further details concerning Scaif's activities are provided by two others. Scaif's brother Thomas, said that George had told him how he

did go along with Edward Bradrick last Whitsunday (a little before sun-setting) from the house of Henry Smorthwait in New Hutton unto John Walker's house at the Elm Tree at Far Crosbank near Kendal, alehouse keeper, where Bradrick lent him (as he told this examinate) £20 to bet at an horse-race on Hay Fell the Tuesday next following. And upon Whitsun Wednesday last Bradrick came unto this examinate's father's house at Ashes vapouring and threatening to shoot George Scaif whensoever he should meet him, he having not met Bradrick that morning at Henry Smorthwait's and repaid him his money. Upon the hearing of which this examinate did go to the place where his brother was, and persuaded him to go to Bradrick, which he then did perform, and paid Bradrick £10 and he and this examinate gave him bond for £8 (which was taken in the name of John Walker) and the others 40s (which made up the £20) this examinate's brother was to pay to John Walker by Bradrick's appointment.

There are also notes concerning Scaif's activities in the Fleming papers:

There came William Beck of the Bleaze in Old Hutton and enquired of Simon Mount's son where he picked the packs and he told Beck in the stable. Afterwards Beck came to George Scaif at Michael Beck's house at Stricklay in New Hutton about eleven o'clock of the night and called him out and discoursed him about half an hour, and returned into the house again and desired to borrow a horse of Michael Beck to ride to his father's house at Hutton Park who denied to lend him one, but Richard Harrison master to Scaif told him that he would lend him his horse if he had any urgent occasion, but that it was to little purpose for they should go thither the next morning to work. Scaif replied he might either go that very night to his father's house or never, for another time would not serve. Then William Beck proffered to lend Scaif his horse if he would give him a shilling, Scaif replied he would give him 6d. The other would not but said they would agree of it. Scaif came to Kendal within a day or two after John Jackson was taken upon the warrant and rid of Henry Smorthwait's mare, and was with Jackson the most part of Sunday. And when Smorthwait was taken of the Saturday, Scaif went to Edward Bainbridge to give him notice, as is believed, of Smorthwait's being apprehended and rid of Smorthwait's mare. Now Scaif never came at his father's house that night as both his father and mother affirmed to Simon Mount.

A final impression of one of the incidents is also contained in Fleming's papers:

> Will. Adland of New Hutton husbandman said one came to knock (with a horserod, or other stick) at Henry Smorthwait's window (the same night that Simon Mount's packs were stolen) and Henry did go forth, and coming in again he said it was an old friend that was come to borrow some money. Adland did that night see a horse tied on the back of Henry Smorthwait's barn. This he told to Edward Tarn about a fortnight ago.

Another important role was that of informant about likely victims for thefts and burglaries. Sometimes this was a single piece of information, as with Lodge, Joseph Cartmel or the Cumberland butcher. Others, for example John Jackson, were offered bribes to give information whenever they could. Those who were particularly well placed to do this were alehouse or innkeepers. Bryan Thompson was such an alehouse keeper, and it was probably he who provided information concerning the wealth of Richard Myles. Another informant in Kirkby Londsdale was 'one William Briscoe of Keastwick in Westmorland who was one that did give notice what way any man did carry money'. As well as these sources of information in his home parish of Kirkby Lonsdale, Smorthwait had another such source when he moved to the parish of Clapham. Bradrick deposed that

> Isabel Taylor of Eldroth Lane near Clapham in Yorkshire mother of John and William Taylor, keeping a tippling or alehouse hath several times resetted goods and other things which she hath known to be stolen and also hath given her two sons and others of their accomplices notice of persons that she knew was travelling that way with any charge of money, that so they might take such moneys and rob the persons who had the charge or care thereof.

Here we have the other major role, that of 'resetter' or 'recettour' a disposer of stolen goods or clipped money. Isabel Taylor's activities in one particular theft are given in more detail by Bradrick:

> And particularly this examinate remembers that at the breaking of John Stout's shop, he and the other persons concerned therein did (over and above the goods before mentioned) take near a pack of tallow candles

which were conveyed to Isabel Taylor's house, as also were several other of the goods so stolen. And Isabel Taylor knowing the goods to be so stolen did melt down most part of the candles into tallow.

One possible reason for Isabel Taylor's involvement may have been that her own sons were the burglars, for Bradrick confessed that he 'with William Smorthwait and one John Taylor of Eldroth Lane and William Taylor his brother with Richard Mitton did in or about the month of March last in the night time break the shop of one John Stout of Keasden-head in Yorkshire and thereout took some flax, hemp, brandy, and about five horse loads of iron.' The candles could be disposed of by an alehouse keeper, but it was more difficult to get rid of the other goods. The flax, hemp and brandy could only be sold by a mercer. The person chosen to 'reset' them was also alleged to be a Kirkby Lonsdale man. Bradrick said that he and Smorthwait sold the flax and hemp to one John Tyson of Kirkby Lonsdale in Westmorland and that 'John Tyson very well knew how the flax and hemp was come by, and hath confessed to him that he had several times clipped or diminished his Majesty's coin.' Tyson, when examined, admitted the same, but denied being aware of how the flax and hemp had been obtained. He said

> that he hath heard that one Stout in Yorkshire had his shop broken and several goods taken out of it, and that afterwards William Smorthwait . . .with another man who called himself Wilson sold unto this examinate the ninth of April last eight stones of flax and nineteen stone of hemp. And this examinate did then allow and pay unto William Smorthwait for the same the sum of thirty-six shillings for the flax and after the rate of eight groats a stone for the hemp.

But there was still the iron to dispose of. According to Bradrick this was sold in the full knowledge of its origins to the blacksmith and clipper Alexander Guy who 'did pay to William Smorthwait for the same the sum of forty shillings in new half crowns of his own counterfeiting and promised twenty-five shillings more which is not yet paid.' Guy's account of the transaction stresses his innocence:

> Going towards the town of Settle about a month or five weeks ago, he called at an alehouse in the country of York where was William Smorthwait, and he enquiring of this examinate whither he was then going to, he answered to Settle, to buy some iron, upon which William Smorthwait said he would sell him a load or two or iron, and thereupon he did buy of him four and twenty stone of Danae iron at the rate of 15s the hundredweight (being eight stone to every hundred). And he did then pay him for the same all but 25s, which this examinate hath now in his hand. He saith, that he never heard that William Smorthwait had sold any iron before, and he did not enquire of him where he got iron. He also saith,

that he paid to William Smorthwait but 20*s*, in which sum there were but two half-crowns, and he denies that they were new ones, or of his own counterfeiting.

Another receiver and abettor was Gerard Scaif of Westhouse near Thornton in Yorkshire, 'who hath several times resetted stolen goods knowing them to be so, and also harboured and given encouragement to those persons who were accustomed to steal and rob.'

Other informers in Kirkby Lonsdale also acted as channels for the distribution of stolen goods. Bainbridge claimed that 'Bryan Thompson. . . did several times exchange thirty or forty shillings of broad money for clipped money.' Bradrick added that William Briscoe of Keastwick 'did reset any goods that were conveyed from any man'.

Finally, the network included comrades and companions, men and women who might help in evading the law. Those of Edward Bainbridge, apart from his brother John, seem to have been Robert Benson and John Barker, and they may also have been involved in various offences. Of Barker, for example, Fleming made a note: 'Jo. Barker of Killington, mill-wright, a great comrade of Edward Bainbridge, enquire why the doors of Jo. Bainbridge's were not forthwith opened when the two constables came to search of Edward Bainbridge of what the said Jo. Barker did in Jo. Bainbridge's house then at that time of the night.' Another 'comrade' was Alexander Guy of Mallerstang, blacksmith and suspected clipper, who fairly frequently encountered members of the gang and bought them an occasional drink. The sort of relationship here is described by Guy himself, who recounted how he

about three years ago did see Edward Bradrick in Mallerstang, at the house of Anthony Ward an alehouse keeper there, where this examinate did drink a while with him and then he did go unto Christopher King's house in Nateby in this county, where Edward Bradrick did stay a week or ten days with his aunt who was wife of Christopher King. And he did also see Edward Bradrick about two days before last Whitsun Eve at an alehouse called the Highway in the parish of Aysgarth in Yorks, together with William Smorthwait and one Richard Huggison, where this examinate continued drinking with them about an hour and a half; and they being looked upon as dangerous persons and saying they had no money, he persuaded a neighbour of his called Henry Shaw of Mallerstang to pay 12*d* of their reckoning, and this examinate paid the rest thereof being 2*s* 6*d*. And then he and Henry Shaw going homewards into Mallerstang, Edward Bradrick, William Smorthwait and Richard Huggison did call at his smithy and one of them having lost a shoe he did set on a new one, for which Bradrick paid 3*d* and then they rid towards Kirkby Stephen and William Smorthwait told him that they would go to Appleby.

On a final occasion, Alexander Guy 'did see Edward Bradrick about a month ago upon a moor called Dent's Cross in Yorkshire where this examinate was going homewards and Edward Bradrick travelling with some stockingers the other way.'

The loyalties of these 'comrades' were not, however, reliable, and they sometimes turned against their accomplices under examination. One vivid instance of this is the examination of John Barker, who gave very strong evidence against Bainbridge, as well as providing an insight into the behaviour of one of the toughest of the robbers. He said that he

> together with Edward Bainbridge and divers others of his neighbours, were all together in a close within Mansergh cutting of broom soon after Christmas last. At which time the constable of Killington with two other men came into the close, and Edward Bainbridge so soon as he discovered the constable and the other two men, did go away. And then Edward Bainbridge did return again to his work of cutting of broom in the close. He also saith, that he observing the great trouble and discouragement of Edward Bainbridge, discoursed with him alone in the evening, desiring to know why he did go away so hastily as aforesaid; to which he would give his examinate no satisfactory answer and he would then confess nothing.

But shortly after Bainbridge confessed a good deal to Barker, which he duly recounted.

This reminds us that while there were perhaps a dozen or so people in Kirkby Lonsdale who may have been involved as friends and accomplices of the Smorthwaits and Bainbridge, many in the population found their behaviour unacceptable. These were the people who finally prosecuted them and helped to search their houses. Not everyone was convinced by Bainbridge's attempts to claim that the robbery at Robinson's house 'was the stoutest deed that ever man did, and they deserved commendation for it'. For example, the man to whom this boasting speech was made, Robert Ward, a neighbour in Killington, reported that 'having heard many reports of Edward Bainbridge's being an ill liver, and of his riding much abroad, generally going from home and returning thither in the night, he advised him several times to give over his ill course; which he took very thankfully, and confessed he had been a very ill liver, and said he would mend.' One reason for the lack of sympathy among the surrounding population was the fact that, as we have seen, the thefts and the crimes were most often directed against near neighbours. The motivation was simply that a neighbour with property worth stealing was considered a reasonable target, even if he was a relative or confidant, as in the Hawkin Hall case. The anger thus caused is beautifully summed up in the previously quoted remark of Dorothy Stainbank at the time of the Robinson burglary: 'Woe be unto Edward Bain-

bridge of Mansergh. . .if he come hither to affright me.' The general irrita-
tion was increased by the violent riding about the country, armed and
disguised, late at night. This led to one particular incident, recounted by
the same Robert Ward who had 'advised' Bainbridge several times to give
up his evil life:

> A little before Christmas last about eleven of the clock in the night his
> father and he having walked a little out of their dwelling-house in
> Killington, did see two horsemen disguised (who speaking as if they had
> something in their mouths) unto this examinate demanded who his
> father and he were, to which he (being constable) answered, that it was
> fitter to know who they were, whereupon they both rid towards this
> examinate. And one of them discharged a pistol at him, upon which his
> father did fetch a fowling-piece out of the house, which this examinate
> discharged towards them, and they soon after rid away. He also saith
> that he believes the horsemen were William Smorthwait and Edward
> Bainbridge, but doth not certainly know it.

Even when they were not disguised and armed, members of the band were
not always welcome. The ambivalence and apprehension, as well as the
pressures towards hospitality, is well shown in an account given by Henry
Yeats:

> The seventeenth day of November last William Smorthwait and Edward
> Bainbridge and another person unknown came to his house at Old
> Hutton in the night time, and desired his housekeeper to fill them some
> drink, but she being alone in the house durst not let them in at that time
> of the night being betwixt eleven and twelve of the clock of the night as
> his housekeeper told and related to him. He further saith that about a
> fortnight after one John Jackson of Old Hutton called at his house about
> ten of the clock of the night and asked if the persons called not at his
> house the time abovesaid, to which he replied he thought they did; and
> thereupon Jackson enquired what they drunk, to which he replied they
> drunk nothing at all, whereupon Jackson desired him to entertain them
> when they came again, and let them have ale and make much of them for
> they would pay well though they would not sit down, but drink it
> standing, being for the most part in haste.

Yet despite the threats and other nuisances, there is no sign that the
neighbours went outside the law and set up vigilante groups or tried to mob
or attack Bainbridge and his accomplices directly. There is some evidence
that the threats from the Bainbridges, particularly to set fire to people's
houses, were effective and saved them prosecution. But even in the middle
of the affair, when rumours were circulating, Edward Bainbridge and his
neighbours were out cutting broom. Edward is never known to have been

physically assaulted, while his brother John, a harbourer of thieves, accused of clipping and coining, and a threatener of his neighbours, was never indicted during the major period of prosecutions.

10
Final Trials and Legends

Fleming and Judge Jeffreys rode into Carlisle on 6 August 1684, where Henry and William Smorthwait awaited trial. Later they would proceed to Appleby to deal with Bryan Thompson and Joseph Cartmel. Bradrick had already been condemned to death at the York Assizes, as the Clerk mentioned to Fleming (see p. 114). Ironically, after all his highway robberies, he had been found guilty and sentenced, according to an indictment surviving in the Assize files, for stealing a grey horse valued at £5.[1] We may now look at the fate of the two Smorthwaits and their accomplices. Once again the evidence of the actual trial is tantalizing: despite a search of the numerous pamphlet accounts printed at the time, nothing has yet been located describing the court-room scene.[2] Only two indictments against the accused at the Carlisle Sessions have survived, dated 6 August.[3]

> Jurors for the King present on their oath that William Clarke late of Morton in Cumberland, miller, William Smorthwait late of Clapham in Yorkshire, yeoman, and Henry Smorthwait late of New Hutton in Westmorland, yeoman, on 19th October 34 Charles II between the hours of 11 and 2 in the night did feloniously and burglariously break and enter the mansion house of Richard Hindson at Ling in the parish of Heskett and took £9 in money away of his goods. . . .
> Witnesses [on back] Richard Hindson, Andrew Bell, Elizabeth Hindson, Edward Bainbridge, Edward Huetson, Richard Bunting all on oath. [See illustration 12]

Two other names, Arthur Birkbeck and Richard Walker are crossed through in pencil with *juratus* against them. There is another indictment,

---

[1] ASSI/44/30, where it is wrongly placed (PRO).
[2] A search of D. Wing, *Short-title Catalogue of Books printed in England, Scotland, Ireland, Wales. . .1641–1700* (New York, 1945–51), 3 vols, revealed no relevant pamphlets. Nor were there any in the additional trial pamphlets, in the Bodleian Library, Oxford or British Library, London, not yet incorporated into Wing.
[3] ASSI/44/32. For a reproduction of this, see illustration 12.

12 *The indictment against William and Henry Smorthwait at Carlisle Assizes on 6 August 1684 upon which they were finally convicted.*
(For translation, see p. 160 of text.)

exactly the same in plea and time as above, with the same witness, though not sworn, for taking 18*d* from Andrew Bell.

Bainbridge had not withdrawn his confession. The trial occurred on 8 August, as Nicholson noted. The two bills were examined by the Grand Jury and found to be technically accurate and a *prima facie* case to exist. Thus 'true bill' was written on the back. They went forward to the Jury of Life and Death. We have a list of the juror's names; none of them has appeared in the depositions or other evidence, and none of them came from the area where the accused lived. The verdict of the jurors is written in different ink above the names of the two Smorthwaits, the simple Latin abbreviation *cul* for guilty. The situation was desperate and the same day Henry Smorthwait wrote to Fleming, begging for his intercession.[4]

> Most Worshipful Sir Daniel,
>   Although God knows I be casten for my life by Edward Bainbridge's oath, my poor wife and children ruined, contrary to a good conscience, for which God will undoubtedly show his judgement immediately upon him, God is my record Sir Daniel, I never designed any man or woman should have received wrong by me, or from any that concerned me upon any account, neither was ever I confederate with those misdemeanours that had been done to the King and country. Therefore good Sir Daniel I humbly implore and beg your worship's good assistance and favour and that your worship would be pleased to desire the Lord Chief Justice to take it into consideration to grant me a reprieve or that I might die in the King's service rather than be put to this ignominious death, God knows I may blame my relatives wickedness upon several accounts for this sad misfortune for which all along I have been a great sufferer. Good Sir, I know you have a good influence with

---

[4] Fleming Letters, 2788. For a reproduction of this see illustration 13.

the Judge, good Sir Daniel be my cordial and true friend in this great and weighty concern, and your servant shall pray as in duty bound whilst I am

[signature in same hand as letter] Henry Smorthwait
August the 8th 1684. [See illustration 13]

13 *The letter from Henry Smorthwait, then a prisoner in Carlisle Castle and awaiting sentence having been found guilty of burglary. Written on 8 August 1684 to Sir Daniel Fleming, pleading for Smorthwait's life.*

Henry's plea that he had been led into evil ways by his brother William was not a totally new one. In the one previous examination of Henry which survives he explained that 'the reason why he is so often in his brother William Smorthwait's company is because William is indebted to him and he doth what he can to secure the same.' This probably refers back to their father's will in 1669 which had the following clause: 'I do give my son Henry Smorthwait forty pounds to put him to an apprentice and an hundred pounds when he shall be free of his apprenticeship to be paid him by my son William Smorthwait, and if my son Henry die before he accomplish the age of one and twenty years the hundred pounds to return to my son William again.' Given all the evidence he had collected, it is unlikely that Fleming could have accepted such an excuse, but we do not know whether he attempted to intercede with Jeffreys. What we do know is that the following day the Judge gave sentence. Under 9 August William Nicholson recorded: 'Two Smorthwaits. . .sentenced to die.' On the indictment is written the single letter 's' with an abbreviation sign. This stood for the Latin word *suspendatur*, that is suspended or hanged.

If a reprieve was attempted, it was not successful. In his 'Memoirs' on the events of 1684 Daniel Fleming made a note against the indictment for stealing money for Andrew Bell: 'Will. Smorthwait and Henry Smorthwait being found guilty upon the former indictment they were not hanged upon this. They were hanged Aug. 16. '84.' [See illustration 14] Their deaths are confirmed by other evidence and while other accomplices continue to be very visible in local records in later years, neither William nor Henry ever appear again. A fortnight after the execution, on 30 August, the Clapham parish register includes the baptism of one of William Smorthwait's children. It was customary to give the father's name in the baptism register, but on this occasion the christening was of Jane Smorthwait, daughter of Jane, of Orcaber, Clapham.[5] Evidently the widow returned to Middleton, for three years later the same child, again stated to be 'daughter of Jane' was registered as buried in the Middleton register. The family remained in Middleton for at least forty-five years after William's execution. When a list of all the inhabitants was made in May 1695 it included 'Jane Smorthwait widow'. With her in the house were her children William, Sarah and Alice. During the thirty years there are frequent references to the son William, who married and brought up his family in Middleton. His will, made in October 1727, survives, showing that the family still lived at Abbey in Middleton.[6] There is no hint of his father's disgrace.

For Henry Smorthwait there is no evidence, for the Old Hutton registers

[5] I am most grateful to the County Archivist of the North Yorkshire County Record Office, Northallerton, for finding this baptism.
[6] William Smorthwait's will is among the Lonsdale wills of the Archdeaconry of Richmond at the LRO.

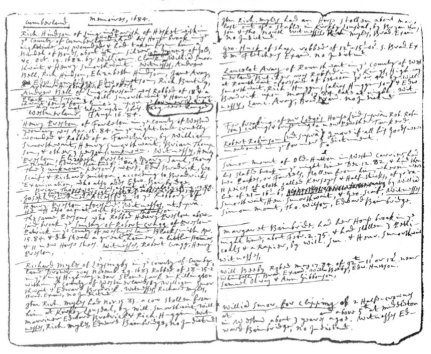

14 Part of the memoirs of Sir Daniel Fleming concerning the trials in 1684. The words 'They were hanged', which indicates the fate of the Smorthwaits, have been ringed by us, near the top of the left-hand page, to make them easier to identify.

do not survive for 1684 and there is no listing of inhabitants. But about the other accomplices we can learn more. Bryan Thompson and the supposed provider of information, Joseph Cartmel, were awaiting trial at Appleby when Judge Jeffreys, accompanied by Fleming, rode there. There are two surviving indictments:

> That Bryan Thompson of Kirkby Lonsdale, labourer, Henry Smorthwait of New Hutton and William Smorthwait of Austwick on 15th April 1684 between the hours of 10 and 12 in the night, with force and arms at Farleton, did break the mansion house of Henry Preston, with the intention of committing a burglary, putting him in fear, and that Joseph Cartmel had consulted with them to do it.

The witnesses were Henry Preston, Elizabeth Preston, Richard Preston, Thomas Thexton and Mary Saule [crossed out]. There was also another indictment, with similar place, date and people, though omitting Cartmel, for wounding Henry Preston with a sword worth 2s. The witnesses were Henry Preston and Mary Saule.

Fleming noted in his 'Memoirs' a few days later that several other possible indictments had never been made. They consequently do not appear in the Assize records. The one concerning Lodge's house we have already quoted.

> The same persons who robbed Henry Preston, broke the smithy of Robert Cragg of Preston Patrick blacksmith Apr.15.84. & did steal a great iron hammer, a little hammer, and 11 new horse shoes. Witnesses, Robert Cragg, Henry Preston.
>
> No indictment for Stonepark robbery, no indictment for theft of cow at Kirkby Lonsdale Novemb.15, no indictment for theft of horse at K.L. from Rich. Myles, no indictment for theft of £12 at Shapp from Geo. Huck, no indictment for theft of 30s from Lancelot Aray of Roundthwait.
>
> For breaking of Mr Lodge's house (vide supra Rob. Robinson) cutting and bruising a new pewter tankard. Robert Robinson. Query if all his goods were mentioned in the former indictment.
>
> Will. Beeby robbed May 17.84. of £92 11s or 12s near Whinfell. See Brad. exam. William Beeby, Edw. Huetson.
>
> William Smor. for clipping 2 half crowns at [blank] and above £5 at Middleton in Westmorland about three years ago. Witnesses Edward Bainbridge. No indictment.

The whole case against Thompson rested on the attack on Henry Preston. Above the names of Thompson and Cartmel in the surviving indictments is written 'not guilty'. In his private memoirs Fleming noted: 'Bryan Thompson was acquit at Appleby Aug.12:84 by a favourable Jury of life and death. The Judge suppressed his being an alehouse keeper' and that Cartmel 'was also acquit with Bryan Thompson'. This would have confirmed Fleming's relief that he had managed to transfer the Smorthwaits to Carlisle.

This trial does not seem to have deterred Bryan Thompson. During the next couple of years he was further involved in various illegal activities, including clipping and coining. Two years later at the Assizes Thompson was again indicted, this time for clipping. In further memoirs, Fleming noted that 'Appleby, Aug.18, 86. Thos. Addison & Geo. Waon received their sentence, as in cases of high treason; they, and Bryan Thompson of Kirkby Lonsdale being found guilty the day before.' This would appear to be the end of Thompson. He had escaped once, then had been found guilty of high treason. In Kirkby Lonsdale manor court book a surrender of property under the date October 1686 mentioned that 'Bryan Thompson was attainted for high treason on 30th August 1683', which had led to the first trial. In December 1686 the same source included a certificate of the possessions of Thompson's wife Bridget, namely those things which on 17 December were her private property. The implication is clear. In cases of high treason, the felon's goods were confiscated. We, therefore turn to the local records, expecting to see either a recorded burial or, at the least, no further references to Bryan. Instead, we find, he lived on. This is explained by the gaol delivery roll for 14th August 1686 'Geo. Waon, Thomas Addison, Bryan Thompson [bracketed together]. Waon and Addison executed, Thompson reprieved.'[7] Thompson continued to live in Kirkby Lonsdale, though his growing poverty is shown by the fact that he received small sums of money from the poor law officers in the last three years of his life. He was buried in 1699, leaving behind a wife who did not die until 1722 and various children, including a son who was frequently presented for various minor offences.

The other figure whose fate we should follow is Edward Bainbridge. Fleming and the other Justices had pleaded for him as a less hardened criminal than the Smorthwaits. He had escaped the gallows three times, in 1679, 1683 and 1684. We may wonder whether he was driven out of the village by local pressure and whether the decision of the Justices was a wise one. In 1686 Bainbridge was back at the Assize for felony, though we do not know for certain on what charge. A gaol calendar for 14 August 1686 lists, among several others we know to be clippers and coiners, Edward Bainbridge. Against him and some of the others is written 'not guilty, delivered'.[8] He continued to worry his neighbours to such an extent that eighteen years later, when he was a man of nearly sixty, the Justices of the Quarter Sessions made an order that he was to give sureties for his good behaviour and to appear at the next court

> the court being fully satisfied upon the information of several very substantial persons that Edward Bainbridge of Gillfoot is and hath been for these many years last past a very notorious person of a disorderly life insomuch that the whole neighbourhood is in great fear of some mischief to be done to their house and goods by Bainbridge.[9]

At the same court Bainbridge was indicted for poaching two salmon from the River Lune in the preceding November. No punishments for these offences are recorded, and it is clear that Bainbridge remained to harrass not only his neighbours but his wife. We know that he finally married in his late fifties, his wife Margaret having a child baptized in the very year when these complaints were made. Four years later we hear of the Bainbridge brothers again in two further orders at the Quarter Sessions. The brothers were both aged over sixty, but they clearly caused trouble to the end.[10]

---

[7] ASSI/47/20, part 6.
[8] *idem*.
[9] Kendal Order book, 1696 to 1724, January 1702, p. 73.
[10] *ibid.*, p.198.

Christmas 1706.

Whereas it appears to this court upon the oath of Margaret wife of Edward Bainbridge and several of the neighbourhood that Edward and John Bainbridge his brother are very dangerous persons, and have threatened the death of Margaret and the burning of the houses of some of the neighbourhood, and they having refused to enter recognizances with sufficient sureties for their appearance at the next general Quarter Sessions of the peace to be holden at Kendal for the county and in the mean time to be of good behaviour towards Margaret. It is therefore ordered that the keeper of the common gaol for the county do take into his custody to keep until they shall be from them enlarged by due course of law and hereof he is not be fail at his peril.

But even to take them to gaol was not an easy matter, as a further order in the same sessions testified.[11]

Christmas 1706.

Upon the humble petition of James Bainbridge [not known to be related] constable of Mansergh showing that by warrant from Christopher Hilton Esq. one of her Majesties Justices of the Peace for this county he was commanded to apprehend the bodies of John Bainbridge and Edward Bainbridge within his constablewick and convey them before Mr Hilton to answer very great misdemeanours laid against them by the wife of Edward Bainbridge. And they John and Edward being very troublesome persons, he the constable was forced to employ two persons to assist him in the conveying the parties to the Justice. And he not having money to discharge the expenses they were at in conveying them, he the constable paid the sum of ten shillings for the charges of two nights and three days, before they could be conveyed to the Justice by reason of their obstinacy. And that the two persons that assisted the constable deserve to have for their attendance of the constable the sum of ten shillings more. And this court having considered and examined the truth thereof, do hereby order that John Bainbridge and Edward Bainbridge upon sight hereof to pay unto James Bainbridge the sum of twenty shillings and the charge of this order, and upon their refusal so to do, that then James Bainbridge shall and may levy the same by distress of the goods and chattels of John Bainbridge and Edward Bainbridge and either of them. And the distress so to be taken to apprize and sell for the said times rendering the overplus if any be and for his so doing this shall be his warrant.

But even after this, the Bainbridges returned to live at Gillfoot among these same neighbours. Edward finally died in Mansergh in 1715, aged 71. His

<hr>

[11] *ibid.*, p.196.

neighbours duly came into the house and made an inventory of his property. They noted no weapons, just a few personal items, some farming tools and a little money. Born eleven years after Sir Daniel Fleming, Bainbridge outlived him by fourteen years.

Since dramatic events like highway robberies and public executions usually attract popular attention, we may wonder whether any legends grew up concerning the Smorthwaits. These would be of interest in themselves, showing how oral traditions alter and distort historical events, and they might also provide clues to the question of where the Smorthwaits were executed. But do they exist?

As far as we know, the Smorthwait trial never became enshrined in a pamphlet or ballad of the time — hence its obscurity until recently. When the antiquary Machell rode through the Lune valley in 1692 he met a number of the participants in the drama, including Sir Daniel Fleming and the whitesmith James Dawson. Although Machell noted many local legends and strange events, he made no allusion to the affair.[12] In fact, it would seem that all had been forgotten, for there is no mention of these events for the next hundred years in the written sources known to me. Yet an oral tradition kept the stories alive, transmuting and embellishing them in various ways. This is a process which can be seen in other parts of the same area. For instance, Thomas Lancaster was hanged as a mass arsenic poisoner in 1672 in north Lancashire and his body was carried from the Assizes at Lancaster and hung in chains in his parish of Hawkshead. Over a hundred years later the young William Wordsworth recalled coming upon the stump of the gallows tree and a hundred years after this a local antiquary reported that people were still telling the story.[13] This illustrates both the power of local traditions and the possibility that a man could be hanged at one place and his body then taken to his home parish to be hung in chains as a warning to his accomplices. This may well have happened in the case of the Smorthwaits and, if it did, would help to reconcile the different accounts of their supposed fate.

The most detailed legend concerning the Smorthwaits was published in 1897 by a local inhabitant of Barbon, Miss Margaret Gibson. The story she tells, written in Yorkshire dialect, is as follows:[15]

A family of the name of Smorthwait lived at 'Abbas' sometime about this

[12] Jane Ewbank (ed.), *Antiquary on Horseback* (Kendal, 1963).
[13] William Wordsworth, *The Prelude or Growth of a Poet's Mind*, ed. E. de Selincourt (Oxford, 1933), p.214; book 11, lines 285ff. H.S.Cowper, *Hawkshead* (1899), pp. 43–4, 225, 326.
[14] A case of hanging in chains at the scene of the crime to deter others is recorded by Pepys, *The Diary of Samuel Pepys*, edited by Robert Latham and William Matthews (1970) II, pp. 72–3.
[15] Margaret Gibson, *A Glimpse into Lunesdale 200 Years Ago* (Kendal, 1897). There is no copy of this rare book in the British Library or Cambridge University Library. I am therefore doubly grateful to Mrs Janet Mason of 'Abba', Middleton, for transcribing the whole book for me and for bringing it to my attention in the first place.

time (two hundred years ago?). A father, mother and two sons. Their history makes me think of those moss-trooping, cattle-lifting days, on the Solway Firth, when no property was safe, if an ill-disposed neighbour could carry it off. This mother certainly had taken a leaf from their book. The father, half reprovingly , would say:

"Yee'll lead t'lads tout gallows!"

A prosperous row of bee-hives was then at Borrens. Said Dame Smorthwait to her sons, "Twould be nowt but a trick o'youth if ya' brought y'ane away", and away the lads went one moonlight night and they carried off the hive and drowned the bees in 'Wammas Dyke'.

Then, as now, fine ducks straddled in and out of the water at Beck-foot, "T'wad be nowt but a trick o'youth if ya' brought one away"!

Once as the story goes on Middleton rose to check these marauders, and its inhabitants flocked to 'Abbas', some of them with pitch forks and other rural weapons of defence in hand, but cunning did not fail the young Smorthwaits, and through an opening in the thatched roof of the house, they had a communication with the stable. Their blood horses were mounted soon and away they went! They swam across the Lune, then in flood and the other side reached, the Smorthwaits cheered and clapped their sides that they were more than a match for their neighbours.

But old Dame Smorthwait's rapacity for plunder grew with her sons' thievish success. So the sheep in the meadows across Lune were the next thing to try for, and very bold and successful the young men were!

But stop. . .!

A search warrant is issued and the lofts visited and the search-officer comes upon fleece after fleece packed away. As each is lifted 'T.G.' (Thomas Godsalve, squire of Rigmaden) is stamped on this, 'T.G.' on that, and so on. "Ye need fash no more aboot it, they're all T.G.'s" cried the Dame.

The curtain falls on these mother-trained thieves, and "Moother mun do what fayther allus said she sud do — lead us tout Gallers so she mun come." And do it she did!

And each son taking an arm, she walked with them up Gallows Hill.

There are many fascinating aspects to this account. The various stories are still told by local inhabitants of Middleton. They remember that the reason the bees were drowned was because they were beginning to escape and sting the young Smorthwaits. The site of the ditch where the Smorthwaits were said to have thrown the bees is still known and it is called 'Wammas dike' ('wamma' being a bee in local dialect). The remains of an opening in the wall of the main bedroom in 'Abba' or Abbey farm, through which the Smorthwaits escaped from the angry mob, is still to be seen. The through-stones down which they climbed to mount their horse in the nearby stable were only recently removed.[16] Furthermore, the important role given to the parents, particularly the mother, has a ring of truth in it. It will be remembered that the Smorthwaits' father died when they were relatively young and that their stepfather Dixon was believed to be an instigator and accomplice of thieves and a petty pilferer. As for their mother, there are several hints of criminality on her part. Fleming has a note in his papers: 'Q. How Mr Middleton died, it being reported that he was poisoned, he having got part of a salmon and bid his wife (now Dixon's wife) make it ready for his supper, which eating, he that night died.' Unfortunately it has been impossible to establish which Mr Middleton this was, or whether the suspicion was ever followed up. We also know that Alice Dixon took away some of the clippings from a servant, who had discovered them in her son's house; and it was Alice who had asked widow Bainbridge what time she would be going to bed the night the widow's house was burgled. Alice Dixon may well have attended the execution, for she was still alive in 1684. She was not buried until 1703 in Middleton, her husband Henry making his will in 1716. The curious overlap of historically verifiable fact and possible invention is further shown in the final discovery of fleeces marked 'T.G.'. There was indeed a Thomas Godsalve at Rigmaden Hall just across the river from the Smorthwaits at the time of the robberies. Though we have seen no mention that his packs were stolen, the legend may be alluding to the fact that the packs of cloth stolen from the carrier Simon Mount were hidden in Godsalve's wood. It is probable that the execution took place at Lancaster Castle. It is known that on the 16 August, when the Smorthwaits were hanged, the judges had reached Lancaster. It seems likely that they had taken the Smorthwaits with them to Appleby and Lancaster in case they should turn out to be useful as witnesses. The facilities for executions, including the presence of an executioner, were probably far better at Lancaster than the other two Assize towns. Certainly, a number of contemporary inhabitants of Kirkby Lonsdale remember stories that the Smorthwaits were hanged at Lancaster.[17]

Their bodies may, like Thomas Lancaster's, have been taken by cart from Lancaster back to their home parish of Kirkby Lonsdale. If this were the case, it would explain a number of other local legends. One of these has been published, in a book written in 1930 by the country solicitor and local

---

[16] Again I am grateful to Mrs Mason for showing me round her house, 'Abba', where Smorthwait once lived, and for providing photographs of 'Wammas dike'.

[17] Mr Jonty Wilson of Kirkby Lonsdale kindly wrote to inform me that the executions probably occurred at Lancaster. Mrs Mason also informs me that Mr Richard Bownass of Middleton Head, whose family has lived in the parish for a number of generations, has heard that the executions took place at Lancaster.

historian Alexander Pearson. Reminiscing about his youth, some fifty years before, he writes:[18]

> When the writer was a little boy, he remembers being told that his grandfather always had a pistol at the ready when he got to the hill on the road close by where Middleton railway bridge now stands, which was a favourite haunt of highwaymen. . . . Anywhere in the neighbourhood of the Crook of Lune was also considered a dangerous place. He said that at one time there were so many highwaymen in the district, that the farmers who used to go to Kendal market would hand over their money to one of their number, who left in such time as to be able to get home before dark, while the rest would return at their leisure. The most unsafe place between Kendal and Killington was one on Hutton Fell called Gillsman Nook. . . . It is said about Killington that some of the highwaymen had their horse hoofs shod backwards so as to confuse those who followed their footprints.

Moreover, at Gillsman Nook according to Pearson, 'a highwayman, who had been caught and executed, formerly used to hang in chains.' This legend appears to be the conflation of two incidents. In 1780 a highwayman was said to have ridden armed out of Kirkby Lonsdale, being seen by Pearson's great-grandfather. It seems likely that this was one of the two men who were described in the *Newcastle Courant* for that year as committing highway robberies between Kendal and Kirkby.[19] But the location of the danger-points and of the last hanging suggest a reference to the events of the 1680s. Certainly Gillsman Nook was an appropriate place to hang Henry Smorthwait. It was near the scene of the robbery of Richard Myles at Stone Park, it was on the border of Henry's parish of Old Hutton, and it was only a couple of miles from the house of John and Edward Bainbridge, which might serve as a warning to them.

Another legend places the actual execution spot elsewhere. An ex-inhabitant of Kirkby Lonsdale, Mr T.E. Aray, was told by his grandfather Edmund Fawcett, who had been born at 'Abba' in 1847, that the Smorthwaits were hanged in a tree in a field called Little Holme, on land belonging to the manor of Rigmaden in Mansergh.[20] It was supposed that this was where the Smorthwaits had been caught. It would be a suitable place as it was across the river from William Smorthwait's house and just down the road from Edward Bainbridge's and it fits well with the legend that the Smorthwaits were finally apprehended for thefts from Thomas

[18] Alexander Pearson, *Annals of Kirkby Lonsdale* (Kendal, 1930), p. 204. Mr Jonty Wilson informs me that it was decided to leave out the names of the highwaymen in the *Annals* in order to avoid offending their descendants, who still live in the valley.
[19] Pearson, *Annals of Kirkby Lonsdale*, pp. 49, 65; J.F. Curwen (ed.), *Records of Kendale* (Kendal, 1926) III, p. 286.
[20] Again I owe the local memories of Mr Aray to the kindness of Mrs Mason.

Godsalve of Rigmaden. Perhaps William's body was hung in chains there. Another possibility is a place still marked on the maps as 'Gibbet Hill', at the extreme north tip of the neighbouring parish of 'Sedbergh. A contemporary inhabitant of Middleton remembers being told by her mother that the hanging occurred at this spot on the 'Fair Mile', the old road leading to Tebay.[21] The position is exactly on the border between Westmorland and Yorkshire and for this reason might have been considered appropriate for a criminal who comitted offences in both counties.

Wherever the hanging occurred, the stories of the Smorthwaits live on in the valley. No other competing legends of either highwaymen or hangings before the nineteenth century, with the exception of the 1780 highwaymen mentioned by Pearson, have survived. The Smorthwaits and Bainbridge were obviously exceptional people in their own way, as was Sir Daniel Fleming in his. When the Justice and the purchasers of the mare's ale clashed in the 1680s they created a unique set of documents which provide an un-rivalled insight into the interplay between personalities, institutions and social forces in the past. The conflict that ended on the gallows reverberates in the popular memory up to the present. Through the lives and deaths of these few men we are able for a moment to dip into the past, to fulfil the prophecy which Maitland made so many years ago: 'Above all, by slow degrees the thoughts of our forefathers, their common thoughts about common things, will have become thinkable once more.'[22]

---

[21] Mrs Mason tells me that Mrs Martindale of 'Borrens', Middleton, heard this from her mother, the late Mrs Conder.

[22] F.W. Maitland, *Domesday Book and Beyond* (Cambridge, 1921), p. 520.

Conclusion: English Violence in Context

How are we to interpret the events brought to light by Fleming? In other words, with what are we to compare them? Do they suggest that England was a violent place characterized by the presence of a brutalized peasantry who were suffering from the side-effects of a massive social, economic and political revolution? One approach would be to compare the records with our own notion of our present society. This would be fruitful, but we need to relate like to like, which would mean using depositions and verbatim reports from a recent criminal trial. If we selected one of the most sensational cases in the central criminal courts, the levels of reported violence would probably seem at least as great as those for seventeenth-century England. An alternative strategy is to compare the preceding narrative with other accounts based on roughly comparable types of documentation for other societies. This would help to stress the special features of the case. Furthermore, since an implicit and sometimes an explicit analogy is often drawn between England in the past and other 'peasantries', it would be useful to consider what is behind the analogies. When certain historians speak of the violence of past societies, what do they have in mind?

The choice of comparative cases is not easy. There are thousands of nations and societies in the world and we could select any of them at almost any point in their history. Fortunately, our choice is limited to studies of violence, crime and order in societies which might be broadly classified as 'peasant'. I have taken three cases recently documented by historians and anthropologists. The first is from China, chosen because it describes a period in the second half of the seventeenth century which is exactly contemporaneous with the events analysed in England. The second is from France during the eighteenth and nineteenth centuries, selected because the country was one of England's closest Continental neighbours. The third example is from Sicily in the nineteenth and early twentieth century, and is used because a recent study has specifically attempted to document from that country the very type of transition with which we are concerned, namely that from peasantry to capitalism, and its supposed reflections in the fields of crime and violence. Three objections, at least, could be made to these choices. Firstly, it could be argued that to compare Europe and China is absurd. At one level this is true, but only if we take the comparisons too literally. The aim is to give an idea of the *bounds* of violence, to answer the question, what does real violence in a pre-capitalist society look like. In other words, what *could* England have been like if it had been a truly violent society? A second objection concerns the accuracy of the observations in our selected cases. Is it not possible that the historians and anthropologists who have studied them have exaggerated the violence and brutality? This may well be the case; if so, readers may wish to take these accounts as 'ideal types' rather than fully established historical analyses. But I doubt whether anyone who reads the descriptions from which the extracts are taken will feel that the whole picture of violence can be explained away as a construction of the investigator. A third objection is that I have selected extreme cases, which is true again. Probably none of the historians quoted in the introduction would envisage England in the past as being quite like nineteenth-century Sicily, though they might go so far as to recognize its similarities with France. Yet I believe that it is important to take fairly extreme cases in order to impress on ourselves what real violence means — for many people in the past and in much of the world today. Furthermore, it is not the particular excesses which are most interesting, but the numerous general features which seem to emerge from these studies.

Our first comparative example is China. Jonathan Spence has published a study of country life in an 'unremarkable backwater' in later seventeenth-century China. The county of T'An Che'Eng, with a population of some 60,000 in the 1670s, was more heavily peopled though smaller in geograph-ical area than the county of Westmorland in England at the same period. The main focus of Spence's study is the years 1668–72, whereas ours is the years 1680–84. His sources are somewhat inferior to those for England at the same period, and he admits the absence of the detailed records which would normally be available to a historian of Europe.[1] Yet the author has access to a full county history, the memoirs and handbook of a local magistrate, and fictional essays and short stories written by P'u Sung-ling. These enable Spence to describe both the general and specific nature of order and violence in a corner of a traditional peasant society.

[1] Jonathan D. Spence, *The Death of Woman Wang: Rural Life in China in the Seventeenth Century* (1978); a wider general study that gives a broadly similar picture is Roland Mousnier, *Peasant Uprisings in Seventeenth-Century France, Russia and China* (1960; 1971 edn), translated by Brian Pearce, pp. 281–301.

The general picture is one of overwhelming suffering and violence and, as described in the first chapter, confirms the realities of existence in a real 'subsistence' economy. Many of the inhabitants of the country had died in risings in 1622 caused by mass misery. 'Many more from T'an-ch'Eng died in the 1630s from hunger, from banditry, from sickness.' In the 1640s locusts destroyed the crops and famine spread. As a local proverb put it, 'To have the bodies of one's close relations eaten by someone else is not as good as eating them oneself, so as to prolong one's own life for a few days.' Bandits followed the famines, an army of several thousand strong moving through the county looting and burning and even besieging the main city. Then the Manchu troops entered the country and slaughtered tens of thousands of inhabitants. The horrors continued with massive flooding in the late 1640s which destroyed crops and caused further famines. Large bandit bands roamed the countryside and sacked the city. We are told: 'The *Local History* has poignant stories about each of the raids: woman Yao, aged seventeen in 1648, cursing the bandits as they dragged her out of her house, still cursing as they cut off her arm and killed her.' There was another famine in 1665 and a massive earthquake in 1668, after which 'over half the people were dying of starvation, their homes were all destroyed and ten thousand men and women were crushed to death in the ruins.' There were many suicides, cannibalism, mass executions of rebels and bandits, dire poverty and enormously heavy taxation.[2]

It will be well to bear this background in mind when we come to compare China with England, for it alone can help to explain the stories of daily life which Spence narrates, of intimidation and thuggery and beating up of witnesses at the court door, of beating a little boy to death in order to get his inheritance, of the strangling of woman Wang by her husband.[3] The general impression is of a very insecure and violent society, while the presence of family vendettas is shown in the Legal Code, which specified that, of the many different kinds of murder, the killing of three persons in one family was the worst.[4] Such feuding is best illustrated in a chapter called 'The Feud'. There are two accounts, which make an instructive comparison with the English evidence. The first is based on a short story by P'u Sung-ling, who had observed in real life how 'misery spawned recklessness and sudden, unreasoning violence that were almost impossible to deal with.'[5] Only two incidents from this complicated story can be given here. It describes a violent man named Ts'ui who hated to see injustice. When he found a vicious wife mistreating her mother-in-law, he was enraged and cut off her nose, ears, lips and tongue and left her dead.[6] The

[2] Spence, *Woman Wang*, pp. 4–9.
[3] *ibid.* pp. 57, 75, 131–3.
[4] *ibid.* p. 89.
[5] *ibid.* p. 79.
[6] *ibid.* p. 80.

whole affair was kept out of court. On a later occasion he went to a wife-stealer and ripped him open, also murdering the stolen wife.[7] The wrong man was caught and was tortured for over a year before the matter was resolved. The background to the story was a world of brigands and bandits, and a gang led by the Wang family terrorized the region. The family was rich and ravaged other substantial families; any who protested were slaughtered on the road. Sometimes a member would be imprisoned, for strangling his wife perhaps, but the culprit would bribe the magistrate and be set free. Other gangs of robbers 'sprang up everywhere' at this time, 'pillaging the villages and grazing grounds in the area'. Finally, a group of villagers in desperation resisted one of the gangs and there was a mass slaughter, 'robbers with severed heads and shattered limbs lay piled in confusion on the valley floor.' Twenty remained alive and begged for mercy; their noses and ears were cut off and they were set free.[8]

All this could be dismissed as exaggerated fiction if it were not for the records of very similar events at the time. Spence describes the activities of a gang based on a real family Wang, who purchased a fortified farmhouse. Groups of horsemen rode out at night armed with swords and bows, but no one dared report the matter to the authorities. Finally, a local inhabitant in a quarrel accused the Wangs of being thugs. Eight of them attacked his house, spearing him in the stomach and cutting him to pieces. They also cut down three of his sons and wounded two guests in the house. Even then, none of the attacked family or neighbours accused the gang publicly. When a magistrate found out the truth, there was some doubt as to whether he had enough troops to deal with the gang. In theory he had three detachments of regular soldiers, 150 soldiers in the garrison, and troops in other smaller garrisons, as well as his own personal staff of 103, 50 militia and eight police constables. But the forces squabbled, they were undermanned and their horses were in terrible condition. The magistrate had to attack by stealth and still found the place fortified and impregnable. He was only able to kill the Wangs in a pitched battle, after luring them out of their hideout. Even when the two Wangs had been killed, there was universal terror, and 'the gentry packed their possessions, fearing there might be a general rising of the Wangs' supporters.' Indeed, eighty households probably connected with the gang fled the next day.[9]

Although one could object to the remoteness of China, this study has been quoted at length, because it is one of the very few to describe the activities of particular bands of robbers in the seventeenth century. In this way, it provides many interesting features of comparison with the robbers of Westmorland in the same period. And, though Spence has chosen the

---

[7] *ibid.* p. 83.
[8] *ibid.* pp. 84–8.
[9] *ibid.* p. 97.

seventeenth century, it is clear that similar events continued until the end of the nineteenth.[10] Apart from the geographical distance the major defect for our purposes is the fact that the local records, particularly criminal depositions, have not survived in the Chinese case. Both these shortcomings are remedied if we turn to France.

It is obviously difficult to represent fairly such a large and diversified country over several centuries, but the substantial agreement between three studies of patterns of crime and justice in France is encouraging. They are all based on the fact that the quality of documentation is particularly good for parts of France from the eighteenth century. As the authors of the first study explain, 'In an English investigation and trial, rumour, hearsay and much superfluous detail about the background of a crime are elicited and used by investigators but are inadmissable or irrelevant in court' and are therefore seldom recorded. In France, however, the judges ran the investigation in criminal trials and consequently 'depositions, examinations and confrontations of witnesses, and lengthy interrogations of suspects formed an integral part of the judicial dossier.'[11] In their examination of patterns of violence in the rural community of eighteenth-century Brittany, Le Goff and Sutherland have used this 'wealth of direct testimony by ordinary people' as a 'unique kind of listening devic: to reveal the day to day tensions within rural society'.[12]

They find that external authority was 'resisted tenaciously' and 'appealed to only in certain circumstances'. [13] Fear, as in the case of the Chinese peasantry, partly explains this reluctance to prosecute. There were gangs of thieves roaming the countryside, one of which threatened to burn the houses of victims who informed on them. This was so effective that though they were held responsible for at least four murders and thirteen violent robberies over a period of twenty-three years, nobody could be induced to come forward to witness against them. The cases which did finally come to a court seem to have been 'a terminal stage in long-standing family feuds'.[14] It required a very large amount of illegal activity before the courts were used and instances are given of considerable violence and harrassment going unpresented. The authors believe 'that much of rural crime went unpunished by legal authorities', the local community resisting the national law and the formal legal officers.[15]

[10] Barrington Moore Jr, *Social Origins of Dictatorship and Democracy* (Peregrine edn, 1969), pp. 214–15.
[11] T. J. A. Le Goff and D. M. G. Sutherland, 'The Revolution and the Rural Community in Eighteenth-Century Brittany', *Past and Present*, 62 (February 1974), p. 97.
[12] *idem*.
[13] *ibid*. pp. 100–101.
[14] *ibid*. p. 103.
[15] *ibid*. p. 104. For a good anthropological account of some of the justified reasons for peasant suspicion of outsiders, see F. G. Bailey, 'The Peasant View of the Bad Life', reprinted in *Peasants and Peasant Societies*, edited by Teodor Shanin (Penguin, 1971).

As well as the opposition between the community and the national law, there was another notable feature — the internal divisions between groups in the village and between villages. Feuds between families could last over a number of years, with pitched battles between groups of kin,[16] and 'in the same sort of way, little wars between neighbouring parishes or sections of larger parishes could occur.'[17] This was all part of a very easy resort to physical violence. Instances of assault appear for very small offences and it is the authors' opinion that the 'countryside was a turbulent world which had its own ways.' Even football matches were 'little more than a ritualized battle between parishes'.[18]

The authors do not believe that this was a state of things restricted to Brittany. Again, stressing the opposition between the local community and the national law, they write:

> It is hard to escape the conclusion that under the old regime as it had existed in Brittany, perhaps in most of rural France, as long as the violence. rowdyism, feuding, petty thieving and the like . . . did not interfere with the collection of taxes and general order, the state preferred not to interfere. The old regime had governed largely by not governing; it allowed rural communities to settle the bulk of their own affairs.[19]

A study of Languedoc in the south of France supports the view that this was not a specifically Breton phenomenon and, as the author writes, 'this marked propensity of Breton communities for going their own way was clearly not unique.'[20]

Olwen Hufton's study is based on an analysis of 350 cases for the 28,000 inhabitants of the diocese of Lodeve in Languedoc, taken from the written complaints made to the military governor. The author stresses the absence of any effective central police force, as in Brittany. But in Languedoc the position was even worse because of the widespread possession of firearms, which the mounted police had totally failed to curb. This added an edge to the bullying and brutality described at length by Hufton and vivid detail is given to support the remark that 'there were communities . . . in which seigneur-baiting was part of the ritual of leisure.'[21] Battles between the servants of the seigneur and the villages were frequent, and in one instance they took place almost weekly, over a period of nearly fourteen years,

[16] *ibid.* p. 105.
[17] *idem.*
[18] *ibid.* p. 107.
[19] *ibid.* pp. 107, 119.
[20] Olwen Hufton, 'Attitudes Towards Authority in Eighteenth-Century Languedoc', *Social History* III, no. 3 (October 1978), p. 283.
[21] *ibid.* p. 287.

between the assembled youth of the village and the baron's servants.[22] Much of the violence was connected with the presence of 'youth groups', that is associations of young unmarried men, who held drinking bouts and organized 'rough music' or public noise against those who offended community sensibility. Hufton ends by referring to the dilapidated state of the prisons, from which offenders often escaped, and to the 'more anonymous groups of bandits, armed thugs and malicious vagrants who periodically terrorized particular localities'.[23]

How exceptional was this picture of local violence? Hufton believes there is evidence that Languedoc was not unusual in its 'ritualized constant bitter friction between seigneur and vassal, the frequent baiting of the parish priest . . . the over hasty recourse to the gun and the steadfast ignoring of government decrees'. Loathing of the seigneur and the use of guns were widespread, and 'the public hatred was the most constant and powerful expression of community solidarity, a binding force in a society often otherwise marked by private altercation and fragmentation.'[24] She maintains that the work of Le Goff, Sutherland and Carstans would impress anyone with 'the degree to which the vendetta could monopolize private leisure'.[25] What is particularly useful for us is that this picture of France is based on depositions, examinations and interrogatories which, although they necessarily distort the amount of violence and crime, are directly comparable to the evidence collected by Fleming.

Hufton is describing part of France in the eighteenth-century pattern. But when did this pattern begin and end? About the ending we know more than the beginning, and the most interesting finding is that this eighteenth-century world, as portrayed above, continued until almost the end of the nineteenth century in France. This can be seen in a recent study by Eugene Weber, who has described how a basically 'peasant' society changed into a unified French nation only in the last quarter of the nineteenth century, when weights and measures, dialects, costumes, transport, the economy and many other features became standardized. We may look briefly at his characterization of the field of law and justice in the 'traditional' society. He finds the same opposition to outside law and outside law-enforcement officers which is so striking a feature of the eighteenth-century studies. He writes: 'One solid reason for the peasant's abiding suspicion of all comers lay in the devastating intrusions of the alien law and its representatives into his world.' Gendarmes were frequently attacked when interfering with local crime, and peasants prayed 'My God, deliver us from all ill and from justice.'[26] This was not because the local community was able to deal

[22] *ibid.* p. 289.
[23] *ibid.* p. 300.
[24] *ibid.* p. 301.
[25] *idem.*
[26] Eugene Weber, *Peasants into Frenchmen: the Modernization of Rural France, 1870–1914* (1977), pp. 50–51.

effectively with violence:

> The War Ministry Archives fairly bulge with reports of thefts, rapes, robberies, fires set in vengeance or out of spite, infanticide, parricides, and suicides; with fights, scuffles, brawls, frays, even pitched battles between poachers and gendarmes, poachers and gamekeepers, smugglers and customs men, peasants and forest guards, rival villages, youth gangs, and conscripts; and with countless homicides, premeditated murders, and attempted murders.[27]

There is a pattern to this activity: crimes against poverty, especially theft, were more frequent in the towns, while in the countryside[28] crimes of physical violence, including sexual assaults and attacks on children, were more common and thefts were very often of trivial objects like a handkerchief or a few sous. The countryside was unsafe, particularly the forests and the lonely roads and especially at night;[29] gangs of bandits roamed the countryside, notably in the wilder regions of Corsica.[30]

Violence was not just caused by outlaws and professional bandits, however. The same internal disputes documented by eighteenth-century historians continued. Battles between villages took place until the start of the First World War; for instance 'the Lot archives contain a very fat file on the subject — bloody scenes, combats, disorders, serious wounds, treaties of peace, and rumours of war.'[21] Traditional rivalries 'between gangs, generally youthful, representing wards of the same village, rival hamlets of the same parish, or rival villages of the same district' survived until the end of the century.[32] The disorders were worst in remote and mountainous regions, such as the Auvergne, where the 'slightest squabble could end in murder and mayhem.'[33] They were exacerbated by the presence of bands of roaming peasants, either self-consciously attacking gendarmes or forest guards, or merely driven to desperation by crushing poverty. We are told of the 'persistence of beggars and begging vagrants as one of the major social problems of the nineteenth century. . . . Hordes of starving peasants swarmed into the towns and tried to intimidate the city folk into charity. . . .By Jules Méline's estimate, there were around 400,000 beggars and tramps in 1905 (1 per cent of the total population)' and consequently 'battalions of the famished' were a 'real scourge for our countryside'.[34]

---

[27] *ibid.* p. 51.
[28] *ibid.* pp. 53, 58, 62.
[29] *ibid.* p. 54.
[30] *ibid.* p. 55.
[31] *ibid.* p. 57.
[32] *idem.*
[33] *ibid.* p. 58.
[34] *ibid.* pp. 62, 63, 65.

It could be argued that the records of military and judicial institutions necessarily convey a picture of disorder and violence. It is not difficult to see what impression we would have of present society if we merely used such sources, in conjunction with certain newspapers. But this again makes the findings comparable to the English evidence. Our final example is indeed an extreme case — a study by Anton Blok of the mafia of a Sicilian village for the period 1860–1960 — but it has been chosen for three reasons. First, it deals explicitly and theoretically with the central question of the effects of the transition from 'traditional', 'peasant' societies, to the modern nation-state, making certain predictions about the supposed features of this transition. Secondly, it is based on a combination of historical and anthropological work, and includes first-hand experience of what it is like to live in a society which still contains many vestiges of the world documented for China and France in the past. Thirdly, it is basically a village study and hence makes a good comparison with the parish of Kirkby Lonsdale.

Blok's argument is that we see in Sicily the side-effects of the dislocation of a feudal or peasant society under the impact of a market economy and the centralizing tendencies of the nation-state.[35] We are able to observe in the nineteenth century a nation-state imposing itself 'on a marginal peasant society which was still largely feudal in its basic features'.[36] The development in some parts of Europe in the sixteenth century, by which the nation-state replaced 'churches, clans, empires, cities, federations etc.', occurred in Sicily only during the nineteenth and twentieth centuries.[37] Corruption, and the mafia for that matter, are inherent parts of societies in a relatively early phase of state-formation', and *mafiosi* are a structural 'concomitant with the gradual transformation of a feudal, dynastic state-society, into that of a nation-state'.[38] The argument stresses that, while bandits are completely outside the law and are one side-effect of the transition, the *mafiosi* are just as important, acting as 'brokers', as middle-men, tolerated by the law and the landlords as the informal agents of order. They inhabit the interstices between landlord and peasant, city and country, the 'Great' and the 'Little' traditions which are central features of peasant societies. They rise and decline in relation to the central power, for there is an 'inverse relationship in a given setting and acceptance of private violence and the level of state control over the means of coercion'.[39] The weakness of the state in Sicily throughout most of the last 150 years, together with great poverty, an adverse climate and terrain, and the social

---

[35] Anton Blok, *The Mafia of a Sicilian Village, 1860–1960: a Study of Violent Peasant Entrepreneurs* (Oxford, 1974), pp. 39, 55.
[36] *ibid.* pp. 6–7.
[37] *ibid.* p. xxi.
[38] *ibid.* pp. 228, 213.
[39] *ibid.* p. xxviii.

atomism caused by a cognatic kinship system, have combined to produce, we are told, a situation where informal violence has flourished.

Only by reading Blok's book can one appreciate the full magnitude of the violence, comparable in scale to that of seventeenth-century China. Violence was ingrained: 'The recourse to violence prevalent in this part of Sicily and expressed in theft, extortion, ransom, arson, shooting, and homicide was taken for granted and accepted rather than questioned.'[40] Peasant uprisings were common, and the countryside was frequently infested by bandits and mafia, whose brutality and feuds are described in numerous passages in the book.[41] The police fought pitched battles with the bands, but were often unable, though heavily armed, to round them up. In one successful purge in 1946, 'ten main bands and 200 minor criminal associations were eliminated. . . . Hundred of bandits were arrested or killed in the inland areas.'[42] Bandits were only the most conspicuous part of the phenomenon, for the *mafiosi* usually managed to avoid being brought to court. Every gesture, every organization, every activity was saturated by violence; even everyday language reflects 'the part played by unlicensed violence in Sicilian peasant society'.[43] Some indication of the dimensions of such violence is contained in the figures for crime from the village where Blok worked as an anthropologist.

The province of Palermo, with a population of about half a million in the 1870s, was rich in criminal activity: during six months in the year 1871, there were 81 recorded murders, 164 cases of highway robbery, 65 cases of cattle rustlings, 18 cases of arson, and continuous assaults on mail coaches.[44] The village of Genuardo provides a microcosm of the province, though figures are given only for the twentieth century. The village population fluctuated between roughly 2,000 and 2,500 persons, making it only slightly smaller than the Westmorland parish of Kirkby Lonsdale.[45] We are told that 'From 1916 to 1966 no less than 93 homicides were reported in the territory of Genuardo'; how many were unreported we do not, of course, know. This village was not exceptional. The nearby village of Godrano, with a population of roughly 1,500 persons, had some 49 assassinations during the period 1918–56.[46] Homicide is only the most extreme form of violence. In an appendix which describes cases of private violence in Genuardo since 1945, Blok outlines numerous instances of serious assault

---

[40] *ibid.* p. 174.
[41] For example, *ibid.* pp. 103ff.
[42] *ibid.* p. 204.
[43] *ibid.* p. 211.
[44] The 1871 figures are derived from an estimate for 1861 that the province had 584,000 inhabitants, of whom 194,000 lived in the principal city. I am grateful to Dr Blok for providing these figures.
[45] *ibid.* p. 244, appendix B.
[46] *ibid.* p. 160.

and kidnapping. As well as these, 'in the period from 1944 through 1962, the territory of Genuardo was afflicted by scores of cattle raids.'[47] These were not just thefts of individual animals, but whole flocks of sheep and goats and herds of cows being driven off, with the culprits very rarely caught.

What is particularly interesting in Blok's book is that he advances certain hypotheses for a country undergoing the transition from feudal or peasant to the modern, capitalist, nation-state. Blok assumes that this transition is always accompanied by the violence, bandits, mafia, corruption and feuding that we find, possibly in an exaggerated form, in Sicily. Although he does not develop this theme much in the text, he does allude to Elias's theoretical model of the 'civilizing process', which postulates that 'the level of socially permitted physical violence and the threshold of repugnance against using it or witnessing it, will differ in specific ways at different stages in the development of societies.'[48] If England had gone through such a transition in the sixteenth and seventeenth centuries, then we should observe these side-effects. That it did undergo a revolutionary change and that the side-effects are indeed visible, appears evident to Blok. After citing Elias he proceeds to quote Lawrence Stone's study of the English aristocracy which, he says, 'demonstrates these interconnections very clearly', showing how the Tudors, 'after a long and sanguinary struggle', managed to promote forcibly 'the development of elite civility'.[49]

Blok's work is concerned chiefly with semi-legitimate mafia. Another feature of peasant violence, social banditry, is only discussed in passing. Yet we have seen that this was of central importance in China and possibly in France. Fortunately, E. J. Hobsbawm has provided a succinct summary of this phenomenon in his book on bandits. This again puts forward some useful suggestions about what we might find in England in the past. Hobsbawm draws a sharp distinction between bandits and other kinds of robber: social bandits, as he calls them, are 'not regarded as simple criminals by public opinion', but represent 'a form of individual or minority rebellion within peasant societies'.[50] 'The point about social bandits is that they are peasant outlaws whom the lord and state regard as criminals, but who remain within peasant society, and are considered by their people as heroes, as champions, avengers, fighters for justice, perhaps even leaders of liberation, and in any case as men to be admired, helped and supported.'[51] They are not just gangs from the professional 'underworld', or mere

---

[47] *ibid.* p. 239.
[48] *ibid.* p. 176, citing the work of Norbert Elias.
[49] *ibid.* p. 177n.
[50] E. J. Hobsbawm, *Bandits* (Pelican edn, 1972), p. 17.
[51] *idem.* The danger of sentimentalizing bandits is suggested by Barrington Moore, *Dictatorship and Democracy*, p. 214.

common robbers; for example they do not steal from other neighbouring peasants, for 'it would be unthinkable for a social bandit to snatch the peasants' . . . harvest in his own territory.' They are explicitly of peasant origin, sharing the traits of their fellows: 'peasant bandits, like most peasants, distrust and hate townsmen.'[52]

For Hobsbawm, banditry and peasantry are causally connected. Obviously the intensity of banditry will vary with the level of political integration, but the general association is clear. Thus banditry, like peasantry, is a universal feature of agricultural societies just before they become capitalist. We are told that 'social banditry . . . is one of the most universal social phenomena known to history', and its amazing uniformity is 'the reflection of similar situations within peasant societies, whether in China, Peru, Sicily, the Ukraine, or Indonesia'. It is to be found 'throughout the Americas, Europe, the Islamic world, South and East Asia', while it 'seems to occur in all types of human society which lie between the evolutionary phase of tribal and kinship organization, and modern capitalist and industrial society.'[53] Banditry is at its worst in times of political or economic dislocation, and so 'tended to become epidemic in times of pauperization and economic crisis', as in the sixteenth century in the Mediterranean region, or seventeenth-century Germany during the Thirty Years War.[54] While it is endemic in peasantries, it becomes epidemic during the transition from peasantry to capitalism. The presence of banditry on a large scale 'may reflect the disruption of an entire society, the rise of new classes and social structures, the resistance of entire communities of people against the destruction of its way of life'. This clearly happened in much of Europe with the change from one type of system to another between the sixteenth and eighteenth centuries, and it is not surprising that, according to Hobsbawm, these centuries were 'probably' the 'great age of social banditry. . . in most parts of Europe'.[55] The connection with peasantry is very deep: 'Bandits belong to the peasantry. . . . They cannot be understood except in the context of peasant society.'[56] One reason for this is that, as stressed for France and elsewhere, weak political integration makes the 'peasant community' largely autonomous. The central government is unable to eradicate bandits for 'in the pre-industrial period the eye of central government does not penetrate too deeply the undergrowth of rural society, unless its own special interests are involved.'[57]

Thus we have several hypotheses. Peasantry and banditry are inter-

[52] Hobsbawm *Bandits*, pp. 17, 18.
[53] *ibid.* p. 18.
[54] *ibid.* p. 22.
[55] *ibid.* p. 23.
[56] *ibid.* p. 130.
[57] *ibid.* p. 90.

connected in general and banditry will be especially prevalent as the clash between peasantry and capitalism intensifies. The watershed between these two systems in western Europe, including England, is the fifteenth to eighteenth centuries, and this should be a peak time for banditry. They will be particularly active in periods of political or economic uncertainty, weak government, uncertain harvests. Geographically, they lurk on the margins, in forests, fens, mountains, in the 'Water Margin', for they are outside the law and need to be able to evade the officers of the state. But it is not just because of the remoteness and inaccessability of the mountains that we find bandits congregated there. Upland regions are usually suited only to a pastoral economy, but animal rearing requires a small amount of human labour and so there is often a surplus of population, impoverished and seeking a bi-occupation. Some migrate to the towns, others become mercenary soldiers, but 'Nothing is more natural than that some of them should become bandits, or that mountain and pastoral regions in particular should become classical zones for such outlawry.'[58]

It is obviously extremely difficult to generalize about 'peasantry'; each society is different and changes over time. Nor would it be fair to leave the impression that 'pre-modern' societies are universally characterized by the phenomena described in the case studies we have selected. It would, no doubt, be possible to show not only that many simpler societies have a remarkable absence of violence, but even that certain well-governed peasantries have at certain periods been largely free of endemic violence. Yet we cannot dismiss these recent studies altogether. They do suggest that we should expect certain features in a country like England, if it really was going through the widely believed transition from peasant/feudal society to capitalist/modern during the three centuries from about 1450 to 1750. We should find bandits, something akin to *mafiosi*, youth gangs, family feuds and vendettas, a high level of physical violence but low level of theft, wandering bands of vagrant beggars and the other traits already described. As we have seen a number of historians of the period have believed that they have, indeed, discerned many of these signs. But before we accept their view, perhaps it is worth looking once more at the evidence. In doing so, we will attempt to go beyond E. P. Thompson's *Whigs and Hunters*, where a similar venture was hampered by the mysterious destruction of the crucial court depositions.

We have examined the longest, best-documented set of violent events recorded in the northern Assizes in the period 1650–1750. They occurred at a time of particular economic and political dislocation and in a broad period which saw the supposed final triumph of a new political, economic

---

[58] *ibid.* p. 31. For a similar thesis, linking banditry with peasantry and the weakness of central control, see Barrington Moore, *Dictatorship and Democracy*, pp. 213–15.

and social system over a previously peasant and feudal one. To what extent did the patterns of violence and order conform to the general descriptions given of the other societies?

The nature of the crimes for which inhabitants of northern England were prosecuted is in striking contrast to that recorded for the other peasantries we have cited. Elsewhere, the major offences were physical assaults, often homicides, and included sexual assaults and attacks on children. These types of crime are almost totally absent for Westmorland. We encounter less than half a dozen persons suspected of murder or homicide during the fifty years 1650–99 for the county. Of really serious and brutal assaults involving the loss of limbs or serious injuries, there are very few indeed. Even the Smorthwaits and their associates do not kill or maim; in their worst attack, on Henry Preston, they left a man unable to walk for three weeks, but normally they just pricked their victims on ears or nose. A comparison of Blok's figures for homicides in Sicily with those of Westmorland shows an entirely different world.

Nor is there much evidence of the other major offences mentioned in the studies of peasantries, namely rape, arson and large-scale cattle rustling. There are no documented cases of any of these for Kirkby Lonsdale in the hundred years after 1650, and scarcely a case for the whole of Westmorland in the surviving records for 1650–99. Though the Bainbridge brothers threatened to set their neighbours houses on fire, there are no records of attacks on the haystacks or outbuildings of a hated landlord. There are no recorded assaults on young children, apart from the occasional murder of a new-born bastard child. I have not come across a single prosecuted rape for Westmorland for this period and there is not even a hint of sexual violence in the Smorthwait affair. Nor is it possible to classify the odd thefts of a single sheep, cow or horse as cattle- or sheep-rustling, which involves the driving away of whole herds or flocks of animals, as described for Sicily. The 'peasant' crimes are very weakly represented.

On the other hand, what might be termed 'capitalist crimes', those to do with money and private property, are more numerous. The most obvious of these is counterfeiting coins — an offence which is not mentioned for any of the money-scarce peasant economies in our sample studies, but is of central importance in England. It presupposes a very widespread use of and demand for coinage at the lowest levels. Secondly, the various forms of theft of property were very common. This was not just a matter of stealing food or the odd handkerchief, as described for France, but premeditated theft, intended to obtain money or valuable goods which could be sold. Burglaries and highway robberies were planned to bring in hundreds of pounds, even though the robbers were often misinformed, and there were considerable sums of money, in cash, or bills and bonds, to be had. Theft, a characteristically 'bourgeois' or capitalist crime, has been the central and most prosecuted criminal offence in England since at least the fourteenth century. This is no coincidence.

The nature of the crimes is related to the motives of the criminals. Bandits or 'peasants' tend to commit crimes out of anger or present need. The physical attacks are often the result of wounded honour or as defence against supposed aggression by another party, while the occasional thefts arise out of desperation. But there is no evidence of either of these types of motive in the Smorthwait case. Superficially, if we had only the indictments, we might have believed that the thefts of veal or heifers, or even of money and clothing, were the reactions of a starving peasantry reacting to dearth. But the added information from depositions and local documents enables us to see, from the position of those involved and their other activities, that this was far from the case. It is clear that crime was considered a short-cut to greater wealth, rather than an attempt to stave off starvation. Only this can explain the involvement in such activities of people of the level of the gentlemen William Foster, the wealthy yeoman William Smorthwait, or the clergyman Edmund Lodge. Their behaviour puzzled contemporaries as well. A reported conversation in 1688 concerning coin clipping gives some clue as to the motives. A man said to another: 'I wonder you should follow this course of life having a good estate, to whom William Atkinson replies, thou art a fool in so saying, for I can live better than thee.'[59] It is perhaps easiest to interpret the crimes as stemming from a combination of greed and adventurousness. There is not a hint of the desire to steal from the rich to give to the poor, nothing of political or social criticism, beyond the fact that Bainbridge tried to claim that it was no crime to steal from Robert Robinson, possibly implying that he was rich. It seems that clipping and theft were merely thought to be easier ways to make money than other activities. The risks involved were worth taking and, as in other diversions, may have added to the pleasure. Such activities were bi-occupations: one could combine farming or blacksmithing or alehouse keeping with a little burglary or clipping, just as others would combine it with hunting or knitting stockings.

The lack of social motivation is also shown in the nature of the victims. Bandits and peasants, we are told, seldom rob from their near neighbours; they steal from landlords, townsmen or other more distant and socially superior persons. Yet the Smorthwaits and their associates did not act in this way: they stole from each other, from very close neighbours, from relatives, and from those poorer and weaker than themselves, servants and carriers and drovers. The nearest they came to stealing from the gentry was from the aged Robinson or the widow Bainbridge. It was not Sir George Fletcher's house or park that Bradrick and his associates robbed, though

[59] Fleming, WD/Ry/57.

Bradrick had inspected the house during his supposed courtship of a servant there, but a husbandman's cottage nearby, where they stole small sums of money. They even stole from next-door neighbours, as at Old Hutton or Hawking Hall — hence the need to wear vizards and to alter their voices. Bandits are supported by their fellow-villagers and do not need to disguise themselves since they are known outlaws. But the Smorthwaits carried their vizards in their pockets; they rode armed and at night, as much to avoid their neighbours as the Justices of the Peace.

Thus the pattern of violence reveals no split between town and country or between social classes. There are no hints of battles between peasants and 'landlords', as reported for the other peasantries we have looked at, nor of anything similar to the seigneur-baiting of Languedoc, or the running battles between poachers and gamekeepers described for nineteenth-century France.[60] In the absence of any clear-cut distinction between 'landlords' and others in Westmorland, it would have been surprising if there had been such battles. The Smorthwaits and others were themselves landlords, though minor ones, and they did not attack any of the higher gentry, for example Fleming or Sir George Fletcher or any of the other Justices. The difficulty of deciding who were gentry and who ordinary commoners is indicated by the fact that Willaim Smorthwait himself was styled 'gentlemen' on certain occasions and yeoman or husbandman on others.

If the violence does not highlight clashes between supposed classes, nor does it do so between family groups. The long-standing feuds and vendettas, the answering of blood with blood, which are a central feature of the situations described for France, China and Sicily, are totally absent in the English evidence. Where kinship ties are strong but national justice weak, retaliation and the keeping of the peace is often in the hands of kin, and violence and kinship are closely linked. But in the English evidence from the Smorthwait case there is no suggestion of blood feuding, long-lasting vendettas or anything of that nature. The Bainbridges and Smorthwaits do not emerge as traditional rivals of other specific families, and there is no sign that the wrongs supposedly suffered in this case were passed on to be righted in the next generation. Nor is there any hint of family feuds in the other legal records for the whole period 1650–1750 for Kirkby Lonsdale. Obviously, there were animosities between specific individuals, and even between one family and another, but the character is so different from the violent, inter-generational, feuds described elsewhere as to belong to a different order of things. The absence of feuds and vendettas is marked,

---

[60] Certain parts of southern England in the early eighteenth century had something vaguely approaching these battles, which have been documented in E. P. Thompson, *Whigs and Hunters, the Origins of the Black Act* (Peregrine edn, 1977): see also Douglas Hay *et al.*, *Albion's Fatal Tree: Crime and Society in Eighteenth Century England* (1975).

central and important, and it is difficult to believe that the legal and other records would have completely overlooked such a phenomenon if it had been widely present. For example, the opportunities for retribution against the robbers or members of their families in this case are never recorded as being taken.

This situation helps to explain the apparent absence of fear of assault. Even towards the end of the nineteenth century in rural France, or up to the present in Sicily, many parts of the countryside were unsafe for travellers, especially in mountainous or forested regions and at night. The events described in the Smorthwait case seem to illustrate that, normally, this was not the case in northern England. The abnormal conditions created by the Smorthwaits, who were frightening tradesmen and others, were given as justification by Fleming for particularly stern action against the associates. A great deal of the material in the depositions suggests that it was quite usual for women to travel by themselves, or for individuals to cross the moors alone, with money and at night. This impression is corroborated by the accounts of many of the seventeenth-century travellers in this region, who seem to have journeyed without fear of assault or robbery. There is ample documentation of a vast amount of movement throughout the region, with people driving large trains of pack horses, or herds of cattle, or carrying money back from the market, without apparent fear of robbery.

Nor is there evidence that travellers or the inhabitants of remote hamlets and farmhouses lived in daily dread of bands of wandering, half-starved peasants. Such bands, some of them endemic, others caused by the terrible natural disasters chronicled for many parts of the world before the twentieth century, were a constant threat to law and order in the other peasantries we examined. Moreover, it has long been held that gangs of beggars and vagabonds, partly attributed to the supposed dislocation brought about by the capitalist revolution of the sixteenth and seventeenth centuries, were a central feature of England at this time. One of the very few parish registers mentioning death by starvation comes from just to the north at Greystoke in Cumberland, and it has been suggested that 'crises' of subsistence in this area lasted until at least the middle of the seventeenth century.[61] And although the worst might be over in terms of sheer starvation, it was notably in the hundred years after the Civil War that these extreme regions would have suffered the full effects of the economic revolution which had begun in the south and east. Westmorland, therefore, should have been the ideal setting for organized vagabondage, yet there is not a hint, in either the depositions or any other other records, of such a phenomenon at this period. We know of no such bands entering Kendal or

---

[61] Andrew B. Appleby, *Famine in Tudor and Stuart England* (Liverpool, 1978), especially chapters 7 and 8.

Kirkby Lonsdale. Given the very detailed manor court records for the latter, which list all persons trying to gain settlement in the town, the church-wardens' accounts, which give payments to the poor, the full reporting by constables to the Quarter Sessions, and the careful supervision by the Justices of the Peace, it seems certain that if there had been a perennial or recurrent problem of vagabondage, we should have heard about it. These records do show that there were individual vagrants and beggars. But there is absolutely no sign of a major threat to law and order from wandering beggars, either individually or collectively.

Another potent cause of popular disorder in peasantries — fights between gangs of youths who represent different groups within the parish, or different villages — is also absent. A central feature of many traditional peasantries is the strong boundary between neighbouring communities, with a concomitant hostility towards outsiders, most fully described in the French instances we have cited. If in Westmorland there had been similar inter-village pitched battles, or gangs of wandering youths from different hamlets, there can be little doubt that the legal records would have alluded to them. And if the activities of the Bainbridges of Mansergh had enraged the inhabitants of Killington and they had reacted with force, we would have heard about it. Yet the records of this parish over the hundred years after 1650, as well as those for the rest of Westmorland for the first fifty years of this period, give no indication of anything like the gang-warfare described for France at a later time. There are no reported gangs of youths fighting after drinking or at football matches, no weekly battles. Of course there were disputes between parishes, particularly over boundaries, grazing rights, responsibility for the settlement of the poor and other matters. But these were settled in court, not by physical force. The whole dimension of battles between communities, or between groups within communities, appears to be missing in this region.

The absence of physical violence and everyday fear in Westmorland is reflected in the nature of weapons and defensive fortifications. Widespread violence, with marauding bandits, bands of vagabonds, or family feuds, is usually accompanied by large numbers of weapons, particularly firearms, daggers and swords, fortified houses and fierce mastiffs. The huge proliferation of firearms is described for eighteenth-century Languedoc and nineteenth-century Sicily. But if we look at the Smorthwait depositions and other local documents, it is a different picture. It is true that the Smorthwaits and their accomplices had rapiers and pistols, but their riding around armed was remarked upon as exceptional. The victims of their attacks were usually unarmed, or very lightly defended, Margaret Bainbridge's husband had an old rapier, but widow Bainbridge did not even bother to put it in her bedroom though she suspected there might be robbers. Henry Preston had a sword, and the constable of Killington had an old fowling piece. But on other occasions when assaults and burglaries occurred, there is no mention of weapons in the victim's possession, as in the robbery at Robert Robinson's or in Cumberland. None of those attacked, with the exception of Preston, defended themselves with cudgel, sword or dagger. Nowhere are we told of fierce dogs defending a house, or attacking intruders, though the barking of dogs woke the household in two of the burglaries. Nor is there any evidence that houses themselves were heavily defended, though many were remote farmhouses. The most they had were shutters on the windows, which in the Robinson house were normally left open, and an iron-bar through the front door. The building of fortified houses had ended at least 120 years before the 1680s in this part of Westmorland and there is no trace in the architecture of a defensive need.[62]

To take a more detailed look at the presence of weapons, out of a sample of 412 inventories for the parish of Kirkby Lonsdale in the period 1500–1720, only 24 mention weapons; over nine tenths of the population had no noted weapons. Looking at the inventories by decade, it is possible to see that there was no appreciable change in weapon ownership over the period. In the 33 inventories for 1610–19 there are no weapons mentioned. For the other periods we can express the ratio of 'weaponless' inventories to the total number of inventories mentioning a weapon as follows:

before 1590, 17:1	1660–69, 20:1
1590–99, 11:1	1670–79, 12:1
1600–09, 25:1	1680–89, 16:1
1620–29, 21:1	1690–99, 18:1
1630–39, 15:1	1700–09, 37:1
1640–49, 6:1	1710–19, 22:1
1650–59, 11:1	

As we might expect, the decade including the Civil War in the 1640s produced the highest ratio of weapons. Under-registration would be due to the fact that not all small weapons such as daggers or bows were listed, although three daggers and several bows do appear in inventories; but this is compensated for by the fact that many of the 'weapons' were obviously primarily for hunting rather than fighting. Thus, of the sixteen 'guns' mentioned in these 412 inventories, four are explicitly said to be 'fowling pieces' and another is an 'old' gun. Several of the swords are also said to be

---

[62] Thus, for example, when the antiquary Machell travelled round southern Westmorland in 1692 he found that the fortifications had long decayed; Jane Ewbank (ed.), *Antiquary on Horseback* (Kendal, 1963). C. M. L. Bouch and G. P. Jones, *The Lake Counties, 1500–1830: a Social and Economic History* (Manchester, 1961), p. 36, state that 'from the middle of the sixteenth century to the end of the seventeenth the large house. . .made little or no provision for defence.'

'old', implying that they were basically family heirlooms.[63]

One of the reasons for this conspicuous absence of offensive weapons seems to have been their effective regulation through law. In the warrant against John Bainbridge it was stated that he 'hath divers guns, pistols and other arms (although he is not qualified by law to keep them)'. This was a reference to the laws concerning the keeping of weapons, summarized in Fleming's copy of the *Statutes* under 'Guns and Cross-bows' as follows (Fleming's additions are shown in italics):

> I. Stat.33.H.8.6. None shall shoot in, or *use to* keep in his house or *elsewhere* any cross-bow, handgun, hagbut, or demy-hake, unless his lands be of the value of £100 per annum, in pain to forfeit £10 for every such offence. *Dags, pistols, & stonebows within this act. . .*
>
> III. None shall travel (*save £100 men*) with a cross-bow bent, or gun charged, except in time *and service* of war, nor shoot *in a gun* within a quarter of a mile of a city, borough, or market town, except for the defence of himself or his house, or at a dead mark, in pain of ten pound.

£100 *per annum* income from real estate was a high sum in this area, and it is doubtful whether more than one or two inhabitants of the parish of Kirkby Lonsdale were at this level.

Fleming then summarized some of the exceptions: for example, lords spiritual and temporal and inhabitants of cities, boroughs and market towns could keep large guns. But no one was to shoot, carry or have any gun under the length of three quarters of a yard on pain of forfeiting £10. Anyone seeing such a weapon having £100 of property was to seize it and destroy it within twenty days. None below the degree of a baron was to shoot a gun in a city or town. Of course, the extent to which the law was effectively enforced requires further investigation.

The apparent absence of weapons and of frequent recourse to physical violence is related to two other notable features. The first is that there were no pitched battles between the robbers and the forces of order. This is in striking contrast to the situations described for China, France and Sicily where highly armed, often mounted, police and military forces controlled the countryside, and used to fight pitched battles with gangs of robbers and bandits. Although Fleming did at one time envisage using the trained band, an amateur organization of footmen and horsemen, there is no evidence that it was called upon. The arrests of the arch-suspects on various occasions were made by constables or Justices who were, as far as we know,

---

[63] It is interesting to compare this to a muster held in 1569 by the bishop of Durham. Even for such a warlike occasion, in this border region, 'just over 4,000 out of the total number of 6,477 were without weapons of any kind.' Mervyn James, *Family, Lineage and Civil Society* (Oxford, 1974), p. 37.

either unarmed or equipped only with sword or staff. The robbers some-times fled, but there is no evidence that even William Smorthwait, who talked boastfully of being able to raise as many men as Fleming and the other Justices, ever used his sword or pistol to prevent arrest. Certainly no one is reported as being wounded in any of the arrests. It has long been noted as a characteristic of England that there was no standing army and that when a regular, professional police force developed in the nineteenth century, it was without weapons apart from truncheons. This continued a tradition dating from well before the seventeenth century. Although they caused unusual alarm by being armed and riding and attacking in small groups, the robbers were basically individuals who acted separately. They, and even less minor criminals, did not present a threat which had to be met by strong punitive forces.

Secondly, people did not need to be protected from violence or given access to justice through the less formal channels of patronage and protec-tion, as described in Blok's work on the mafia and *mafiosi* of Sicily. There, amidst the violence of everyday life, and with the huge gap between countrymen on the one hand, and the bureaucracy and power of the towns and of the landlords on the other, a set of intermediary protectors has grown up. More generally, anthropologists have documented the importance of protection by means of patron-client ties throughout the peasantries of the Mediterranean.[64] The weakness of central government and of national law leads to the importance of political protection by 'godfathers' and other patrons. There is scarcely a hint of such political patronage in the Smorth-wait events, and no mention of godparenthood or other 'constructed' kinship ties being of any significance. The person who would most surely have revealed such a system in his own dealings was Fleming, who was in a prime position to act as a patron. It is true that he was once offered money for favour, and some of the letters, particularly those of Robert Robinson and Henry Smorthwait, asked for his protection. But this is a far cry from the deeply ingrained and institutionalized patterns we observe in studies by anthropologists and sociologists. And the Smorthwaits themselves, though they threatened people, apparently never took the opportunity of the fear they aroused to obtain protection money or become political patrons. When protection was needed, it was bought on the open market with cash, by the hiring of professional attorneys or barristers, as is illustrated in several places in the affair.

In fact, the methods by which disputes were settled outside the criminal courts is highly significant: rather than resorting to threats or force, people would use the other legal courts as well as informal negotiators. The depositions give us an unusual insight into a number of cases which

[64] Ernest Gellner and John Waterbury, *Patrons and Clients* (1977).

normally would never have come to our attention. Here we find people hiring attorneys and taking each other to the civil courts, or settling matters out of court for the payment of cash, after influential local inhabitants had been called in to arbitrate. Both these methods are illustrated in the reactions to Bainbridge's theft. In other more minor cases, such as Scaif's pickpocketing, people were prepared to accept their money back again. In general, it seems many were loath to bring criminal charges, which caused bad feeling, cost money and might well rebound. If possible they would settle out of court; if not, they would use another part of the highly elaborate judicial system. This confirms the belief of historians that many crimes do not appear in the surviving legal records. In the particular case of the Smorthwaits, it would seem that at least half the major crimes would never have been prosecuted if the case had not developed into such a serious one.

The unwillingness to prosecute, and the resort to negotiation and money fines rather than to physical violence, is again at odds with what we find in many peasantries. When supposed wrongs are righted there, the punishments are often of a physically brutal kind. The slitting off of noses and ears, the maiming and killing described for China, Sicily or France, are the natural counterpart to the viciousness of the crimes themselves. This violence is a feature both of the informal vengeance of neighbours and kin at the local level, and of the punishments inflicted by the state. Just as the cruelty of peasant rebellions is characteristically quenched by enormous brutality on the part of the landlords and the state so the only way to check violent crimes is by savage penalties.

But in the Smorthwait affair, at the informal level, there is not a single example of 'mob' vengeance, the only trace being in the nineteenth-century legend that the people of Middleton had risen up against the Smorthwaits. This absence of popular retaliation is most marked in relation to Edward Bainbridge. He molested his neighbours for over thirty years, stealing from them, threatening them, leaving their gates open. Yet all they appeared to do was to try to reason with him, urging him to give up his evil ways or, finally, to prosecute and complain about him in the courts. There is scarcely any evidence that people used physical threats or brutal attacks to punish each other. Of course there were assaults, and there were many affrays concerned with the right to particular ownership of houses and fields. But these were on a scale and of a nature which places them in a different class to those we observe in our other societies.

It could well be argued that this was because the state monopolized violence, just as the upper classes monopolized the use of serious weapons. If we read only legal textbooks and the statutes, it would appear that this was indeed so. The official penalties for what seemed to us fairly trivial offences, especially those concerned with property, were very harsh. But if the potential punishments were grave, how many people were actually convicted of such offences, how many were pardoned though convicted, and to what extent were the penalties mitigated in practice? This is not the place to undertake such a study in detail, but the Smorthwait affair lends support to the view that, while the sanctions of the law were severe in theory, in reality it bore less heavily on the population. The reluctance to convict is well shown in this case, for despite the apparently immense evidence, the major figures escaped once and Bainbridge and Thompson escaped again and again.[65] It is well known that, when convicted, perhaps half the condemned escaped execution through a reprieve or pardon.[66] Both Bainbridge and Thompson received pardons and reprieves and, according to Fleming's letter to the Clerk of assize, attempts were being made to obtain a pardon for the Smorthwaits. Gaol calendars for Westmorland frequently contain 're-prieved' or 'transported' against the names of those who one would have assumed, from the indictment, were to be executed. Even when a person was to be executed, the penalty was often lightened. For instance, clip-ping and coining were high treason and, in theory, a man convicted of these offences was to be drawn to the scaffold, hanged by the neck and then cut down, dismembered while alive and his entrails burnt before his eyes, and finally cut into four pieces. In practice, it would seem, those executed for this offence were hanged in the normal way, or at least hanged until dead before the later stages began. In the case of women, for whom the penalty was burning alive, they were usually strangled before being burnt.[67] Perhaps the best characterization of the formal system would be to say that a harsh legal code existed, but that a great deal of flexibility and compromise was permitted in its application. Thus for the whole of Westmorland for the second half of the seventeenth century, perhaps half a dozen persons were hanged for normal criminal offences.

Numerous other indices could be used to point out the difference between the situation revealed in studies of rural violence and banditry in other societies and that shown by the Smorthwait affair. For example, one of the centrally defining features of bandits as opposed to ordinary

[65] Dr Baker estimates that the acquittal rate in the sixteenth to eighteenth centuries was 'between one quarter and one half of those indicted' in J. S. Cockburn (ed.), *Crime in England, 1550–1800* (1977), p. 23.

[66] Citing the work of Cockburn and Radzinowicz, Baker states that 'it has been estimated that the number of convicted felons actually condemned to death, throughout our period, was between 10 and 20 per cent; while the proportion of those condemned who were actually executed probably averaged about one half.' In Cockburn (ed.), *Crime in England*, p. 43. Taking all the figures in this and the previous note into account, it would appear that between 2.5 per cent and 7.5 per cent of those indicted for felony were actually executed.

[67] C. M. Atkinson, 'Trial at York for Counterfeiting', Thoresby Society, IX (1899), p. 225n.

robbers, according to Hobsbawm, is that social bandits are admired and helped by their fellow peasants. While Bainbridge and the others would have liked to encourage others to support them and argued that it was no sin to rob Robert Robinson, they seem to have failed to gain popular favour. There is some evidence that a few young men went around when drunk imitating William Smorthwait, and the reluctance of the juries who were too 'favourable' to them may indicate a certain sympathy. But as we saw in chapter 9, it would be difficult to argue that the Smorthwaits and their accomplices really approached the position described by Hobsbawm. By attacking the houses and persons of their near neighbours, frightening local women late at night, causing general dislocation and anxiety, they alienated many. While their clipping and coining may have fostered no general resentment, it is clear that they were commonly regarded as ordinary, if flamboyant, criminals, whether pickpockets like Scaif, stealing petticoats and sides of veal, or robbing from aged gentlemen, carriers and drovers. Search warrants were taken out by the villagers and local inhabitants did the prosecuting. These were not full-time bandits, shielded from the law, but part-time robbers, threatening those around them not to betray them. We are a long way indeed from social bandits.

We must now try to answer the difficult question of why the English case should be so exceptional. We can find a clue in the English legal and social system, and a striking feature which differentiates it from those of other countries we have documented. One of the most marked characteristics of peasant societies is the opposition between the culture and controls within the local community, what is often known as the Little Tradition, and the rules and norms of the wider society and the state, of the Great Tradition. Combined with vertical gaps between the peasantry and the other estates of lords, clergy and professions, and between the county and the town, this tends to produce a very marked opposition on the part of villagers to the agencies and even the premises of the national law. For instance, in eighteenth- and nineteenth-century France we saw that the formal apparatus of courts and officers was resented and kept at a distance by the villagers; justice and gendarmes were seen as evil threats, and the central government was forced to accept that its hold over a village was weak and superficial.

The documents for Westmorland give an entirely contrary picture. Informal mechanisms of dispute settlement might be widespread, but even they involved attorneys and recourse to courts of law. Constables might be reluctant to present cases but, when they were summoned by Justices, they appeared. There is no indication of a popular opposition to national laws or to the activities of Justices or other law-enforcement officers. There were many reasons for wishing to avoid appearance at court or as a witness, but the system of recognizances, whereby people were bound in large sums of money to appear at court as witnesses or prosecutor, seems to have been effective in making them do so. Likewise, the technique of binding people under pain of similarly large sums not to break the peace seems also to have been observed, on the whole. Furthermore, most adult men were themselves minor legal officials, as we saw for Kirkby Lonsdale. Furthermore in the Smorthwait case they included the major criminals as well as the law-abiding; this means that any analysis in terms of opposition between a Little Tradition of local custom and informal control rejecting the Great Tradition of professional lawmen and law officers is mistaken. The self-policing involved in the English system had long been one of its distinguishing and crucial features.[68]

The experience which people gained of the law is reflected in the depositions and letters in this case, and these, alongside other legal records, show a very considerable awareness of how the law worked, what the laws were, and a general consensus that they were locally applicable and to be observed. There was not one law for the nation and another for the community. Occasionally we find a servant such as Esther Craven perhaps overstressing her ingenuousness, saying that she was not sure whether a certain activity was unlawful. But the total impression is that the multitude of overlapping courts and laws penetrated right down to the level of the lowest inhabitants, and that a Bryan Thompson or George Scaif had a good working knowledge of the national system of criminal law. Such a picture certainly fits well with the other recorded legal activities of the Westmorland inhabitants at the time. In France, China or Sicily, it would be inconceivable that large numbers of villagers should personally initiate complex legal actions against their fellows to be heard in the capital city of the nation, over two hundred miles away, by the highest judges in the land. Yet this is exactly what happened in Westmorland. Between 1550 and 1720, in just one of the central courts, that of Chancery, dozens of cases from Kirkby Lonsdale were heard, each one extending to a large number of written pages of evidence. They concerned small pieces of landed property and other goods in the parish. To people engaged in such litigation, not only in Chancery but in King's Bench, the court of Common Pleas, the ecclesiastical courts and elsewhere, the complexities of the Smorthwait affair would

[68] John P. Dawson, *A History of Lay Judges* (Cambridge, Mass., 1960), provides an excellent account of this legal and law-enforcement system from early times. The Justice of the Peace was clearly a crucial figure here. Fleming may be exceptional, but the case does lend support to the contested theory of John Langbein, namely that Justices had important prosecutorial and investigative roles in preparing cases for the judges in felony cases, as well as in cases of misdemeanour. In fact, the Smorthwait affair and Fleming's activities in it are exactly what Langbein would have expected, though he himself was unable to find conclusive evidence in support of his case. John H. Langbein, *Prosecuting Crime in the Renaissance: England, Germany, France* (Cambridge, Mass., 1974), part 1.

not have seemed great. English society was based on, and integrated by, two principal mechanisms — money and the law. The twin pillars of justice and economics were mutually supporting and avoided the necessity for recourse to either physical or religious persuasion. As Edward Thompson has nicely put it, the rule of the eighteenth-century gentry and aristocracy 'was expressed, above all, not in military force, not in the mystifictions of a priesthood or of the press, not even in economic coercion, but in the rituals of the study of the Justices of the Peace, in the Quarter Sessions, in the pomp of Assizes and in the theatre of Tyburn.'[69]

If it is indeed true that herein lies the key to the difference between England and many other contemporary societies, we are again drawn to the peculiar and exceptional development of the Common Law of England from the twelfth century onwards. For we have already seen that the system of Justices of the Peace, Quarter Sessions and Assizes was established in principle by the thirteenth century, though some features were not formally instituted until the middle of the fourteenth. This is not the place to pursue this story back to those times, but perhaps we can end with citing just one small example from an earlier period.

It has been frequently suggested, as we have seen, that banditry and peasants are associated; it could furthermore be argued that bandits are only the most extreme and visible feature of a whole system of informal violence, which had disappeared in England by the time of the Smorthwaits. If we could find when banditry ceased, we might well gain some clue to the disappearance of the whole pattern of peasant violence. Hobsbawm's book on bandits is a starting point. Many bandits from throughout the world are cited, over 120 names in all, but only two English 'bandits' are included in the name index, Robin Hood and Dick Turpin. Hobsbawm willingly concedes that Turpin, whose behaviour is rather like Smorthwait's, is not a bandit at all but a highway robber who has been accidentally romanticized.[70] This leaves Robin Hood, a particularly important figure since 'the country which has given the world Robin Hood, the international paradigm of social banditry, has no record of actual social bandits after, say, the early seventeenth century.'[71] This is an interesting statement, implying that there are documented bandits for England before the early seventeenth century. Yet none is cited and I know of no historian who has ever discovered any, either for the sixteenth, fifteenth, fourteenth or thirteenth centuries.[72] Of course one can play tricks with words and try to turn

---

[69] Thompson, *Whigs and Hunters*, p. 262.

[70] Hobsbawm, *Bandits*, p. 39.

[71] *ibid.* p. 19.

[72] For example, see John Bellamy, *Crime and Public Order in England in the Late Middle Ages* (1973), especially chapter 3 which shows a state of affairs very different from that predicted by Hobsbawm. The robber gangs seem quite unlike 'social bandits', and for example,' for the

any robber baron or outlaw into a bandit. One can even attempt to transform the whole of feudal society into one vast system of banditry made outwardly legitimate.[73] But if we take Hobsbawm's definitions seriously, we are left with one figure for all those centuries — Robin Hood.

Yet even Robin Hood vanishes in our gaze. Hobsbawm himself admits that while Robin Hood is 'in most ways the quintessence of bandit legend', in 'many other respects. . .[he] is also rather untypical.' Moreover, 'no real original Robin Hood has ever been identified beyond dispute.' This is somewhat deflating: we do not know that such a person ever existed, and even if he did, or in the legends about him, he does not behave as a bandit should. There is no explicit cross-reference by Hobsbawm here, but he may be thinking of the famous controversy in the pages of the journal *Past and Present*, where an attempt to turn Robin Hood into a kind of social bandit, a hero of the peasantry attacking the rich and giving to the poor, failed to demonstrate that there ever was a real Robin Hood, that he was any kind of a peasant or that his victims were the landlord class.[74]

The absence of bandits in England is consistent with the fact that, as I have argued elsewhere, from at least the thirteenth century England has not had any peasants.[75] And just as the word 'peasant', from the French *paysan*, was not used in English of Englishmen before the seventeenth century, so the word 'bandit' from the Italian is of foreign, and late, importation. The Oxford English Dictionary shows that it was not used of English criminals until well after the last possible bandit had disappeared. These foreign words would seem to have been imported in order to re-invest the past with characteristics which it never had and therefore never needed a word for. Thus we end the trail that started at Robert Robinson's burglary and arrive at the strange conclusion that, for several centuries, Englishmen obstinately refused to behave in the way in which many modern academics would like them to have done.

---

most part the leaders were drawn from the gentry, the knights, and esquires' (p. 72), and many of them were subsequently elected to parliament (p. 82) and given local offices (p. 86). Likewise, though James Given uses the words 'bandits', 'robbers', 'burglars' and 'thieves' as synonyms, it appears that the thirteenth-century criminals he describes are very different from Hobsbawm's social bandits. For example, we are told that 'organized groups like Robin Hood's were largely a figment of myth and legend' and rather than attacking lords, townsmen and merchants, the robbers attacked 'peasants' particularly women and children who were present in the houses they robbed. James B. Given, *Society and Homicide in Thirteenth-Century England* (Stanford, 1977), p. 111 and chapter 6 *passim*.

[73] 'European feudalism was mainly gangsterism that had become society itself and acquired respectability through the notions of chivalry.' Barrington Moore, *Dictatorship and Democracy*, p. 214.

[74] The controversy has been republished, with an additional and important recantation by M. Keen (p. 266), in R. H. Hilton (ed.), *Peasants, Knights and Heretics: Studies in Medieval English Social History* (Cambridge, 1976).

[75] Alan Macfarlane, *The Origins of English Individualism* (Oxford, 1978).

Appendix A
Calendar of Major Events

1633   Sir Daniel Fleming born.

1644   Sir George Jeffreys born.
          Edward Bainbridge born.
          William Smorthwait born.

1647   Bryan Thompson born.

1655   Sir Daniel Fleming married.

1664   Robert Robinson High Constable of Kendal ward.

1670   Bryan Thompson married.

1673   William Smorthwait married.

1674   Edward Bainbridge constable of Mansergh.

1676   January or February: burglary at Hawkin Hall, Middleton. Clippings said to be found in William Smorthwait's house.

1677   May: Edward Bainbridge steals veal and a coat in Kendal.

1677–8   William Smorthwait High Constable for Lonsdale ward.

1678   Edmund Lodge goes to live with Robert Robinson in Old Hutton.

1679 or
1680   William Smorthwait goes to live in Clapham, Yorkshire.

1680   Edmund Lodge suspected of stealing a silver cup.
          November 3: burglary at Robert Robinson's in Old Hutton.
          November: Justices warned of armed men and send out warrants.

1681   July 22: William Foster gives information about clipping.
             26: Foster and Stephen Woodworth give information about clipping.
          October 28: two heifers stolen out of a close at Barbon.

1682   April: Esther Craven sees clippings in Old Hutton, she later claims.
          April or May: warrant sent out in Lancashire for arrest of Smorthwaits.

October: Smorthwaits and others commit burglary at Ling near Penrith.

November: Edward Bradrick and others steal horses in Leeds district.

December 12: theft of Simon Mount's pack of cloth.

1683 January 12: Quarter Sessions at Kendal, first informations come in

13: John Jackson taken and committed.

February 12: John Jackson confesses and implicates Smorthwaits.

15: Justices issue warrants for arrests of malefactors.

17: Henry Smorthwait apprehended and committed to gaol.

28: local worthies write to Fleming urging him to further action.

April 20: Quarter Sessions at Kendal, warrants and hue and cry sent out.

June 27: George Scaif committed to prison.

July 10: William Smorthwait apprehended and committed by Henry Bouch, JP.

August 10: Edmund Lodge committed to prison.

13–28: northern Assize circuit of Carlisle, Appleby, Lancaster; Smorthwaits, Lodge and Bainbridge all tried and freed.

November: burglary from widow's house in Killington.

November 15: Richard Myles has cows stolen at Kirkby Lonsdale.

29: Richard Myles robbed on Killington Fell near Stone Park.

December: Edward Bradrick and others rob on the highway near Shap.

1684 Edmund Lodge goes to Clapham as vicar.

March: burglary from a shop at Keasden Head.

theft of a horse from Richard Myles at Kirkby Lonsdale.

April: Edward Bradrick commits various highway robberies in Yorks and Lancs.

April 15: attempted burglary and assault at Henry Preston's in Farleton.

16: theft of John Bainbridge's mare.

May 12: Henry Preston gives information concerning attempted burglary.

17: William Smorthwait and others rob a drover near Penrith.

18: the same ride south and assault and rob near Rounthwaite.

20: Henry Smorthwait and Bryan Thompson examined and committed to gaol.

26: Edward Bradrick and John Lyley ride to Carlisle.

June 1: William Smorthwait, Bradrick and others apprehended at Padiham.

6: Edward Bainbridge makes his first confession.

10: Edward Bradrick makes a confession in Lancaster gaol.

23: second confession of Edward Bainbridge.

July: Edward Bradrick condemned to death at York Assizes.

July 10: Fleming writes to Clerk of northern Assizes at York for advice.

25: Henry and William Smorthwait moved to Carlisle gaol.

August 5: Fleming rides to Carlisle.

6: Assizes commence with arrival of Judge Jeffreys at Carlisle.

8: trial of William and Henry Smorthwait.

8: Henry Smorthwait writes to Fleming pleading for his help.

9: the two Smorthwaits sentenced to be hanged.

11: Assizes at Appleby, Bryan Thompson freed.

14: Assizes at Lancaster.

16: Smorthwaits hanged, possibly at Lancaster.

1689   Sir George Jeffreys dies in the Tower of London.

1699   Bryan Thompson dies a pauper in Kirkby Lonsdale.

1701   Sir Daniel Fleming dies at Rydal.

1715   Edward Bainbridge dies in Mansergh.

Appendix B: Examinations and Signatures

1683

These are based on part of a manuscript in Daniel Fleming's hand among the Fleming papers (WD/Ry/31). The following amendments have been made:

> Fleming always states whether the examinations were upon oath or not: since almost all were upon oath, only those instances where the examination was not upon oath have been noted as such.

> Fleming took most of the examinations at Rydal Hall in Westmorland and this is mentioned throughout; only where the examination was taken elsewhere is the fact noted here.

> Fleming always gives the county for the places he refers to: these can be assumed to be Westmorland unless otherwise stated.

> Fleming uses the old style of dating, and so some of the dates are given as 1682 when by modern style they would be 1683; since all dates are in 1683, the year date has been omitted.

> Most of the examinations were taken before 'Sir Daniel Fleming, Knight': only in cases where they were taken before someone else is the fact recorded.

> Where only a copy of mark or signature is given, this is indicated in square brackets.

> Surnames have been standardized in line with the text.

Henry Yeats of Old Hutton. yeoman, taken at Kendal January 12, before Sir Geo. Fletcher Bar. & c.

[signature]

Robert Robinson of Old Hutton, Gent. at Kendal Jan. 13, before Sir Geo.
Fletcher Baronet &c.

Another examination of his at Rydal Hall. Apr. 14, before Sir Dan. Fleming
Knight & William Fleming Esq.

[*as above*]

Will. Speight junior of Old Hutton, yeoman, at Kendal Jan. 13. before Sir
Geo. Fletcher Bar. &c.

James Dawson of Old Hutton, whitesmith, at Kendal Jan. 13, before Sir
Geo. Fletcher Baronet &c.

Another examination of his, Apr. 16, before Sir Daniel Fleming Knight &
Will. Fleming Esq.

[*as above*]

Jo. Jackson of Old Hutton, yeoman, taken without oath at Kendal Jan 13.
before Sir George Fletcher Baronet & c.

Edmund Lodge of Old Hutton, clerk, Febr. 10, committed Aug. 10. 1683.

Tho. Cowperthwait of Bleaze in Old Hutton, shepherd Apr. 10, before Sir Dan. Fleming Knight & Will. Fleming Esq.

Margaret Blakeling of Chappel-houses in Old Hutton, spinster, Apr. 10 1683, before Sir Dan. Fleming Knight and William Fleming Esq.

Margaret wife of Edmund Lodge of Old Hutton, clerk, Apr. 14, before Sir Dan. Fleming Knight & Will. Fleming Esq.

Margaret wife of John Dickonson of Lupton Row, yeoman, Apr. 14, before Sir Dan. Fleming Knight & Will. Fleming Esq.

Dorothy Stainbank of Killington, spinster, Apr. 16.

Geo. Holme of Old Hutton, linen-webster, Apr. 16.

Richard Rigg of Old Hutton, waller, Apr. 16.

George Scaif of Hutton Park in New Hutton, tailor, taken without oath at Kendal Apr. 21.

Another examination of his, taken without oath, June 4. He was committed at Kendal June 27.

Simon Mount of Old Hutton, carrier, June 13.

Tho. Wilson of New Hutton, husbandman, July 23.

Tho. Robinson, junior, of Old Hutton, yeoman, July 24.

Tho. Clark of Holme, yeoman, at Kendal, Aug. 11.

John Jackson aforesaid, taken at Appleby, Feb. 12. before Edward Musgrave, sworn to June 30.

[*as above*]

Esther Craven of Hebden in Craven, taken at Kilnsay, Aug. 6, before Cuth. Wade Esq.

One further examination, which Fleming does not list, is
William Smorthwait of Austwick, yeoman, before Henry Lord Fairfax and others, 11th July.

1684

Less details are given by Fleming in his list of examinations for 1684. Most of the information therefore comes from the examinations themselves, copies of which are to be found in Fleming's manuscripts and in the Public Record Office (with the exception of those indicated). The same conventions concerning repeated standard information will be followed as for the 1683 examinations.

Andrew Bell of Ling in the parish of Hesket, husbandman, 4th July.

Edward Huetson of Penrith, chandler, 17th July.

Edward Bainbridge late of Mansergh, yeoman, 23 June, before Sir Daniel Fleming and three other Justices.

Further examination of Edward Bainbridge, at Kendal, 10th July, before Sir Daniel Fleming and four others.

Henry Preston of Farleton, yeoman, before Edward Wilson and Henry Wilson, Esq., 12 May.

Henry Preston

Edward Bainbridge of Mansergh, yeoman, at Kendal, 6th June, before Sir Christopher Philipson and Edward Wilson.

[*as above*]

Edward Bradrick late of Leeds, now a prisoner in the castle of Lancaster, 10 June before William Kirkby.

Ed. Bradrick

Henry Smorthwait of New Hutton, yeoman, taken at Cowbrow in Lupton the 26 May before Edward Wilson & Henry Wilson.

Henry Smorthwaite

Alexander Guy of Mallerstang, blacksmith, 4 June.

Alexander [mark] Guy

Lancelot Aray of Rounthwait, butcher, 7 July.

Lancelot [mark] Aray

Tho. Scaif of Ashes in Hutton in the Hay, husbandman, 14 July.

Lancelot Dennison of Greenholme in Orton, alehouse keeper, 25 July.

Jo. Barker of Killington, mill-wright, taken on July 30.

Robert Ward of Killington, clothier, July 30.

Samuel Otway of Barbon, yeoman, July 30.

Edward Stainbank of Middleton, butcher, July 30.

Robert Newby of Little Hutton, hatter, July 31.

Jo. Fisher of Old Hutton, carrier, July 31.

Giles Helme of Old Hutton, blacksmith, July 31.

Margaret wife of Jo. Walton of Natland, carrier, July 31.

Robert Benson of Mansergh, husbandman, Aug. 4.

Margaret Bainbridge of Middleton, widow, Aug. 6.

Jo. Harrison of Middleton, yeoman, Aug. 6.

Bernard Edmundson of Kendal, butcher, Aug. 8.

Tho. Bland of Sedbergh, whitesmith, Aug. 10.

Tho. Inman of Sedbergh, haberdasher, Aug. 10.

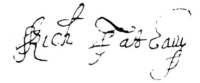

Rich. Tatham of Ireby, husbandman, taken at Kendal, Aug. 11.

Margaret wife of Edward Bradrick late of Leeds, 23 June, before Sir Daniel Fleming and three other Justices.

Joseph Dawson of Old Hutton, whitesmith, 23 June, before Sir Daniel Fleming and three other Justices.

John Tyson of Kirkby Lonsdale, mercer, 23 June, before Sir Daniel Fleming and three other Justices.

John Gathorn of Holmescales, stapler, 23 June, before Sir Daniel Fleming and three other Justices.

Richard Myles of Lazonby, drover, 30th July.

Robert Benson of Mansergh, husbandman, at Kendal, 16th July before Sir Daniel Fleming and four Justices.

[*see 1683*]

John Jackson of Old Hutton, maltster, at Kendal, 16th July before Sir Daniel Fleming and four Justices.

[*see 1683*]

John Jackson of Mansergh, husbandman, 18 July.

John Bainbridge of Gillfoot in Mansergh, yeoman, 2 Aug.

Examinations (copies of signatures only) found only in Fleming papers (WD/Ry/36)

Elizabeth Preston wife of Henry Preston taken at Cowbrow in Lupton 26 May before Edward Wilson and Henry Wilson Esq.

[mark]

Mary Saule wife of Richard Saule of Hincaster, taken as above.

[signature]

Bryan Thompson of Kirkby Lonsdale, yeoman, taken as above.

[signature]

Thomas Thexton of Farleton, taken as above.

[mark]

Joseph Cartmel of Farleton, yeoman, taken before Edward Wilson Esq., 16 May.

[signature]

Robert Cragg of Preston Patrick, blacksmith, taken as above.

[signature]

Examinations in Palatinate of Lancaster depositions (PL 27/1)

William Foster of Tatham, gentleman, taken before William Kirkby and others, 31st July, 1681 at Lancaster gaol.

Stephen Woodworth of Little Newton, taken before William Kirkby and others, 27th July, 1681, at Lancaster gaol.

Appendix C: The Method of
Counterfeiting Coins

Among the depositions in the Palatinate of Lancaster papers (P.L.27/ 1,PRO) is a paper headed 'The ingredients and materials these rogues use and the manner'. This is very unusual and, for example, nothing like it has been found in the prosecutions against counterfeiters to 1700 in the MINT prosecutions at the PRO. It is therefore reproduced here.

> The ingredients of the coining stuff called spawd (spelt) and the way they make it:
> 1 Alumen plumosum[1] 1 lb. worth about 4*s* or 5*s*,' tis a light stuff and in the form of a feather and is burnt and bruised to powder.
> 2 Alabaster burnt and bruised to powder about 6 lb. of that.
> 3 Bole armoniac[2] also burnt and bruised to powder twixt 1 lb. and 2 lb.
> 4 Sal ammoniac[3] dissolved in water to which water the aforementioned powders so mixed and sifted very fine were put and when to be used they were wrought like dough or paste.
> The materials they have to coin with and the manner of using them:
> 1 Copper whitened with white arsenic.
> 2 Silver clipped off his Majesty's lawful coin, two parts silver and three parts whitened copper.
> 3 A pair of flasks, a pestle all made of iron. These flasks are round or oval at top and bottom, so made with a pin in the top falling into a hole made to fit it in the bottom. When laid together they fall fixed and [illegible] to close always even and alike. Then in their bottom flask laid upon a place for the purpose, they first lay their patterns, any piece of money they will have counterfeited and so seven or eight half crowns or shillings at a time

---

[1] Plumose alum, feather or plume alum, i.e. *Ferroso-alumic sulphate*.
[2] Soft friable salty earth, usually of a pale red colour.
[3] *Ammonium chloride*.

or more. And these they cover with the stuff called spawd, which they thrust very hard down with the iron pestle. And this leaves in that stuff the impress of one side of the money to be counterfeited. Then they turn this stuff which retains the impressions upon a smooth board and set the top flask filled with the same stuff in like manner prepared and closed with the bottom flask takes the impression of the other side of the money to be imitated. And then again part the top and bottom and take out the money laid for their pattern. And then make with a knife a hollow place for the metal to run in to fill the hollows prepared for the metals to run into. And then having again closed the top and bottom flasks, out of the iron melting pot cast their mixed metals melted down, which when taken out of the flasks is at first very black. And to alter the colour, they lay it upon an iron plate, which plate they set upon a very red hot fire, which changes the colour to blue. And then they take it off the fire, and boil it in tartar bruised, which they call argol,[4] mixed with salt, and this makes it over white. Then they rub it in sal ammoniac, which makes it somewhat black again, and then they rub it with clay and after wash off the clay with water. And when so brought to the colour they would have it, wipe away the clay and water with a cloth. And this makes it very passable and if cut into the colour is as all silver.

[4] Tartar.

Appendix D: Major Manuscript Sources

1 PUBLIC RECORD OFFICE, CHANCERY LANE, LONDON

The major set of documents upon which this book is based are the depositions filed among the northern circuit Assize papers in the class ASSI 45. The examinations and informations before the trial in August 1683 are contained in ASSI/45/13/3 folios 79–91. Those for the trial of August 1684 are in ASSI/45/14/1, folios 134–40. Other relevant material is contained in ASSI 44, the Assize indictments, especially in the period 1650–99, and in ASSI 47, miscellaneous documents partly covering the same period.

Palatinate of Lancaster: depositions, 1663 to 1750. P.L.27/1,2.

2 LANCASHIRE RECORD OFFICE, BOW LANE, PRESTON

Wills and inventories for the parish of Kirkby Lonsdale, approximately 2500 documents for the period 1500–1720 from Lonsdale deanery, Archdeaconry of Richmond.

Quarter Sessions papers: petitions, 1680–85. QSP.

3 KIRKBY LONSDALE PARISH CHURCH

Register of baptisms, marriages and burials, 1558–1750.

4 CUMBRIA RECORD OFFICE, THE CASTLE, CARLISLE

Court rolls, surveys and rentals for Lupton and Kirkby Lonsdale, 1598–1750. Musgrave and Lonsdale papers.

5 CUMBRIA RECORD OFFICE, COUNTY HALL, KENDAL

Quarter Sessions Papers: Kendal Indictment and Order Book, 1669 to 1691.
Kendal Order Book, 1669 to 1696.
Kendal Indictment Book, 1692 to 1724.
Kendal Order Book, 1696 to 1724.

Fleming manuscripts: WD/Ry.

The general description of these papers in the *Historical Manuscripts Commission, 12th Report, Appendix, part 7* (1890) is inadequate. Because extensive quotation has been made, without specific references being given, it is necessary to list the relevant papers in the separate boxes.

Some six thousand letters to and from the Fleming family, many of them concerning Sir Daniel Fleming, are kept in separate boxes. Specific references to these numbered letters have been given in the text. A few of the missing letters are in the Lancaster Public Library.

Sir Daniel's large account book is in box 119.

Sir Daniel's annotated copy of *The Statutes of the Peace*, broken into three parts, has now been reunited and is in box 36.

The rest of the relevant material is best described by box number.

Box 31

Examinations and informations, 1683: Robert Robinson, William Speight, James Dawson, John Jackson, Esther Craven, Thomas Cowperthwait, Margaret Blakeling, Edward Stainbank, Robert Newby, John Fisher, Giles Helme, Margaret Walton, Robert Benson, Margaret Bainbridge, John Harrison, Bernard Edmundson, Thomas Bland, Thomas Inman, Richard Tatham, Thomas Clark, Robert Robinson, Margaret Lodge, Dorothy Stainbank, James Dawson, George Holme, Richard Rigg, Thomas Robinson, John Barker, Robert Ward, Samuel Otway, Edmund Lodge, Henry Yeats.

Examinations and informations, 1684: Andrew Bell, Edward Huetson, Thomas Scaife, Lancelot Dennison, Edward Bradrick.

Recognizances for appearance: of all those above, except Edward Bradrick, Esther Craven and Henry Yeats.

General charge to petty constables, surveyors of highways, churchwardens etc. 1684.

Warrants to constables of Farleton, Mansergh, New Hutton, Mallerstang, Old Hutton, Kirkby Lonsdale, Barbon and Mansergh to apprehend suspects and to bring in witnesses.

Memoirs of Fleming, June 1684: questions to ask Edward Bainbridge.

Rough draft of *mittimus* to keeper of gaol at Appleby, committing Henry Smorthwait.

Account of constables of New Hutton, for charges in carrying Henry Smorthwait to gaol.

Original copy of bills of indictments at Appleby Assizes, 1683.

Table of examinations in 1683 and 1684, copy by Fleming.

Rough drafts of indictments concerning Robinson burglary, and lists of witnesses to each offence.

Memoirs by Daniel Fleming concerning the various burglaries and the stages in the prosecution.

Box 34

Warrants to constables of Old Hutton, Middleton, Barbon, Mansergh, Killington, to apprehend felons and to bring in witnesses.

Copy of questions to Grand Jury, Appleby Assizes 1683.

Rough draft of *mittimus* to gaoler at Appleby to commit Edmund Lodge to gaol; similar *mittimus* for George Scaif, 1683.

Box 35

Calendars of prisoners in gaol at Appleby, for 1683 and 1684.

Box 36

Examinations and informations, 1684: Henry Preston, Elizabeth Preston, Mary Saule, Henry Smorthwait, Bryan Thompson, Thomas Thexton, Joseph Cartmell, Robert Cragge, Edward Bainbridge, Joseph Dawson, John Tyson, John Gathorn, Richard Myles, Margaret Bradrick, John

Bainbridge, Robert Benson, John Jackson of Old Hutton, John Jackson of Mansergh, William Speight, Alexander Guy, Lancelot Aray, Richard Hindson, Elizabeth Hindson, Jane Arey.

Recognizances for appearance: for all the above persons, except the first six and the last three; also recognizances for William Fairer, Thomas Wilson, Simon Mount.

Letters: to the Deputy Sheriff concerning the removal of Henry Smorthwait to Carlisle; to the keeper of Lancaster Gaol, for the removal of William Smorthwait; from the Deputy Sheriff concerning William Smorthwait's removal; to and from the Clerk of the Assize at York; from Thomas Lodge schoolmaster at Lancaster.

Copy of writs from the Lord Chief Justice, for removing William and Henry Smorthwait to Carlisle gaol.

Warrant to constables of Old Hutton to bring in witnesses, 1683.

Calendar of prisoners in Lancaster gaol, 1684.

Box 57

Information by William Becke, 1683.

List of persons named in Bradrick and Bainbridge's examinations.

Assorted 'Memoirs' by Daniel Fleming concerning William Smorthwait and the various thefts and burglaries.

Glossary
(based mainly on the *Oxford English Dictionary*)

affray	a disturbance, a noisy or tumultuous outburst, especially caused by fighting.
ague	an acute or violent fever.
bindings	joists.
bodystead	central room of house; living room.
carrier	one who undertakes for hire the conveyance of goods and parcels.
chandler	retail dealer in provisions, groceries and especially candles.
corruption of blood	the effect of an attainder upon a person attainted: his blood was said to have become tainted or corrupted by his crime so that he and his descendants lost all rights to rank and title and he could no longer retain possession of land which he held, or leave it to heirs.
counterfeit	to forge.
deponent	one who deposes or makes a deposition under oath; one who gives written testimony to be used as evidence in a court of justice.
dower	the portion of a deceased husband's estate which the law allows to his widow for her life.
drawers	trousers.
drover	person who drives horses or cattle.
engrosser	one who buys in large quantities, especially with a view to being able to secure a monopoly.
falchion	a sword, particularly a broad sword.

fardel	a bundle, a little pack, a parcel.
fog	aftergrass, aftermath, the grass that comes after a crop of hay.
forestaller	one who buys up goods before they reach the public market.
gavelock	iron crowbar, chiefly used for making holes for hedge stakes.
groat	coin worth approximately 4*d*; ceased to be issued in 1662.
hue and cry	a proclamation or outcry for the capture of a criminal or the finding of stolen goods.
indictment	the legal document containing the charge; 'a written accusation of one or more persons of a crime or misdemeanour preferred to, and presented upon oath by, a grand jury' (Blackstone).
kersey	a kind of coarse narrow cloth, woven from long wool, usually ribbed.
ling	heather.
maltster	a maker of malt.
mercer	one who deals in textile fabrics, a small-ware dealer.
messuage	dwelling house.
mittimus	a warrant under the hand and seal of a JP or other proper officer, directed to the keeper of a prison, ordering him to receive into custody and to hold in safe keeping, until delivered in due course of law, the person sent and specified in the warrant.
plack	any coin of little value.
present	to bring or lay before a court, magistrate, or person in authority, for consideration or trial, to make presentment of.
press	large, usually shelved, cupboard, especially one placed in a recess in the wall, for holding clothes, books etc.
puncheon	pointed tool for piercing.
recognizance	a bond or obligation, entered into and recorded before a court or magistrate, by which a person engages himself to perform some act or observe some condition (as to appear when called on, to pay a debt, or keep the peace).
regrater	one who collects commodities from the producer and brings to market in order to sell again at a profit.
resetter	a receiver of stolen goods.
sad	dark, deep, dull, sober (of colour).

sojourner	a temporary resident.
spell	a chip or splinter of stone or ore.
spelder	splinter.
spelks	small strips of wood for thatching etc.
stanchion	an upright bar, stay, prop or support, specifically of a window.
stapler	a trader who buys wool from the grower to sell to the manufacturer.
teste	the authenticating clause of a writ used with the name of a witness etc.
trainband	a trained company of citizen soldiery, organized in the sixteenth to eighteenth centuries.
ward	an administrative district, peculiar to the north of England.
webster	a weaver.
whitesmith	one who works in white iron, a tinsmith.
yeat	a gate.
vizard	a mask.

Index

Page numbers in italics refer to maps and illustrations.